I0105457

SPECIAL ECONOMIC ZONES IN THE INDONESIA–MALAYSIA–THAILAND GROWTH TRIANGLE

OPPORTUNITIES FOR COLLABORATION

Aradhna Aggarwal

FEBRUARY 2022

ADB

ASIAN DEVELOPMENT BANK

Notes:
In this publication, "$" refers to United States dollars.
ADB recognizes "America" as United States of America, "China" as the People's Republic of China, "Korea" as the Republic of Korea, "Russia" as the Russian Federation, and "Hanoi" as Ha Noi.
This publication is produced by ADB Technical Assistance (TA) 9572: Enhancing Effectiveness of Subregional Programs to Advance Regional Cooperation and Integration in Southeast Asia which has funding support from the People's Republic of China Regional Cooperation and Poverty Reduction Fund and Republic of Korea e-Asia and Knowledge Partnership Fund.

Cover design by Judy Yñiguez.

On the cover (from left to right): An electronics engineering student of Batam State Polytechnic in Indonesia design printed circuit boards inside the electronics labs; a worker in the manufacturing workshop in Malaysia operating a hole punching machine; and a manufacturing engineer in Thailand using a socket hand tool to adjust industrial equipment in the factory (photos by Lester Ledesma/ADB, iStock and iStock).

Printed on recycled paper

Contents

Tables, Figures, Boxes, and Maps

Tables

Figures

Boxes

Maps

Foreword

The Indonesia–Malaysia–Thailand Growth Triangle (IMT-GT), supported by the Asian Development Bank (ADB), has long adopted special economic zones (SEZs) as a policy tool to foster the development of regional and cross-border production networks and to facilitate global value chains participation. The IMT-GT considers SEZs as potentially effective mechanisms to intensify subregional cooperation; bolster economic linkages to the wider Association of Southeast Asian Nations (ASEAN) Economic Community; and stimulate economic activities, employment, exports, and foreign direct investments. SEZs are also considered prime catalysts for subregional development and inclusive growth, especially in border areas of the IMT-GT economic corridors.

IMT-GT acknowledges that the potential benefits of economic zones development in corridors can only be realized if the participating economies have a coordinated approach that integrates trade expansion and growth strategies with SEZ development. Over the years, the IMT-GT member countries have recognized the need to have a more explicit, collective, and strategic approach in SEZ development and cooperation and concretely identify ways in which economic corridors can be leveraged to set up SEZs and other production hubs to generate network externalities via regional cooperation.

Against this background, during the 24th IMT-GT Ministerial Meeting held on 1 October 2018 in Melaka, Malaysia, the IMT-GT ministers requested ADB, as IMT-GT's regional development partner, to conduct the study on SEZs development and cooperation.

This technical study, a first of its kind, brings together a wide array of literature on economic zones in the IMT-GT member countries and the subregion. Across the IMT-GT countries, there are 2,092 cluster-based economic zones of different types. This proliferation not only in number but also in variety calls for rigorous analysis, answering the following key questions: what are the typologies and characteristics of economic zones and where are they located, how can the strategic relevance of SEZs in IMT-GT be strengthened, and what actions can be taken to promote them. The study identifies the challenges facing IMT-GT economic zones and offers recommendations for policy makers to support active clustering and specialization efforts in the subregion.

The study also proposes a strategic framework for successful SEZs development and cooperation in the IMT-GT. It identifies collaborative and competitive actions that the IMT-GT stakeholders can adopt amid the coronavirus disease (COVID-19) crisis. The COVID-19 pandemic has highlighted the need for more robust cooperation, given that SEZs are critical tools to boost trade, sustain supply chains, attract quality and investment, generate employment, and build economic resilience inclusively.

We hope this study will guide IMT-GT stakeholders as they pursue concrete actions to further develop and intensify SEZs and economic corridors as drivers of growth in the subregion and to maximize benefits for the people in the subregion.

Ramesh Subramaniam
Director General
Southeast Asia Department
Asian Development Bank

Acknowledgments

The technical study forms part of the analytical work produced under ADB Technical Assistance (TA) 9572: Enhancing Effectiveness of Subregional Programs to Advance Regional Cooperation and Integration in Southeast Asia which has funding support from the People's Republic of China Regional Cooperation and Poverty Reduction Fund and Republic of Korea e-Asia and Knowledge Partnership Fund.

Aradhna Aggarwal, an internationally renowned special economic zone (SEZ) expert and professor at Copenhagen Business School, served as the main author and leader of the study team. The team was supervised by Alfredo Perdiguero, director of ADB's Southeast Asia Regional Cooperation and Operations Coordination Division, with support from Gary Krishnan, senior country specialist; Maria Theresa Bugayong, operations officer (Resource Planning); and consultants Pamela Asis-Layugan, Jordana Queddeng-Cosme, and Alona Mae Agustin.

The IMT-GT ministers H.E. Agus Suparmanto, Minister of Trade, Indonesia; H.E. Dato' Sri Mustapa Mohamed, Minister in Prime Minister's Department (Economy), Malaysia; and H.E. Arkhom Termpittayapaisith, Minister of Finance, Thailand, at the 26th IMT-GT Ministerial Meeting held in November 2020, provided overall strategic guidance, which greatly enhanced the relevance and overall quality of the report.

Regular consultations and discussions with IMT-GT senior officials Rizal Affandi Lukman and Raldi Hendro Koestoer, Coordinating Ministry for Economic Affairs of Indonesia; Saiful Anuar Bin Lebai Hussen, Noor Zari Bin Hamat, Mohd Shafiee B. Mohd Shah, and Sarimah Binti Amran, Economic Planning Unit, Prime Minister's Office of Malaysia; and Danucha Pitchayanan, Pattama Teanravisitsagool, and Wanchat Suwankitti, Office of the National Economic and Social Development Council of Thailand provided valuable inputs. Peer reviews and technical guidance from the IMT-GT national secretariats Netty Muharni, Tri Hidayatno, Sonny Ameriansah Soekoer of the Coordinating Ministry for Economic Affairs of Indonesia; Ahmad Zamri Bin Khairuddin, Suhana Binti Md Saleh, Nurul Ezzah Binti Md Zin, Balamurugan Ratha Krishnan, Mohammad Akhir Abdul Rahman, and Mattias Murphy Lai of the Economic Planning Unit, Prime Minister's Office of Malaysia; and Thuttai Keeratipongpaiboon, Chiraphat Chotipimai, Orachat Sungkhamanee, Potcharapol Prommatat, and Puntasith Charoenpanichpun of the Office of the National Economic and Social Development Council of Thailand helped fine-tune the report. The Centre for IMT-GT Subregional Cooperation headed by Firdaus Dahlan and relevant IMT-GT working groups also provided insights.

Fieldwork and interviews by Aradhna Aggarwal and Pamela Asis-Layugan in 2019 in the IMT-GT economic zones were conducted with assistance from the IMT-GT national secretariats and coordinated by the following SEZ authorities: the National Council for Special Economic Zones in Indonesia; the East Coast Economic Region, and Northern Corridor Implementation Authority in Malaysia; and the Industrial Estate Authority of Thailand, and National Committee for Special Economic Zone Development Policies in Thailand.

Pamela Asis-Layugan and Hammed Bolotaolo gave instrumental editorial advice on this study. Judy Yñiguez handled typesetting and graphics generation and designed the cover artwork. Maria Theresa Mercado and Jess Alfonso Macasaet proofed the draft layout. Alona Mae Agustin, Raquel Tabanao, and Hannah Althea Estipona provided overall support for the publication process. The publishing team of ADB's Department of Communications supervised the graphic design and provided production support.

Abbreviations

ADB	Asian Development Bank
AEC	Association of Southeast Asian Nations (ASEAN) Economic Community
ASEAN	Association of Southeast Asian Nations
BOI	Board of Investment of Thailand
CIMT	Centre for IMT-GT Subregional Cooperation
CIQ	customs, immigration, and quarantine
CMGF	Chief Ministers and Governors Forum
COVID-19	coronavirus disease 2019
DFTZ	digital free trade zone
E&E	electrical and electronics
ECER	East Coast Economic Region
EEC	Eastern Economic Corridor
EIT	eco-industrial town
EPZ	export processing zone
ESDZ	eastern special development zone
EU	European Union
FCZ	free commercial zone
FDI	foreign direct investment
FIAS	Foreign Investment Advisory Service
FIZ	free industrial zone
FTZ	free trade zone
GDP	gross domestic product
GEZ	general economic zone
GPP	gross provincial product
GRDP	gross regional domestic product
GVC	global value chain
ICD	inland container depot
ICQS	Immigration, Customs, Quarantine and Security
ICT	information and communication technology
IEAT	Industrial Estate Authority of Thailand
IMT-GT	Indonesia–Malaysia–Thailand Growth Triangle
JBC	Joint Business Council

KAPET	Kawasan Pengembangan Ekonomi Terpadu (Integrated Economic Development Zone)
KEK	Kawasan Ekonomi Khusus (Special Economic Zone)
KHTP	Kulim Hi-Tech Park
KLIA	Kuala Lumpur International Airport
km	kilometer
KPBPB	Kawasan Perdagangan Bebas dan Pelabuhan Bebas (free port and free trade area)
LMW	licensed manufacturing warehouse
LNG	liquefied natural gas
M&E	monitoring and evaluation
MIDA	Malaysian Investment Development Authority
MNC	multinational corporation
MSC	Multimedia Super Corridor
MSMEs	micro, small, and medium-sized enterprises
NESDC	National Economic and Social Development Council
NSTDA	National Science and Technology Development Agency
NTB	nontariff barrier
OECD	Organisation for Economic Co-operation and Development
PPP	public–private partnership
PRC	People's Republic of China
PSC	Project Selection Committee
R&D	research and development
RPJMN	Rencana Pembangunan Jangka Menengah Nasional (National Medium-Term Development Plan)
RPJPN	Rencana Pembangunan Jangka Panjang Nasional (National Long-Term Development Plan)
RSP	regional science park
RSPO	Roundtable on Sustainable Palm Oil
RVC	regional value chain
SBEZ	special border economic zone
SDZ	special development zone
SEC	Southern Economic Corridor (Thailand)
SEZ	special economic zone
SIJORI	Singapore–Johor–Riau
SMEs	small and medium-sized enterprises
STP	science and technology park
TSP	Thailand Science Park
UNCTAD	United Nations Conference on Trade and Development
UNESCAP	United Nations Economic and Social Commission for Asia and the Pacific
UNIDO	United Nations Industrial Development Organization
US	United States
WTO	World Trade Organization

Executive Summary

Background. The Indonesia–Malaysia–Thailand Growth Triangle (IMT-GT) and the Brunei Darussalam–Indonesia–Malaysia–Philippines East ASEAN Growth Area subregional cooperation programs supported by the Asian Development Bank (ADB) highly prioritize developing regional and cross-border production networks using special economic zones (SEZs) and special border economic zones (SBEZs) as the key tools. These programs are potentially effective mechanisms to deepen subregional cooperation; strengthen linkages to the wider Association of Southeast Asian Nations (ASEAN) Economic Community; and stimulate economic activities, employment, exports, and foreign direct investment (FDI). However, very little is known about whether and how economic corridors are leveraged to set up SEZs and other production hubs and how successful the participating countries have been in coordinating their SEZ strategies to generate network externalities in the subregion through regional cooperation. Against this background, the present study is conducted by ADB—a regional development partner to IMT-GT since 2006—on a collaborative approach to SEZ development and cooperation in IMT-GT under the technical assistance project titled Enhancing Effectiveness of Subregional Programs to Advance Regional Cooperation and Integration in Southeast Asia at the request of the member states. To my knowledge, no earlier study has assessed the implementation of the subregional agenda from the perspective of economic zones.

Objectives. The study sets out the following specific objectives:

- mapping the economic zones in the IMT-GT countries;
- mapping the economic zones on IMT-GT economic corridor routes;
- assessing the national and subnational policies, regulations, institutions, and governance relating to IMT-GT economic zones;
- assessing the alignment between the national development agenda on the one hand and the IMT-GT economic corridor and zone development approaches on the other;
- reviewing the subregional economic performance to gauge the success of economic zones; and
- identifying the challenges facing the subregional economic zones and offering recommendations for actions to deepen economic zone development and cross-border cooperation in the IMT-GT subregion.

The study's ultimate objective is to strengthen the strategic relevance of economic zones in the subregional initiative and identify actions for promoting them. Its geographical scope covers all 32 provinces and states under the IMT-GT—10 provinces of Sumatera in Indonesia, 8 northern states of Peninsular Malaysia, and 14 provinces in Southern Thailand.

Data. The analysis is based on both primary and secondary data. The primary data were gathered through field trips to selected economic zones, and consultations and interviews with a cross section of federal governments as well the state or provincial governments' officials, the Centre for IMT-GT Subregional Cooperation management team, economic zones' management authorities, and private entrepreneurs. The primary data were combined with the secondary data, which encompassed an enormous range of sources including nationally and internationally published studies; development plan documents of the three countries since the 1960s; texts of the relevant acts, decrees, and regulations; government reports and press releases; academic and news articles; blogs and books; and the websites of various government agencies.

Methodology. The data were assessed using descriptive, exploratory, and explanatory approaches. The descriptive element includes mapping the economic zones in Indonesia, Malaysia, and Thailand and their policy frameworks. The exploratory part delves into the linkages between the zones and national development strategies, and reviews the zones' economic impacts. Finally, the explanatory part explains the subregional program's relevance using both theoretical arguments and empirical evidence, discusses the challenges, and offers recommendations to strengthen the subregional economic zones.

Typological framework of economic zones. A two-layered classification is proposed to map the economic zones. At the top (level 1) is the typology based on the legal perspective, from which there are mainly three types of economic zones: general, special, and hybrid. The distinction between the general economic zones (GEZs) and SEZs centers mostly around the type of regulatory regime that governs them. The SEZ is a distinct economic zone with a specialized legal regime to overcome the institutional deficit in developing countries. Hybrid zones consist of both GEZs and SEZs. Each type of economic zone further branches out according to its functional characteristics in layer 2. In this typological framework, subregions are classified as cross-border hybrid zones covering contiguous subnational units from two or more nation-states that can drive growth by reinforcing local competencies through regional integration.

Mapping of the economic zones in IMT-GT countries. The governments of Indonesia, Malaysia, and Thailand adopted the economic zones program at different times; followed different policies regarding the designs, types, and names of the zones; and implemented them with different rigor. However, the turning point came in the mid-2000s when all three countries gave a major thrust to their economic zones programs to steer their respective economies to a higher growth trajectory with structural shifts to higher value-added activities. Since then, there has been proliferation not only in the number but also in the variety of zones. The typology presented in the study is employed to map all 2,092 cluster-based economic zones in these countries (excluding the hybrid zones), for which specific information is available. It is found that 497 (24%) of them are general zones; the rest are cluster-based SEZs (1,595) of different varieties. Indonesia has the largest number of SEZs (1,482), followed by Thailand (68) and Malaysia (45). Malaysia leads in GEZs (309), followed by Indonesia (149), and Thailand (39). Overall, Indonesia has the most diverse types and the largest number of economic zones, followed by Malaysia and Thailand. More importantly, however, 91% of Indonesia's zones are SEZs, followed by Thailand (72%), and Malaysia (13%). The analysis also shows that all three countries have been launching ever more ambitious zones initiatives since the mid-2000s. Economic zones have evolved toward larger spatial dimensions, complex structures, more comprehensive high-tech orientation, multisectors, and flexible locations. This evolution reflects a strong commitment, pragmatic approach, and dynamic learning toward economic zones adopted by all three countries, which are critical components of an economic zone policy.

Legal and institutional frameworks of special economic zones and general economic zones. It is shown that the economic zones are evolving not only in terms of their structural features but also in legal and institutional frameworks. Along with the provisions of fiscal incentives, the range of facilities, services, and amenities available within zones has been extended in new ambitious zone programs, particularly in Indonesia and Thailand. The preferential regulatory contents have also been enriched and enlarged over time. The SEZs, which have been the centerpiece of industrial policy of the three IMT-GT countries since the 1970s, have grown in importance with an aggressive drive launched by these countries to build a new variety of zones in recent years to achieve a variety of goals by unleashing their full potential.

Special economic zones and general economic zones in IMT-GT corridors. The IMT-GT corridors' landscape is abuzz with various economic zones at various stages of operation. There are 355 cluster-based zones of different types in the IMT-GT subregion for which there is specific information available. These zones are mainly in Malaysia-GT and Indonesia-GT. Thailand-GT is yet to pick up. In addition, there are 35 projects in the pipeline—19 in Malaysia, 10 in Indonesia, and 6 in Thailand—many of which are large projects involving different types of economic zones.

Assessing the alignment of the national and subnational development policies with the IMT-GT agenda. The linkages between the national development agenda and IMT-GT corridors and economic zones are assessed using two approaches: qualitative and quantitative.

- **Qualitative approach.** The study identifies four forms of linkages between the subregional policies on the one hand and national and subnational development agenda on the other. It explores them one by one based on an in-depth review of the long- and medium-term plan documents at the national level. These forms are (i) alignment between national and IMT-GT objectives, (ii) mainstreaming of IMT-GT spatial approach as a strategic pillar, (iii) mainstreaming of the IMT-GT projects, and (iv) mainstreaming of the development of subregional production networks through SEZs. The explorations reveal a growing recognition of the importance of the IMT-GT subregional program in the national strategic plans and that all three countries have explicitly or implicitly incorporated it into their national development agenda, albeit in different forms and varying degrees. Yet, the role of the IMT-GT spatial approach, particularly that of economic zones in unlocking subregional potential, is not fully recognized. Overall, Thailand has taken the lead, followed by Malaysia and Indonesia.

- **Quantitative approach.** Based on the premise that the integration of the subregional program into national development strategies is crucial for the success of the program, the quantitative approach analyzes trends in five performance indicators of the subregion organized into three categories: immediate (projects completed), intermediate (intra-subregional trade and FDI); and final (shares of IMT-GT regions in national GDP and the ratio of subregional income per capita to the national average). The analysis indicates that the IMT-GT subregional program, or even the proliferation of economic zones, has not made the subregion significantly better off in relative terms. The progress in IMT-GT connectivity projects also falls short of expectations.

The need to mainstream the subregional program into a broader development agenda. All three countries have undergone substantial industrial and social transformation alongside rapid economic growth and development since the 1960s and transformed their industrial base from agriculture to export-oriented manufacturing. This transformation was largely achieved by integrating key manufacturing production into global value chains (GVCs), with economic zones being the linchpin of this strategy. However, since the mid-2000s, these economies have been slowing down, as reflected in gross domestic product growth per capita, structural transformation, and international trade despite adopting an aggressive approach to their economic zones initiatives to promote trade and investment. The linkages between the economic zones and economic growth seem to be weakening in the region. A renewed thrust on zone programs from the perspective of regional integration can infuse a new dynamism to economic growth. The study highlights how the coronavirus disease 2019 (COVID-19) pandemic has further underscored the need for fostering regional cooperation and the regional value chains in which the subregional zones can play a vital role. However, it also recognizes that the subregional economic zones are facing challenges that need to be addressed.

Challenges facing economic zones. These challenges are grouped into three categories:

- **External challenges.** These include intensified competition for GVC-linked FDI with new centers emerging in Africa and Asia; increasing protectionist sentiments across the developed world; the People's Republic of China–United States trade war; the rise of digital technologies; and very recently, the COVID-19 pandemic and lockdowns to contain it.

- **Domestic conditions.** They refer to regional disparities, limited spillover effects, and the proliferation of economic zones.

- **Subregional factors.** Some of these factors are the gaps in physical connectivity and transport facilitation; nontariff barriers and custom barriers; non-differential treatment to economic zones in the subregion; weak alignment between the national development agendas and the IMT-GT economic corridor approach; heterogeneous cross-border policies, regulations, and standards; social and environmental risks; and security challenges.

Policy and strategy development. The study proposes a "coopetition" strategic approach to strengthen the IMT-GT corridors and economic zone programs. It is founded on two pillars: cooperation and competition. The underlying principle of the former is to establish a single market and production base in the subregion through cooperation, while the latter focuses on competition for investment in the economic zones. The central idea is that cooperation enables countries to augment their capabilities by having access to subregional resources and markets, which they can use to compete for more investment in their respective zones.

Cooperative Approach

- **Strategy 1:** Implement effectively IMT-GT economic corridors. This requires mainstreaming IMT-GT into national plans by recognizing regional cooperation as part of the national development strategy and improving physical connectivity, expediting the implementation of priority connectivity projects, and developing robust project pipelines. It is also critical to remove impediments to the mobility of people, vehicles, and goods by pilot testing ASEAN trade and transport agreements in IMT-GT and relaxing labor mobility.

- **Strategy 2:** Augment regional capabilities through cross-border cooperation programs to build micro, small, and medium-sized enterprise (MSME) production capabilities by encouraging large firms to support MSMEs, engaging MSME associations, promoting digitization of MSMEs and their alliances, and initiating industry-specific programs. Build a strong technological base by establishing a research fund, initiating technology collaboration programs, and promoting faculty exchange and internships. Develop research and development (R&D) alliances in palm oil and rubber industries within the region and with international companies, and ensure sustainable development of rubber and palm oil plantations and industries. Besides, local governments and private sector participation are needed to strengthen social capital by instituting small-scale funds for projects and activities to sustain participation in IMT-GT.

■ **Strategy 3:** Promote regional and/or cross-border value chains by leveraging the development ladder formed in IMT-GT and customizing trade and investment policies to generate cross-border economic and institutional synergies, e.g., harmonizing product standards, rules, and regulations. Plan direct policy interventions to promote cross-border chains by identifying leading sectors, encouraging the formation of industry consortia, structuring value chains of select products, and encouraging regional and domestic companies as anchor firms in targeted sectors. Systematic approaches to building capabilities of regional firms to participate in regional value chains can also be adopted.

■ **Strategy 4:** Adopt a rigorous branding and marketing strategy for the IMT-GT subregion to position it as an investment destination for food, palm, and rubber industries and as a global hub for rubber and palm industries. The investment promotion agencies of each member state can develop a national web page on IMT-GT subregional economic zones with regularly updated information.

Competitive Approach

■ **Strategy 5:** Improve the attractiveness of SEZs and industrial zones by promoting sustainable economic zones including logistics parks and incorporating sustainability criteria in site selection and master plans of the zones. Compensate the locational disadvantages through strategic master planning of the economic zones, including innovative on-site solutions, specialized infrastructure to cater to a specific investor, on-site social infrastructure, centers for labor training, and off-site infrastructure. Provide investor-friendly one-stop services via custom facilitation, specialized management services, digitization of services and transactions, and customized incentives. The general investment climate in areas surrounding the economic zones can be improved by enhancing regulatory institutions and promoting urban development. Expediting integration efforts for GVCs' smooth operation, especially amid the COVID-19 pandemic, can be achieved in parallel with the establishment of the ASEAN Economic Community (AEC) by introducing broader economic reforms and experimenting with decentralization of powers.

■ **Strategy 6:** Improve spillovers by adopting a smart approach to identify and promote the production of goods and services required by SEZs and linking subregional companies with regional and extra-regional firms participating in GVCs; and complementing the smart approach with horizontal approaches by implementing initiatives to promote investment in skills, technologies, R&D, and infrastructure in the wider economy to create conditions for spillovers from the SEZs.

Each of the two approaches suggested above consists of strategies broken down into strategic interventions that are further divided into enabling actions.

Policy adoption into planning. For adopting the proposed strategic framework into planning, a fourfold solution is proposed.

- First, adopt a holistic and integrated approach that requires simultaneously adopting all the broad policy prescriptions as a package. A piecemeal approach cannot be effective.
- Second, break down the strategic interventions into three time frames (short, medium, and long term) and focus on the short- and medium-term measures as low-hanging fruits while building consensus for the long-term measures.
- Third, mainstream all proposed strategic interventions and enabling actions for economic zones into the relevant sectoral or thematic strategies of the development plans and the agendas of the seven working groups.
- Fourth, design special programs and initiatives for the subregion to implement them effectively.

Adoption of the proposed strategies for the promotion of rubber cities. The study illustrates how the proposed strategic interventions can be adopted in planning to develop rubber cities. The key recommendation is to adopt the industrial symbiosis approach as a strategic plan, which will ensure the sustainability of rubber cities with efficient utilization of energy, water resources, and waste and improve the industry's image globally.

A sound strategy for implementing the spatial approach. A four-pronged implementation strategy has been proposed with specific enabling actions. These approaches focus on overcoming institutional constraints, human resource constraints, social and environment costs, and external risks in integrating border areas and promoting SEZs. It is also proposed to strengthen the monitoring and evaluation frameworks for both the corridors and economic zones. The study maps the IMT-GT working groups and government agencies that need to collaborate closely to adopt these strategies and deliver the desired results.

Introduction

Background

Since its inception in 1993, the Indonesia–Malaysia–Thailand Growth Triangle (IMT-GT) subregional program has attained remarkable economic growth and shared regional prosperity through concerted policy interventions. Yet, there is a mismatch between the actual achievements and declared objectives. The midterm review of the IMT-GT Implementation Blueprint 2012–2016 observes that the gains in terms of intra-subregional trade and investment are particularly modest, suggesting the limited success of the member states in leveraging on their comparative advantages to make it a well-positioned regional production base (Asian Development Bank [ADB] 2015). To address this gap, the IMT-GT Vision 2036 (Centre for IMT-GT Subregional Cooperation [CIMT] 2017a) supported by the IMT-GT Implementation Blueprint 2017–2021 (CIMT 2017b) adopts the spatial approach that accords a high priority to the development of regional and cross-border production networks in the IMT-GT areas using special economic zones (SEZs), special border economic zones (SBEZs), and other production sites as the key tools. The IMT-GT Vision 2036 places the five priority IMT-GT economic corridors at the center to facilitate cross-border connectivity of these production sites backward with resources and forward with markets and maximize the economic network externalities. The objective is to foster diversification and sophistication of manufacturing, agribusiness, and tourism chains for "an integrated, innovative, inclusive and sustainable subregion by 2036" (CIMT 2017a, 43). However, very little is known about whether and how economic corridors are being leveraged for setting up SEZs, SBEZs, and other production hubs and how successful they have been in generating network externalities in the subregion through regional cooperation. Bearing this in mind, ADB, a regional development partner to IMT-GT since 2006, has conducted this study on a collaborative approach to SEZ development in the IMT-GT subregion at the request of the member states under the technical assistance project titled Enhancing Effectiveness of Subregional Programs to Advance Regional Cooperation and Integration in Southeast Asia.

The study's main objectives are to take stock of the IMT-GT SEZs and other economic zones, review the extent to which these are integrated into national development agendas of the member states, review their performance, identify challenges, and offer recommendations for policy makers to support their active clustering and specialization efforts in the subregion. One of the study's objectives is to map the universe of SEZs and other industrial zones in a comparative framework to harmonize the data on economic zones in the three member countries. Harmonization of data means transforming the data of varying zone types and naming conventions into one cohesive data set by developing a framework for zone typology. To my best knowledge, no earlier studies have assessed the implementation of the subregional agenda from the perspective of economic zones and/or attempted to harmonize the regional economic zone data. This study is the first to address this gap. The study makes three major contributions to the existing literature on economic zones, particularly SEZs. First, it harmonizes the data on economic zones in the IMT-GT member countries. Second, it develops a framework to assess the mainstreaming of the subregional agenda into national and subnational development agendas and proposes a strategy to implement it successfully. Third and most important, it proposes a strategic framework for the success of economic zones in the subregion. While doing so, it underlines the relevance of the collaborative approach for the subregional economic zones and highlights how the outbreak of the COVID-19 pandemic has further underscored the need for the collaborative approach to economic zones. Typically, economic zones are set up as a competitive tool to attract investment and generate employment. However, this study identifies the transborder subregion with a hybrid zone and proposes a coopetition (a combination of collaboration and competition) strategy to improve the attractiveness of the subregional economic zones.

Objectives and Scope

The study sets out the following specific objectives:

- mapping the economic zones in the IMT-GT countries;
- mapping the economic zones on IMT-GT economic corridor routes;
- reviewing the national and subnational development policies. and strategies including incentives, regulations, institutions, and governance relating to the IMT-GT economic zones;
- assessing the alignment between the national development agenda on the one hand, and the IMT-GT economic corridor and zone development approaches on the other;
- appraising the subregional economic performance to gauge the success of economic zones; and
- identifying the challenges and offering recommendations for actions and mechanisms to deepen economic zone development and cross-border cooperation in the IMT-GT subregion.

The study's ultimate objective is to strengthen the strategic relevance of economic zones in the subregional initiative and identify actions for promoting them.

While the study proposal was designed to cover only SEZs and SBEZs, all other economic zones have been included in the study for three reasons. First, there has been a proliferation not only of SEZs but also of other economic zones in the region; any study based only on SEZs would, therefore, present a partial view of trade and investment activity along the economic corridors. Second, the distinction between SEZs and other economic zones is becoming blurred, with many of the advantages of SEZs also being offered in other economic zones. Third, the ultimate goal of the zones, irrespective of the type, is to promote industrial clustering and production networks, one of the planks on which the Vision 2036 strategic framework is based.

The geographical scope of the study covers all 32 provinces and states under the IMT-GT (Map 1):

- 10 provinces of Sumatera in Indonesia (Aceh, Bangka Belitung, Bengkulu, Jambi, Lampung, North Sumatera, Riau, Riau Islands, South Sumatera, and West Sumatera);

Map 1. Indonesia–Malaysia–Thailand Growth Triangle

INDONESIA-MALAYSIA-THAILAND GROWTH TRIANGLE

- ⊛ National Capital
- ◉ Provincial/State Capital
- ● City/Town
- National Road
- Other Road
- Provincial Boundary
- International Boundary

Boundaries are not necessarily authoritative.

This map was produced by the cartography unit of the Asian Development Bank. The boundaries, colors, denominations, and any other information shown on this map do not imply, on the part of the Asian Development Bank, any judgment on the legal status of any territory, or any endorsement or acceptance of such boundaries, colors, denominations, or information.

Source: Asian Development Bank.

- 8 northern states of Peninsular Malaysia (Melaka, Kedah, Kelantan, Negeri Sembilan, Pulau Pinang, Perak, Perlis, and Selangor); and

- 14 provinces in Southern Thailand (Nakhon Si Thammarat, Narathiwat, Pattani, Phatthalung, Satun, Songkhla, Trang, Yala, Chumphon, Krabi, Phangnga, Phuket, Ranong, Surat Thani).

Methodology

The methodology employed in this study involves a combination of secondary and primary research. Extensive country consultations were conducted during July and August 2019. Using semi-structured questionnaires, a study team comprising of the author and project management team of ADB conducted face-to-face interviews with key informants such as government officials at the national and subnational levels, administrative officials of SEZs and other economic zones, the Centre for IMT-GT Subregional Cooperation (CIMT) management team, and private sector entities across the subregion. The field-based consultations offered crucial insights into the implementation of the subregional agenda at the national level. Country consultations were also filled with presentations by various government agencies, discussions, and site visits, yielding rich information on the existing and proposed economic zones in these countries. The primary data gathered during field trips were then combined with the secondary data, encompassing an enormous range of sources, including nationally and internationally published studies; development plan documents of the three countries since the 1960s; texts of the relevant acts, decrees, and regulations; government reports and press releases; academic and news articles; blogs and books; and websites of investment promotion agencies such as the Malaysian Investment Development Authority (MIDA), Indonesian Investment Coordinating Board, Industrial Estate Authority of Thailand (IEAT), and Board of Investment of Thailand (BOI).

The data were assessed using the descriptive, exploratory, and explanatory approaches. The descriptive element includes the mapping of economic zones in the three IMT-GT countries and their policy frameworks. The exploratory part analyzes the linkages between the zones and national development agendas, and reviews the subregional economic performance. The explanatory approach explains the relevance of the subregional program using both theoretical arguments and empirical evidence, discusses the challenge, and suggests approaches to strengthen the subregional economic zones.

Organization of the Study

Since the study's ultimate objective is to identify policy actions for promoting economic zones created within the subregional economic corridors, it is structured using the "stages model framework" of the public policy literature. According to this model, the process of producing public policies can be divided into five to seven stages. This report uses the Howlett and Ramesh model (Howlett and Ramesh 2003), which proposes five stages of public policy: agenda building, policy formulation, adoption, implementation, and evaluation. The agenda building stage establishes the relevance of an issue or topic for public intervention. Policy formulation means strategy building to address the issue. In policy adoption, the third phase of the policy process, policies are adopted by government bodies for implementation. Implementation involves putting the policies into effect.

Evaluation, the final stage, requires an impact assessment of the policy. In the present study, these stages are adapted and reorganized into four stages: agenda building, strategy development, policy adoption into planning, and policy implementation. The fifth stage of monitoring and evaluation (M&E) is grouped into the implementation stage as part of the implementation strategy. The rest of the study is organized into 10 sections covering these four stages and concluding remarks, as illustrated in Figure 1.

Figure 1. Organization of the Study

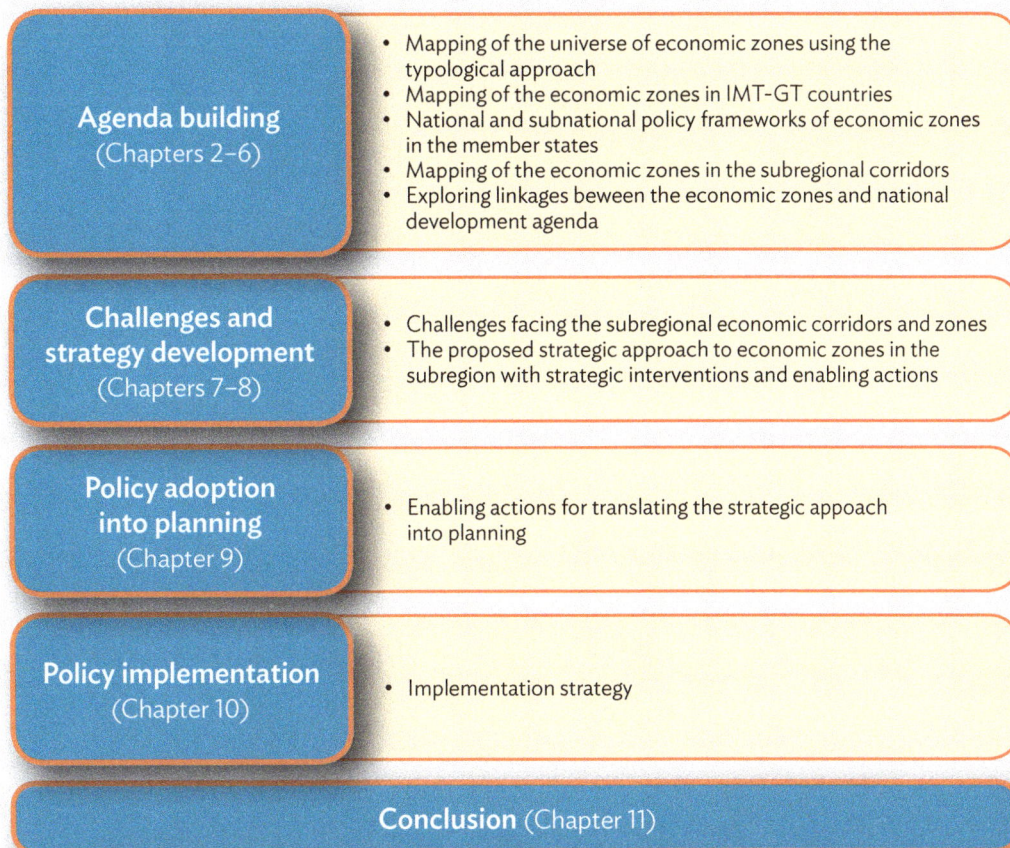

Agenda building (Chapters 2–6)	• Mapping of the universe of economic zones using the typological approach • Mapping of the economic zones in IMT-GT countries • National and subnational policy frameworks of economic zones in the member states • Mapping of the economic zones in the subregional corridors • Exploring linkages beween the economic zones and national development agenda
Challenges and strategy development (Chapters 7–8)	• Challenges facing the subregional economic corridors and zones • The proposed strategic approach to economic zones in the subregion with strategic interventions and enabling actions
Policy adoption into planning (Chapter 9)	• Enabling actions for translating the strategic appoach into planning
Policy implementation (Chapter 10)	• Implementation strategy
Conclusion (Chapter 11)	

IMT-GT = Indonesia–Malaysia–Thailand Growth Triangle.
Source: Author.

Chapter 2

Understanding the Concept of Economic Zones: The Conceptual Framework

Typological Framework of Economic Zones

Economic zones are geographically delimited areas created to offer well-developed industrial spaces with or without special rules and incentives. While the underlying principle for economic zones is clustering general or specialized firms and generating agglomeration economies, they are different from industrial or economic clusters in terms of origin, entry barriers, and composition of enterprises. Clusters are often organically formed geographic concentration of highly interconnected companies, specialized suppliers, and service providers (finance, business consultants and service providers, and academic and technological institutions) linked by commonalities and complementarities without a clearly demarcated geographical boundary (Porter 1998) and as determined by historical legacy (Miller and Côté 1985). They are instrumental in improving the competitiveness of firms in a globalizing world by exploiting the strength of agglomeration economies through collaborative networks developed between economic actors operating within them (Krugman 1991).

In contrast to industrial clusters, economic zones are government-designated or approved industrial areas with specific geographical boundaries. They are developed by public and/or private entities, offering enabling environments in a limited place with a single administrative regime and infrastructure such as roads and power and other utility services (ADB 2018). The zone management authorities determine the type, size, and number of firms operating in them. The collaborative networks and social capital that develop between various economic actors engaged in production processes in natural (organic) clusters may not be seen in these government-designated zones. However, they can evolve and transform into economic clusters to serve as a useful policy tool.

Policy makers across the globe have pinned their hopes on economic zones for promoting agglomeration economies and have been experimenting with innovative designs, features, and incentives to generate the intended effects. This experimentation has led to a proliferation in the number and variety of zones in terms of the objectives, designs, ownership, sectoral composition, and geographical spread. With their evolution, it has become difficult to present any universally accepted, all-encompassing, and comprehensive definition or terminology for economic zones (ADB 2018). Therefore, we use the typological method to understand the concept of economic zones. But there is no uniform typology of economic zones either. They can be categorized in various ways based on their legal regimes or geographical, institutional, and economic characteristics, resulting in diverse typologies, each addressing certain analytical requirements.

In this study, a two-layered classification has been proposed in Figure 2 to map the universe of economic zones. At the top (level 1) is the typology based on the legal perspective, from which there are mainly three types of economic zones: general, special, and hybrid. The distinction

Figure 2. Typological Framework of Economic Zones

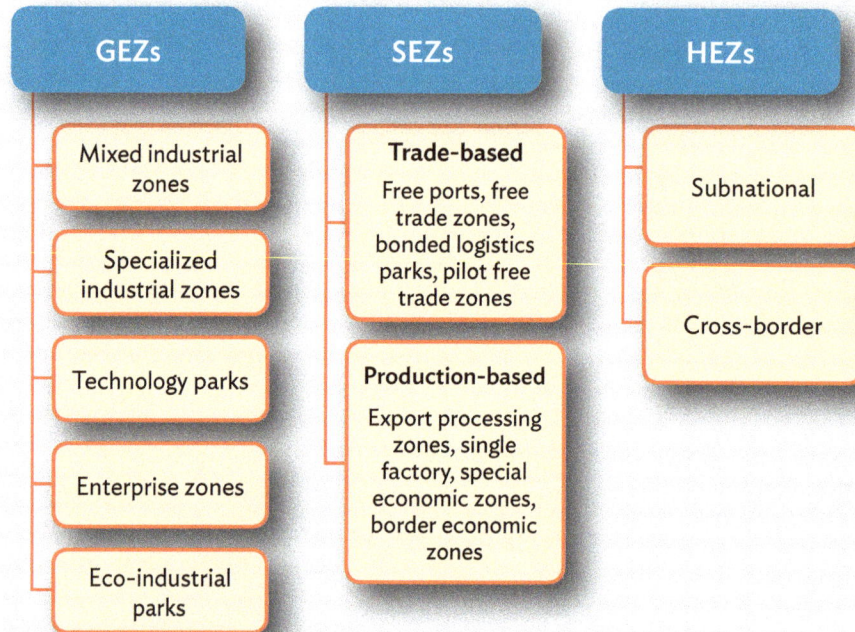

GEZs	SEZs	HEZs
Mixed industrial zones	**Trade-based** Free ports, free trade zones, bonded logistics parks, pilot free trade zones	Subnational
Specialized industrial zones		
Technology parks	**Production-based** Export processing zones, single factory, special economic zones, border economic zones	Cross-border
Enterprise zones		
Eco-industrial parks		

GEZ = general economic zone, HEZ = hybrid economic zone, SEZ = special economic zone.
Source: Author based on various sources.

between general economic zones (GEZs) and SEZs centers mainly around the type of regulatory regime that governs them. Hybrid zones consist of both GEZs and SEZs. Each type of economic zone further branches out according to its functional characteristics in layer 2.

Types of Economic Zones

General Economic Zones or Industrial Zones

According to the United Nations Industrial Development Organization (UNIDO 1997, 10), an industrial zone/park is "a tract of land developed and subdivided into plots according to a comprehensive plan with the provision of roads, transportation, and public utilities, sometimes also with common facilities, for use by a group of manufacturers." Industrial parks started emerging in the early 20th century in advanced countries,[1] and their number exploded post-World War II. The United States (US) alone had

---

[1]   Manchester's Trafford Park, set up in 1896, was the world's first industrial estate (World Bank 1992).

as many as 1,000 industrial parks by 1959, which grew to 2,400 by 1970 (World Bank 1992). In Asia, the first publicly funded industrial estate was set up in Singapore in 1951 (World Bank 1992). The concept spread quickly, with industrial estates emerging and multiplying in other Asian countries. The most common names used are industrial zones, industrial parks, industrial districts, and industrial estates. This chapter uses the term GEZ or industrial zone throughout the analysis. Table 1 provides a second layer typology of GEZs, based on their functions (objectives and forms).

Table 1. Functional Typology of General Economic Zones

GEZ	Description
Mixed type industrial zones	• **Industrial zones of mixed type** accommodate a wide range of industrial activities and firms.
Specialized industrial zones	• **Specialized industrial zones** provide factory accommodations exclusively to industrial units belonging to the same trade in manufacturing or services, with the advantage of common services and facilities organized efficiently and economically for the benefit of the tenants. Some illustrative examples are textile parks, food parks, or halal parks. • A **business park** is a variety of specialized zones with non-pollutive light, high-tech, research-oriented, and service-based businesses clustered in them. They also cover cybercities and centers. • A **specialized business district** is a business hub specialized in a specific type of activity. • **Logistics parks** are specialized zones that provide services related to transport, logistics, and distribution to lower freight and transaction costs, vehicular pollution, congestion, and warehousing costs.
Technology and/or science parks, or science and technology parks	• **Technology parks** are specialized industrial parks with research and development institutions, companies, and markets that facilitate the creation and growth of innovation-based companies through incubation and spin-off processes.[a] • An **innovation district** is a second-generation technology park with a top–down urban innovation ecosystem designed with the ultimate objectives of accelerating innovation and strengthening the location's competitiveness (UNIDO 2015).[b]
Enterprise zones	• **Enterprise zones** are intended to revitalize distressed urban or rural areas by providing tax incentives and financial grants. Most such zones are in the developed countries such as France, the United Kingdom, and the United States.
Eco-industrial parks	• **Eco-industrial parks** are communities of businesses both in manufacturing and services, seeking enhanced environmental and economic performance by sharing common pollution-control services and facilities, and promoting the exchange of goods, services, material, energy, water, waste, and by-products through a process called industrial symbiosis (Lowe 2001, UNIDO 2019).

UNIDO = United Nations Industrial Development Organization.

[a] Science parks are found worldwide, but they are most common in the developed world. According to a United Nations Educational, Scientific and Cultural Organization (UNESCO) list, North America alone hosts 72 science parks. Some of the earliest science and technology parks in Asia were set up in Taipei,China and the Republic of Korea.
[b] Daedeok Innopolis in the Republic of Korea, for instance, has 30 government-funded institutions, 5 universities, over 400 corporate R&D centers, and more than 1,200 high-tech companies. Over 11% of all doctor of philosophy (PhD)-level researchers in the Republic of Korea who specialize in engineering and the natural sciences are residents of this town (Oh and Yeom 2012).

Sources: Author based on the existing literature; D.-S. Oh and I. Yeom. 2012. Daedeok Innopolis in Korea: From Science Park to Innovation Cluster. *World Technopolis Review*. 1 (2). pp. 141–154.; UNIDO. 2015. *Economic Zones in the ASEAN: Industrial Parks,*

Special Economic Zones, Eco Industrial Parks, Innovation Districts as Strategies for Industrial Competitiveness. Hanoi: UNIDO Country Office, Viet Nam; Lowe, E. A. 2001. *Eco-Industrial Parks: A Handbook.* Manila: ADB; and UNIDO. 2019. *Eco-Industrial Parks: Achievements and Key Insights from the Global RECP Programme 2012–2018.*

Special Economic Zones

The SEZ is a distinct variety of economic zone with a specialized legal regime and institutional environment different from the rest of the economy. They are set up to overcome the institutional deficit in developing countries (Aggarwal 2010). Typically, an SEZ is set up for export-oriented enterprises, particularly foreign invested, to offer them a special regulatory regime for exporting activity with a separate customs area, duty-free benefits, streamlined procedures, and its own management authority (Akinci and Crittle 2008). But SEZs can also target import-substituting activity or investment in priority industries. In today's world, they have become a critical tool for developing countries to plug into global value chains (GVCs). According to the United Nations Conference on Trade and Development (UNCTAD) (2019), 147 countries have established nearly 5,400 SEZs within their borders and more than 500 are in the pipeline. Over time, SEZs have evolved into various forms, depending on their objectives (Table 2).

Hybrid Zones

Typically, hybrid economic zones are subdivided into a general zone open to all industries and a separate SEZ area reserved for export-oriented production. Over time, however, hybrid zones have taken a conceptual leap with the emergence of contiguous subnational or transborder economic regions comprising of clusters of SEZs and GEZs.

- **Subnational hybrid zones.** Known as micro-regions, these are groupings of contiguous subnational economic regions being promoted on a premise to create specialized territorial areas that can enable the development of distinct polarities (such as SEZs and GEZs), around which activities, resources, and economic and market relations structure themselves to generate a cumulative process of territorial agglomeration and a virtuous circle of development (Capello 2009). It means that the concept of a single node (a single factory or economic zone) growth pole has been upscaled to a hybrid zone comprising of a cluster of such nodes (SEZs and industrial zones) to exploit externalities generated by them on a larger scale. Regional economic corridors of Malaysia are, for instance, subnational hybrid zones.

- **Cross-border hybrid zones.** The early 1990s witnessed a resurgence of regionalism with an explosion of the number and types of new regional programs across the globe. One of the major developments was extending the concept of micro-regions to transborder regions covering contiguous subnational units from two or more nation-states (Söderbaum 2004, Hutchinson and Chong 2016, Jessop 2003). Originated in Germany, the concept had been in existence since 1958. However, such early regions were in the form of cross-border cooperation by local governments with no formal organizational arrangements (Perkmann 2002). In 1980, the Madrid Convention was signed to provide a legal framework for binational and multinational agreements for cross-border regions between local governments in Europe, which started growing in the 1990s under the Interreg Community Initiative launched by the European Commission.[2] In Europe, these are termed "macro-regions," which are initiated and requested by the European Union (EU) member states (and in some cases non-EU countries) located in the same

---

[2]   By 2002, there were over 70 such zones in Europe (Perkmann 2002).

Table 2. Functional Typology of Special Economic Zones

Trade-Based SEZs	
Free ports	• **Free ports** are a special kind of maritime port or airport where normal tax and customs rules do not apply.
Free trade zone (FTZ)	• An **FTZ** is a small, enclosed area carved out in or adjacent to ports or airports, offering warehousing, storage, and distribution facilities for trade, transshipment, and reexport operations, and located in the ports of entry or airports (UNCTAD 2019).
Bonded logistics parks (BLPs)	• **BLPs** are essentially a variant of free trade zones, offering a range of transport and logistics services to trade, including swift, customer-oriented just-in-time services and value-added logistics services to reduce inventory and raw material procurement costs.
Digital free trade zones (DFTZ)	• A **DFTZ** aims at providing physical and virtual space for SMEs to grow through cross-border e-commerce activities. It is supported by logistics centers set up in selected locations.
Production-Based SEZs	
Export processing zones (EPZs)	• A **first-generation EPZ** is a relatively small, geographically separated area within a country to attract export-oriented processing activity by offering favorable investment and trade conditions. It provides for importing goods to be used in the production of exports on a bonded, duty-free basis. • **Second-generation EPZs** are relatively larger and more sophisticated in terms of the composition of export processing activities, services, and facilities offered than the traditional ones.
Single factory EPZs	• **EPZs** may be promoted as a single firm or factory that is a designated enterprise with EPZ benefits. Mexico's maquilas and Mauritius's EPZs are well-known examples of single factory zones.
Special economic zones (SEZs)	• **SEZs** are mega open industrial towns spread over several square kilometers. The key features of SEZs are that they accommodate all activities, including tourism and retail sales, and permit people to reside on-site with an elaborate on-site social infrastructure. • **Second-generation SEZs** are more specialized and more complex than first-generation SEZs.
Special border economic zones (SBEZs)	• First introduced in Mexico (on US–Mexico border) in the early 1960s in the form of maquiladoras, border economic zones are set up to exploit comparative advantages of border areas that arise due to their climatic conditions, factor endowment, spatial proximity to foreign markets, and the relatively high potential for developing cross-border backward and forward linkages and regional cooperation. • **Cross-border economic zones (CBEZs)** are established by integrating border economic zones on both sides of the border to catalyze economic activity and promote regional cooperation. ADB supports the development of Hekou–Lao Cai and Pingxiang–Dong Dang CBEZs on the PRC–Viet Nam border.

ADB = Asian Development Bank, PRC = People's Republic of China, SMEs = small and medium-sized enterprises, UNCTAD = United Nations Conference on Trade and Development, US = United States.

Sources: Author based on the existing literature; and UNCTAD. 2019. *World Investment Report 2019: Special Economic Zones.* Geneva.

geographical area via the European Council (EU 2017). In Asia, these arrangements arose in the form of growth triangles, growth polygons, and growth areas, which are orchestrated by central governments' policies. One of the earliest subregions in Asia was the Singapore–Johor–Riau (SIJORI) Growth Triangle initiated by Singapore. It was followed by other subregional arrangements in Asia, including Greater Mekong Subregion Economic Cooperation Program, Tumen River Delta Initiative, IMT-GT, and Brunei Darussalam–Indonesia–Malaysia–Philippines East ASEAN Growth Area. Backed by a formal organizational structure, a cross-border subregion is an eco-territorial unit designated to promote economic nodes or zones, which drive growth by accelerating trade, investment flows, and productivity growth, reinforcing local competencies through regional integration. From this perspective, the IMT-GT subregion is a cross-border hybrid zone. Physical integration of institutionally and physically fragmented cross-border areas is necessary to create a contiguous economic spatiality to ensure efficient movement of people, resources, and goods and services. This integration facilitates the promotion of new production hubs and urban centers on the one hand and expansion of the existing one on the other hand. Therefore, economic corridors that support connectivity infrastructure and regulatory reforms are integral to the economic fabric and economic actors (including economic zones of different types) of the subregion (Brunner 2013). In general, the assessment of the subregion (ADB 2015) focuses either on the primary goals (connectivity and regulatory reforms) or the outcomes (gross domestic product [GDP], investment, and trade); the intermediate goal, i.e., the promotion of economic zones, is often ignored. This study deals precisely with this gap.

Chapter 3

General Economic Zones and Special Economic Zones in IMT-GT Countries

Economic zones have been a core element in the economic development strategy of the Association of Southeast Asian Nations (ASEAN) member countries since the early phases of their development. Currently, all ASEAN countries have economic zones of different varieties. The IMT-GT countries were among the first major economies in the region and in Asia that successfully leveraged economic zones to support their manufacturing-centered industrialization strategy (Aggarwal 2019). By the early 1970s, all IMT-GT countries had established both GEZs and SEZs to promote industrial diversification. Since then, GEZs and SEZs remain the centerpiece of the countries' national development strategies. Over time, these countries' economic zones have undergone several transformations with changing macroeconomic contexts. Several types of economic zones have emerged, and their objectives evolved from promoting economic diversification to achieving balanced regional growth to improving competitiveness. This chapter describes the evolution of economic zones in the IMT-GT countries through different economic development phases and maps them using the typological framework outlined in Chapter 2.

Indonesia

Indonesia is known for its abundance of natural resources: spices, wood, rice, copper, tin, gold, coffee, tea, cacao, tobacco, rubber, and—since 1883—mineral oil. At the time of independence, the economy was heavily dependent on commodity trade. In 1949, the government embarked on industrialization as the engine of economic development. Economic development policies evolved with the political regimes and economic crises and can be broadly classified into three distinct phases: 1949–1966, 1967–1999, and 2005–onward (Table 3). Each phase is associated with evolutionary changes in the economic zones.[3]

The first phase of growth (1949–1966) focused on widening the industrial base to support economic development, during which a nationalistic industrialization strategy was adopted with the nationalization of foreign enterprises, extensive foreign exchange controls, and all-pervasive government interventions and regulations as major policy tools (Humphrey 1962). The potential of economic zones in driving industrialization was overlooked. After a short period of industrial momentum, the economic strategy resulted in economic stagnation and structural retrogression. Foreign capital fled while many private companies, dependent on imported materials, shut down or turned to quick-return activities such as trade and currency exchange. In 1967, a change in the political regime led to a series of reforms and marked a shift in the policy regime from nationalist to import-substituting industrialization (Ananta, Soekarni, and Arifin 2011). A systematic approach to

---

[3] 2000–2004 was the recovery period and hence excluded from the analysis.

Table 3. Evolution of Industrial Policy and Economic Zones in Indonesia

Development Phase	Subphases	Industrial Policies Strategic Focus	Industrial Strategy	Evolution of Economic Zones	Evolution of Special Economic Zones
Phase 1: 1949–1966	1950–1966	Widening of the industrial base	Nationalistic industrialization	–	–
Phase 2: 1967–1999	1967–1982	Economic and political stabilization	Import-substituting industrialization	Industrial estates (1970)	Bonded zones (1973) Batam bonded zone (1974)
	1983–1999	Economic growth and regional equity	Export-led growth with selective import substitution	Private industrial estates (1989) Integrated Economic Development Zones (KAPETs) (1996)	Export-oriented production entrepôts (EPTEs) (1993)
Phase 3: 2005–onward	2005–2015	International competitiveness, modernization, and high value-added activities, with regional equity	Cluster development approach	Science and technology park	Free Port of Batam (2007), KEKs (2009)
	2015–onward			Proliferation of industrial estates and improvement in their attractiveness	Bonded logistics Centers (2015) Proliferation of KEKs and bonded zones

– = not applicable, KAPET = Kawasan Pengembangan Ekonomi Terpadu (Integrated Economic Development Zone), KEK = Kawasan Ekonomi Khusus (Special Economic Zone).

Source: Compiled by the author from various sources.

economic planning was adopted with the introduction of the first 25-year development plan from 1969–1970 to 1993–1994. It was implemented through 5-year development plans called Repelita. During this phase, all successive 5-year plans emphasized the importance of redressing regional disparities and spreading economic growth more evenly. It was against this background that various industrial estates and bonded zones were created in Indonesia. However, the growth of industrial estates and bonded zones until the mid-1980s remained limited due to a highly regulated business environment. In the mid-1980s, a series of reforms were initiated to stabilize the economy and promote industrial growth. The functional and geographical scope of both industrial estates and bonded zones was expanded to achieve that goal. The industrial estate business was opened to the private sector.

Further, export-oriented production entrepôts (EPTEs or stand-alone export-processing units) were introduced in 1993. Besides, Indonesia also participated in the SIJORI subregion—comprising Singapore, Johor in Malaysia, and Riau in Indonesia. New types of zones called Integrated Economic Development Zones (Kawasan Pengembangan Ekonomui Terpadu [KAPET]) (Rothenberg et al. 2017) were introduced to accelerate regional development. The emergence of economic zones had transformative effects on the economic structure, as is evident from the share of manufacturing in GDP, which grew from 10% in 1970 to 27% by 1997 (Grabowski and Self 2020). The 1997 Asian financial crisis, followed by political regime change, hit Indonesia hard and took 6 long years to show recovery signs (Tijaja and Faisal 2014). Indonesia entered the third phase of development from 2005 when it scrapped the then planning system and introduced the Rencana Pembangunan Jangka Panjang Nasional (RPJPN, the National Long-Term Development Plan) for 2005–2025 to be implemented through 5-year medium-term plans called the Rencana Pembangunan Jangka Menengah Nasional (RPJMN). The country placed the industry sector at the center of growth to strengthen the economic structure, improve efficiency with modernization, promote local and international competitiveness, strengthen the national industrial base, and achieve more balanced economic development outside Java, focusing on developing resource-based industries. A major thrust was provided to economic zone establishment by envisaging cluster development as the basis of industrial growth. However, the share of manufacturing in GDP did not improve. To give manufacturing a thrust, the government renewed its focus on promoting economic zones in 2015. Since then, efforts to increase the number of economic zones and improve their attractiveness have accelerated. Currently, Indonesia has different types of economic zones, as described below.

General Economic Zones

- **Industrial estates.** The Government of Indonesia started to develop industrial estates in the early 1970s to support the promotion of domestic investment and foreign direct investment (FDI) and encourage regional development. The country's first industrial estate, Jakarta Industrial Estate Pulogadung, was set up in 1970 over 500 hectares of land. In 1971, a presidential decree designated Batam as an industrial estate (Kam and Kee 2009). In 1973, the Batam Industrial Development Authority was established for the industrial development of the island. Subsequently, a series of regulations were issued that formed the legal and technical basis of industrial estate development. A few more industrial estates were set up by public companies, covering 2,596 hectares of land until 1989 (HKI 2019a)—Surabaya Industrial Estate Rungkut (1974), Cilacap Industrial Estate (1974), Medan Industrial Estate (1975), Makassar Industrial Estate (1978), Cirebon Industrial Estate (1984), and Lampung Industrial Estate (1986) (Kwanda 2000). In 1989, the Presidential Decree 53/1989 concerning industrial estates opened industrial estate development to private companies and set the legal and technical standards for their development. This gave an impetus to the industrial estate program. Several local entrepreneurs partnered with foreign companies to set up industrial estates, including Sumitomo, Itochu, and Marubeni from Japan; Hyundai from the Republic of Korea; and Sembcorp from Singapore. By 2007, 40 industrial estates had become operational, 32 of which were on the main Java island (WTO 2007, 57). Since then, the number has further surged. In 2019, 87 operational industrial estates covered over 86,000 hectares of land (HKI 2019a), 45 of which were in Java, 23 in Sumatera, 6 in Kalimantan, and 5 in Sulawesi. In addition, there are 15 industrial estates under construction and 10 in planning.

The most successful, relatively larger, and more diversified industrial estates are in Java, attracting investment in wide-ranging products from technology and knowledge-intensive consumer goods such as electronics and electrical, automotive, and other consumer items to labor-intensive industries (HKI 2015). The concentration of economic activity in Java started with the rise of the colonial economy based on the exports of plantation crops accompanied by the growth of processing industries and infrastructure development. Post-independence, despite the government's transmigration policies, industrial hubs in Java continued to expand and extended to adjacent cities. Java, accounting for 7% of land and home to 57% of the population, contributed 70% of total manufacturing value added in 2014 (ADB 2019a). However, there has been a thrust in promoting economic zones outside Java. New industrial centers are emerging in natural resource-abundant areas outside Java with favorable conditions for growth in processing activities to leverage the opportunities presented by abundant natural resources such as gold, copper, tin, palm, rubber, cocoa, spices, fruits, forests, oil and gas fields, and marine life. The 2020–2024 RPJMN, the National Medium-Term Development Plan, has set the target of promoting 24 industrial estates outside Java by 2024, out of which 9 are strategic priority projects (Government of Indonesia 2020). In the long term (2015–2035), industrial estates in 36 locations are planned, requiring the availability of land of about 50,000 hectares prioritized in areas outside Java and new small and medium-sized enterprise (SMEs) centers so that each district or city owns at least one SME center from 2015 onward (Government of Indonesia 2016).

- ◼ **Kawasan Pengembangan Ekonomi Terpadu (Integrated Economic Development Zones).**
  The Presidential Decree No. 89 of 1996 introduced the Kawasan Pengembangan Ekonomi Terpadu (KAPETs or Integrated Economic Development Zones) to address regional inequality under the program "Acceleration of Development in Eastern Indonesia," which created 13 zones in the island groups of Kalimantan, Maluku, Nusa Tenggara, Papua, and Sulawesi. There is one KAPET in Aceh. These zones are large industrial areas in lagging regions, which are endowed with fiscal and non-fiscal benefits. These are modeled after enterprise zones of France, the United Kingdom, and the US (Table 1). An attractive feature of KAPET is that, along with financial incentives, it offers several nonfinancial incentives, including 31 priority programs in human, economic, and natural resources; facilities and infrastructure; and investment facilitation services (Temenggung 2013). These programs cover business counseling and assistance programs to help small and medium entrepreneurs apply for loans and promote a one-stop shop integrated licensing system. The target is to attract 20% of the national investment to KAPET regions (Organisation for Economic Co-operation and Development [OECD] 2016, 70). However, during 2005–2010, these regions could attract only 3.4% of the national investment (OECD 2016, 70). Several studies have evaluated the performance of KAPET regions, and they all find that, despite attractive features, these zones could not measure up to expectations (Rothenberg et al. 2017, Temenggung 2013, and Rothenberg and Temenggung 2019).

- ◼ **Science and technology parks.** Indonesia took an early lead to promote high technology-intensive industries when supporting aircraft manufacturing and biotechnology research started in the late 1970s. One of the initiatives was to establish the Center for Research, Science and Technology (Puspiptek) in 1976 (Amir 2013), which was developed as a township complex of government-funded research institutes that focused on science and technology development (United Nations Economic and Social Commission for Asia and the Pacific [UNESCAP] 2019). However, the synergies could not be created between institutional science and technology on the one hand and industry on the other. In 2002, the development of technology parks received attention through legislation (Undang-Undang Nomor 18 Tahun 2002), which encouraged the government and private sector to develop the science and technology infrastructure for connecting the industry with institutional research and development (R&D) (Sihotang, Hadian, and Muslim 2019). This led to the creation of Bandung Technopark by the Ministry of Industry (2010); Solo Technopark (2009), Batam Technopark (2018), and Palembang Technopark by their respective city administrations; and Cikarang Technopark (2011) by industry players (Narita 2015). There is no systematic study on these parks or their performance. However, the RPJMN 2015–2019 (Government of Indonesia 2015) gave a major thrust to specialized high-tech parks by proposing 100 science and technology parks (STPs) to support the government's nine-priority agenda called Nawacita. Five ministries or agencies were given the task to build 100 STPs until 2019—(i) Indonesian Institute of Sciences, (ii) Ministry of Agriculture,

(iii) Ministry of Marine Affairs and Fisheries, (iv) National Atomic Agency, and (v) Board for Research and the Application of Technology. The Ministry of Research and Technology—or another appropriate institution—is responsible for overseeing the program at the provincial and district levels. According to the RPJMN 2020–2024, however, there are currently 45 operational STPs with 8 planned for the next 5 years (Government of Indonesia 2020). Many of these STPs are in Java and at public universities.

■ **Halal parks.** A halal zone being built at Modern Cikande Industrial Estate in Serang in West Java is the first industrial estate to receive halal industrial estate status. The 500-hectare halal zone is carved out of the 3,175-hectare Modern Cikande Industrial Estate that PT Modern Group developed in the early 1990s (Winosa 2019). The park will have halal certification facilities with a laboratory for tests by halal guarantee institutions, a halal wastewater treatment plant, and a logistics park with storage facilities. Halal Industrial Park Sidoarjo in East Java Province managed by PT. Makmur Berkah Amanda is another integrated park expected to enter the global market in 2021. Other proposed halal industrial zones are Surya Borneo Industrial Zone in Central Kalimantan, Batamindo Industrial Park (a 17-hectare site for halal cosmetics and pharmaceuticals), Bintan Industrial Park (100 hectares dedicated to halal food and beverages), and Jakarta Industrial Estate Pulogadung (part of a 433-hectare area) (Winosa 2019). The RPJMN 2020–2024 has targeted to develop three areas for halal hubs by 2024.

Special Economic Zones

■ **Bonded zones.** Bonded zones are buildings or confined areas used to process goods and materials for export. These are traditional first-generation export processing zones (EPZs). The bonded zones program was initiated in the early 1970s. The oldest bonded zone is Kawasan Berikat Nusantara on the outskirts of Jakarta set up in 1973 (Table 3). It mainly produces garments for the EU and US markets. Overall, 114 establishments within the Kawasan Berikat Nusantara zone employed 75,551 workers as of 2006 (Sivananthiran 2009). The second major area designated as a bonded zone in 1978 was Batam, near Singapore. It was given the status of an industrial estate earlier. The bonded zone status given to Batam accelerated the growth of this island, transforming it from a fishing village into a hub of electronics, shipbuilding, and oil and gas industries. As of September 2019, there were 1,372 bonded zones in Indonesia (*The Jakarta Post* 2019). Bonded zones are dominated by labor-intensive and medium-technology activities such as electricals and electronics (20%), textile (33%), plastics and rubber (12%), and other items (Damuri, Christian, and Atje 2015). To rebrand bonded zones, the Minister of Finance Regulation No. 131/PMK.04/2018 streamlined the zones' procedures by expediting the permit process, improving the efficiency of online transactional permits, extending the permit's validity period until it is evoked, extending the subcontracting facility, and offering flexible incentives. The government is now seeking to build self-managed bonded zones to promote the efficiency of processes. These zones can run export and import businesses without having to involve custom officers. Of the 1,372 bonded zones, 119 have been granted licenses to self-manage them (*The Jakarta Post* 2019).

■ **Export-oriented production entrepôts (EPTEs).** EPTEs were introduced in 1993. They resemble single enterprise EPZs and enjoy the benefits of bonded zones. They may be set up inside or outside an industrial estate. Their number is not known.

■ **Free trade areas and free ports.** Indonesia has four free trade areas and free ports, officially termed Kawasan Perdagangan Bebas dan Pelabuhan Bebas (KPBPB) or free trade zones (FTZS): Batam, Bintan, Karimun on Riau Islands, and Sabang in Aceh. Batam, Bintan, and

Karimun received the status of free trade areas and free ports in 2007 after having enjoyed that of industrial zone in the early 1970s and bonded zone between 1978 and the early 1990s. Typically, FTZs allow only commercial activities such as sorting, initial or final inspection, packing, repackaging, and repairing or rebuilding machinery (Table 1). However, Indonesia's KPBPB are not traditional commercial FTZs since they allow processing activities. Further, they allow social infrastructure such as housing, condominiums, trade centers, and all related facilities. These zones are, therefore, equivalent to SEZs. The Riau Islands' KPBPB allow the province to attract investment in the shipbuilding and shipyard industry, given its strategic location. More than 150 major maritime, oil and gas, and electronics companies operate in the province (Global Business Guide Indonesia 2014). These KPBPBs also host medical equipment, agribusiness, tourism, metal fabrication, and other sectors. However, technology content is not high in these zones (Rothenberg and Temenggung 2019). In addition to the Riau Islands, there is also a KPBPB at Sabang in the north of Indonesia (Weh Island, Aceh province). The development of a deep seaport in Sabang is a joint venture with India to enhance maritime connectivity to attract investment to the northern part of Indonesia (Roy Chaudhury 2019). However, these KPBPBs will expire in accordance with a predetermined period unless they are subsumed within Indonesia's SEZs program (Article 48, Law number 39 of 2009, concerning SEZs, Government of Indonesia 2009).

- ■ **Bonded logistics centers.** Government Regulation 85/2015 introduced bonded logistics centers (logistics parks) to reduce logistics costs in Indonesia (Hadiputranto, Hadinoto & Partners 2015) (Table 2). Since the launch of the first logistics center in March 2016, the number has grown to 91, spread across various regions of Indonesia (Haryana et al. 2017). The Minister of Finance Regulation No. 131/PMK.04/2018 concerning bonded zones encourages the setting up of integrated bonded zones with bonded logistics centers built within the bonded zone. It is expected to increase the production capacity of bonded zones by optimizing supply chains through bonded logistics centers.

- ■ **Kawasan Ekonomi Khusus.** In 2009, the government introduced a new variety of zones named Kawasan Ekonomi Khusus (KEK or Special Economic Zones) as its most ambitious zone program. These are zones with specific boundaries within Indonesia that carry out economic functions such as export processing activities, logistics (storage, assembly, sorting, packing, distributing, and repairing or rebuilding machinery), and industrial engineering. They are expected to encourage value-added processing activities and exports. They are to be situated in strategic positions (i.e., close to trade and/or maritime routes) and are supported by well-developed external infrastructure. Each SEZ can have different types of zones within them, including bonded zones, export-oriented production entrepôts, and industrial zones, supported by facilities such as ports and logistics services. While there is no export requirement for the units, export-oriented investment is targeted in KEKs. These are second-generation EPZs that focus on processing activity but are characterized by large size and extended facilities and services. The SEZ program took off post-2014; until then, only two SEZs were announced: Sei Mangkei (rubber and palm oil) and Tanjung Lesung (tourism). Currently, there are 15 SEZs, and each one is developed for a set of specific sectors. Of the 15 SEZs, six are tourism zones, while the rest focus on manufacturing. The target industries are essentially resource-intensive, such as palm oil, rubber, fertilizer, logistics, wood, coal, mineral, oil and gas, paper, agro-processing, and energy. In addition to the existing 15, proposals for the establishment of five SEZs are under review.

Hybrid Zones

■ **Economic corridors.** In 2011, the government adopted the concept of (subnational) economic corridors as part of its long-term industrial strategy, the Masterplan for Acceleration and Expansion of Indonesia's Economic Development (MP3EI). One of the key elements of this strategy was developing economic potentials in six economic corridors: Sumatera, Java, Kalimantan, Sulawesi, Bali–Nusa Tenggara, and Papua–Maluku corridors. The corridors are defined as six economic development highways to improve internal connectivity. They are located along coastlines, which would connect the existing economic growth centers and build new economic clusters and business centers on five islands: Java, Sumatera, Kalimantan, Sulawesi, and Papua to support the comparative advantages of the local economies. A study by Berawi, Miraj, and Sidqi (2017) shows that each corridor has its own comparative advantages— Sumatera as national plantation and processing industry corridor, Java as cyber technology innovation and services center, Kalimantan as national energy reserves and processing, Sulawesi as national aquaculture and processing industry, Bali–Nusa Tenggara as national ecotourism corridor, and Papua–Maluku as national ore mining and processing. However, there is no legal framework to implement these corridors. These corridors are to be implemented through medium-term national development programs. Although *Nawacita* replaced the Masterplan for Acceleration and Expansion of Indonesia's Economic Development in 2014, the development of economic corridors continues to be a priority of the government.

In sum, Indonesia started establishing industrial estates and export zones in the early 1970s. The next 3 decades witnessed the emergence of a large and broad-based industry sector. Since 2009, Indonesia has accelerated its drive to attract industrial investment by setting up new economic zones. Post-2015, the drive is given further momentum.

Malaysia

Malaysia, the most rapidly industrializing country in the subregion, has had remarkably high economic growth since its independence in 1957. At the time of independence, Malaysia was an agrarian economy with heavy dependence on rubber and tin exports, and entrepôt trade centered on the free ports of Singapore, Penang, and Malacca. Given the risks associated with the overdependence on commodities trade, the government set out to diversify the economic base by promoting manufacturing with SEZs and GEZs as the centerpiece of its national development strategies. In general, three broad phases of industrial strategies may be identified in Malaysia as manifested in the evolutionary changes in economic zones (Table 4).

Soon after independence, Malaysia embarked on import-substituting industrialization (Rasiah, Crinis, and Lee 2015; Jomo 2013; Rasiah 1996). In the first phase of development (1957–1970), specific industries were promoted primarily through tariff protection and quotas, and the development of basic infrastructure to cater to the domestic market. In 1958, the Pioneer Industries Ordinance Act was introduced, under which companies that were granted pioneer companies' status enjoyed tariff protection along with other tax breaks. Creating industrial areas (GEZs) in Malaysia, unlike in Indonesia, was a critical element of the industrialization strategy in the first phase of growth. The pioneer import-substituting firms grew in number in the 1960s, but widespread unemployment and social unrest in the late 1960s led the government to change the development agenda from

Table 4. Evolution of Industrial Policy and Economic Zones in Malaysia

Phase	Subphase	Strategic focus of Industrial Policies	Trade Regime	Industrial and Spatial Policies	Evolution of GEZs	Evolution of SEZs
Phase 1: 1957–1970	1957–1970	Growth	1st phase import substitution industrialization (ISI)	Pioneer Industries Ordinance Act 1958	1st GEZs developed by state economic development corporations	–
Phase 2: 1971–1990 New Economic Policy	1971–1980	Growth with social restructuring and regional equity	1st phase ISI—1st phase export-oriented industrialization (EOI)	Investment Incentives Act 1968; Industrial Coordination Act 1975	Spread of industrial estates in backward states	Free Export Zone Act 1971. FIZs and LMWs set up.
	1981–1985	Growth with expanding the manufacturing base	2nd phase ISI—1st phase EOI	Heavy Industrial Policy 1981; Look East Policy 1981	Growth of first-generation GEZs	–
	1986–1990	Efficiency and competitiveness	2nd phase EOI	Industrial Master Plan 1 (1986–1995)	Emergence of private industrial parks	Integration of EPZs with the wider economy
Phase 3: 1991–2020 New Development Policy	1991–2000	R&D, innovation, and competitiveness	Knowledge economy	Industrial Master Plan 2 (1995–2005)	Specialized high technology parks 1995, Multimedia Super Corridor 1996	Setting up of free commercial zones for efficiency in logistics
	2001–2010 New Vision	Balanced industrial development with a shift to a knowledge-based economy	Cluster-based industrialization	Industrial Master Plan 3 (2006–2020); Five economic corridors (2005–2020); National Physical Plan 2005	Proliferation of both GEZs expansion of specialized high-tech and halal parks	Emergence of subnational hybrid economic zones
	2011–2020 New Trans-formation Policy	Economic transformation with balanced regional development	High-density cluster-based policy	–	Proliferation of GEZs, specialized high-tech and halal parks	Setting up SBEZ

– = not applicable, EPZ = export processing zone, FIZ = free industrial zone, GEZ = general economic zone, LMW = licensed manufacturing warehouse, R&D = research and development, SEZ = special economic zone, SBEZ = special border economic zone.

Source: Compiled by the author from 5-year development plans.

growth to growth with social restructuring and regional equity (Second Malaysia Plan 1971–1975, Government of Malaysia 1971).

For accelerating economic growth in the second phase (1971–1990), the import-substituting regime was complemented with export-oriented policies in selected sectors, creating EPZs that aimed at attracting labor-intensive assembly-type activity of imported components for trade-based growth and employment generation. To achieve the objective of regional equity, the government set up industrial estates in backward regions. Kedah was the only backward state that had an industrial estate in 1971. However, by the end of 1980, 20 of 76 industrial estates were in the economically backward states of Kedah, Kelantan, Pahang, Sabah, Sarawak, and Terengganu (Fourth Malaysia Plan 1981–1985, Government of Malaysia 1981). Following the Plaza accord 1985, a surge of FDI occurred in the second half of the 1980s from Japan and the Asian newly industrialized economies, intensifying competition for attracting foreign investors. This led to the reorientation of the policy in favor of growth with competitiveness and efficiency. Toward that goal, in the late 1980s, private investment was leveraged to set up economic zones. Further, to improve logistics efficiency, free commercial zones (FCZs) of the FTZ variety were introduced alongside the EPZs, which were initiated in 1971. Alongside, the approach toward EPZs also changed. During the first 15 years, the government kept the EPZs segregated from the rest of the economy, where it continued to follow the import-substituting regime. In 1987, the country adopted the first Industrial Master Plan and attempted to integrate the EPZs with the rest of the economy by facilitating backward linkages of SEZs with the rest of the economy.

In 1991, Malaysia launched Vision 2020, embarking on the third phase of economic development to induce a structural shift from low to high value-added activities through information- and knowledge-led growth along with equity. This led to the creation of high-tech parks and the Multimedia Super Corridor (MSC) modeled after Silicon Valley. Efforts to enhance competitiveness were further intensified following the 1997 Asian financial crisis. In 2006, the Government of Malaysia announced five regional economic corridors to unlock the regions' potential through micro-planning and build competitive cities by integrating economic zones into urban planning. With a thrust in promoting a high productivity society supported by infrastructure, industrial investment, and innovation, a high-density integrated cluster development approach was adopted in the 10th Malaysia Plan 2011–2015 (Government of Malaysia 2011). Based on the principle of concentrated decentralization laid down in the National Physical Plan-2 (Government of Malaysia 2010), this approach has dominated Malaysia's broader industrial strategy since then.

According to the Malaysian Investment Development Authority (MIDA) statistics, over the three economic development phases, Malaysia has created more than 600 economic zones of different types (MIDA), of which 247 are major facilities developed by various government agencies such as the state economic development corporations (SEDCs), regional development authorities (RDAs), port authorities, and municipalities (MIDA, Infrastructure Support).

General Industrial Zones

- **Industrial parks or estates.** As early as 1955, the first industrial site was created in Petaling Jaya in Selangor over 295.42 hectares. It was followed by nine more industrial estates by the end of 1970 (Second Malaysia Plan, Government of Malaysia 1971). Since then, there has been a rapid growth in the number of industrial estates. By the end of 1980, the number of industrial estates rose to 76, covering about 9,650 hectares developed principally by SEDCs (Fourth Malaysia Plan

Government of Malaysia 1981). In the late 1980s, establishing industrial estates was open to the private sector, leading to a proliferation of privately developed industrial estates, particularly in the developed states of Melaka and Selangor. However, no comprehensive statistics are available on the number, type, or location of industrial estates in Malaysia. As stated earlier, MIDA provides information on 247 major economic zones, of which nearly 200 are industrial estates. Most of these parks are in manufacturing and comprise wide-ranging economic activities from light to high-tech ones. Johor hosts the largest number of industrial estates, followed by Terengganu, Melaka, and Selangor. Most parks are mixed in terms of their economic composition. However, there are some parks in single trades as well, including integrated fisheries park (Kelantan), maritime park (Johor), furniture park, biopolymer park (Terengganu), and Aerotech park (Selangor), among others. There are a few business parks (Table 1) for office spaces, but they are concentrated in Johor.

■ **Technology parks.** In the early 1990s, technology parks were launched to cater to technology-intensive industries and R&D activities. Kulim Hi-Tech Park (KHTP), the country's first high-technology park created in 1995, was developed as a self-contained township with a shopping center, a hospital, educational institutions, and recreational facilities. According to MIDA statistics, there are currently 17 public-owned and managed STPs with different nomenclatures and specifications. These include KHTP, Kulim STP, Technology Park Malaysia (Kuala Lumpur), Seri Iskandar Technology Park (Perak), Selangor Science Park (Selangor), Science Park (Penang), and Johor Technovation Park (Johor) (MIDA, Infrastructure Support).

■ **Other Specialized Industrial Parks**

- **Multimedia super corridor.** In 1996, Malaysia set up the MSC as a high-technology business district measuring 15 by 40 kilometers (km) in central-southern Selangor, and anchoring cybercities, cyber centers, and digital hubs, which present an attractive ecosystem to spur Malaysia's information technology industry and digital economy. While digital hubs are the designated areas created for start-ups, cybercities and centers are built to host information technology-related domestic and foreign companies. As of July 2019, 61 cyber cities and centers were within the MSC Malaysia (MIDA, Infrastructure Support). Cyberjaya Technology Park of Malaysia and Technology Park Malaysia (TPM) are two major technology hubs on the MSC. Spread over 2,883 hectares of land, Cyberjaya is an information and communication technology (ICT) city designed to attract world-class multimedia and ICT companies. TPM, spread over 277.61 hectares, is not dedicated only to ICT companies, yet the ICT cluster has recorded the highest tenancy within the park. In addition to companies in cybercities, centers, and digital hubs, eligible ICT-related businesses located outside may also be granted the MSC Malaysia status with the same rights and privileges to promote continuous growth. As of May 2019, the number of active MSC status companies stood at 2,954.[4]

- **Halal parks.** In addition to technology parks and cybercities, a new variety of specialized parks called halal parks emerged when the Negri Sembilan government built the first Halal Products Industrial Park on a 22-hectare land at the Pedas MIEL Industrial Park near Rembau in 2004 (The Halal Journal 2004). A halal park "is a community of manufacturing and service businesses located on a common property with the aim of preserving the integrity of

---

[4]   Malaysia Digital Economy Corporation. Stimulating the Growth of the Nation's Digital Economy. https://mdec.my/what-we-offer/msc-malaysia/.

halal products" (Islam and Madkouri 2018).[5] These are eco-friendly parks for halal products developed with a focus on the green design of park infrastructure, cleaner production, pollution prevention, availability and accessibility of raw materials and ingredients, and energy efficiency. The Halal Industry Development Corporation is responsible for the overall management of these parks, while the Department of Islamic Development Malaysia (Jabatan Kemajuan Islam Malaysia) is responsible for the halal certification. Currently, there are 21 halal parks, of which 14 are HALMAS (accredited halal parks) and the rest are nonaccredited. The largest one is a halal hub in Sarawak, spread over 124,000 hectares of land.

Special Economic Zones

- **Free industrial zones.** Malaysia promulgated its Free Trade Zones law in 1971 to set up traditional EPZs (named FTZs), where the companies had to export 80% of their production to avail themselves of the benefits. The first zone was built near Bayan Lepas airport of Penang in 1971 to revive entrepot trade, attract foreign investment in labor-intensive industries, and promote manufacturing exports. These zones benefited from large waves of foreign investors, particularly from the US, who relocated electric and electronics assembly and processing plants in Penang to avail the advantage of its large, educated pool of English-speaking cheap labor; attractive incentives; and political stability. As a result, the electronics industry grew fast during the 1970s and 1980s and became the main economic growth engine. Encouraged by the success of Bayan Lepas, the government set up more such geographic spaces. In 1990, the name of these zones was changed from FTZs to free industrial zones (FIZs) to reflect their objective better. As of August 2020, there were 22 FIZs located at Johor (Pasir Gudang, Tanjung Pelepa), Melaka (Batu Berendam I, Batu Berendam II, Tanjung Kling), Selangor (Pulau Indah, Sungai Way I, Sungai Way II, Ulu Kelang, Telok Panglima Garang), Perak (Jelapang II, Kinta), Penang (Bayan Lepas I, II, III, IV, Seberang Perai), and Sarawak (Sama Jaya). These zones host electronics and electrical industry, petrochemicals, food products, plastics, medical equipment, general assembly industries, services, logistic, warehousing, e-commerce, etc.

- **Single enterprise zones.** In 1975, Malaysia introduced the scheme of single factory EPZs termed as licensed manufacturing warehouses (LMWs) under Section 65/65A of the Customs Act 1967. An LMW is a factory for manufacturing and warehousing the approved products on the same premise. They enjoy the same benefits of FIZs and can be set up where FIZs do not exist. Companies with 80% or more exports qualify for the status of LMWs.

- **Free commercial zones.** The Free Zones Act 1990 introduced FCZs of the traditional FTZ variety (Table 1). Commercial activities conducted in these zones include trading (except retail trading), breaking bulk, grading, repacking, relabeling, transshipment, and transit. All major ports and international airports in Malaysia are integrated with free zones, which have been instrumental in attracting foreign companies to establish regional distribution centers and turning Malaysia into a major distribution hub by hosting companies such as France's oil and gas giant Technip SA, Deutsche Post DHL, Vale SA (the world's biggest iron ore producer), and Schlumberger Ltd. Currently, there are 21 FCZs at the north, south, and west of Port Klang, Port Klang Free Zone, Pulau Indah MILS Logistic Hub, Butterworth, Bayan Leas, Kuala Lumpur International Airport (KLIA), Rantau Panjang, Pengkalan Kubor, Stulang Laut, Johor Port, and Port of Tanjung Pelepas.

5   Islam R., and El Madkouri, F. 2018. Assessing and ranking HALMAS parks in Malaysia: An application of importance-performance analysis and AHP. *Journal of Islamic Marketing*. 9 (2). pp. 240–261.

■ **Digital free trade zone.** It is a digital export platform for small and medium companies to carry out cross-border e-commerce and benefit from globalization. Digital free trade zones (DFTZs) have three components:

- **e-fulfillment hub.** It helps SMEs and other businesses export their goods easily, with the help of leading fulfillment service providers. Alibaba, a Chinese company, hosts its regional e-fulfillment hub at KLIA Air Cargo Terminal 1, which Pos Aviation has developed.

- **Satellite services hub.** It connects SMEs and businesses with leading players who offer services like financing, last-mile fulfillment, insurance, and other important services in cross-border trade.

- **e-services platform.** It allows for direct communication between Malaysian businesses and Chinese manufacturers. Lazada Malaysia serves as the e-commerce platform for the MSME players.

  Through MIDA, the government has approved eight e-fulfillment projects as of March 2019, with more in the pipeline (Nee 2019). In the second phase, a logistics center over a 24.28 hectare plot will be operational at KLIA to support the DFTZ. In addition, facilities will be created within Penang International Airport, the Subang Airport, and Port Klang (Free Malaysia Today 2019). The number of companies on DFTZ has grown from 1,972 in late 2017 to 13,000 by the end of 2019 (Malaysia Digital Economy Corporation website).

■ **Special border economic zone.** An SBEZ is coming up in Bukit Kayu Hitam, a Malaysia–Thailand border town, as a duty-free logistics hub covering 6,000 hectares of land, which will be developed by the Government of Malaysia jointly with the Kedah state government.

Hybrid Zones

■ **Regional economic corridors.** The idea of national economic corridors was mooted in the Ninth Malaysia Plan (2006–2010) (Government of Malaysia 2006), following which, in the 2008 Mid-Term Review of the Ninth Plan (Government of Malaysia 2008), the government announced five economic corridors for balanced growth and to move the economy up the value chains as a key objective. These corridors are East Coast Economic Region (ECER), Iskandar Malaysia in Johor, Northern Corridor Economic Region, Sabah Development Corridor, and Sarawak Corridor of Renewable Energy (SCORE). Unlike Indonesia, which focuses on subnational connectivity through regional economic corridors, Malaysia develops these corridors as essentially micro-regions that transcend the boundaries of Malaysian administrative states to generate agglomeration economies by upscaling the clusters through factor complementarities and pooling of resources. Iskandar targets creative industries, Northern Corridor Economic Region automobile and aerospace, ECER petrochemical, Sabah Development Corridor tourism and palm oil, and Sarawak Corridor of Renewable Energy hydropower. The overall development of these regions in Peninsular Malaysia is guided by the spatial strategy of concentrated decentralization, aiming to concentrate the resources into a few priority urban areas with the greatest growth potential while protecting the rural areas and natural environment (National Physical Plan-2 2010–2020, Government of Malaysia 2010). In addition to the federal government's extensive subsidies, the state governments have also developed some incentives to encourage investors in industrial areas in these concentrations.

In August 2009, Malaysia introduced an SEZ within the ECER micro-region, which stretches from the district of Kerteh, Terengganu in the north to the district of Pekan, Pahang in the south for integrated development of commercial, residential, education, industries, service, and knowledge components as part of the concentrated decentralization strategy (high-density cluster approach). Four separate zones are to be established within this SEZ to promote and focus on groupings of industries: manufacturing, agro-industry, petrochemical, tourism, ICT, and logistics. Officially named the ECER SEZ, it is a submicro region with no distinct administrative framework.

Thailand

Economic development and modernization started in Thailand when some measures were taken to promote agriculture and major reforms were introduced in the corvée labor system (unpaid labor under the feudal system) and public administration through the late 19th and early 20th century (Kelly et al. 2012). The process intensified when the government launched the first 5-year National Economic and Social Development Plan in 1961 (Government of Thailand 1961), focusing on infrastructure and agricultural extension (Pombhejara 1965). Since then, three phases of industrial development policy could be identified: 1961–1975, 1976–2001, and 2002 onward (Table 5).

During the first phase (1961–1976), economic development was sustained by expanding the agriculture sector and infrastructure development, such as the construction of dams for

Table 5. Evolution of Industrial Policy and Economic Zones in Thailand

Phase	Subphase	National Objectives	Industrial Strategy	Evolution of GEZs	Evolution of SEZs
Phase 1: 1961–1975	1961–1976	Growth (agriculture and infrastructure)	Import substituting	First industrial zone in 1971	None
Phase 2: 1976–2001	Phase 2: 1977–1981	Growth (light manufacturing)	Import substituting complemented by export-oriented regime	Emergence of industrial parks in Bangkok	Emergence of industrial estates in Bangkok
	Phase 3 1982–2001	Growth with industrial dispersal through a zoning system	Step-by-step liberalization	Expansion of industrial parks	Spread of industrial estates across Thailand
Phase 3: 2002–onward	Phase 4: 2002–2014	Competitiveness and regional development	Liberal economic regime, regional development incentives dropped	Science and technology parks	–
	2014–onward	Competitiveness	Liberal economic regime	–	SEZs in border areas, ESDZ

– = not applicable, EEC = Eastern Economic Corridor, ESDZ = eastern special development zone, GEZ = general economic zone, SEZ = special economic zone.
Source: Compiled by the author from various sources.

irrigation purposes and hydroelectric power and other public utilities (Meesook, Tinakorn, and Vaddhanaphuti 1987). In the industry sector, the government adopted selective, protective, and promotional policies to develop domestic industrialization and funded it by foreign exchange earned from the export of primary products. The manufacturing sector was offered a high level of protection combined with tariff exemptions on their imported raw materials and incentives. As a result of the active promotion and protection policy, private investment increased rapidly during this period; the US military bases and foreign aid from the US and the World Bank were other factors that benefited private investment (Meesook, Tinakorn, and Vaddhanaphuti 1987).

In 1971, Banchan Industrial Estate, Thailand's first government-developed industrial estate, was created. Soon after, the first private sector-developed industrial estate named Nava Nakorn Industrial Zone by Nava Nakorn Public Company Limited emerged. In 1972, IEAT was established. However, there was little progress in the evolution of economic zones. In the mid-1970s, a series of crises hit the economy, including the oil crisis of 1973, the closure of the US military base that ended the procurement boom, and a slowdown in agriculture. In 1977, the Investment Promotion Act B.E. 2520 was enacted to bring a favorable climate for investors. It was followed by the IEAT Act (1979), which provided the legal framework to build, manage, and govern industrial estates and industrial ports toward promoting the country's industry sector expansion. Thus, the country entered the phase of cluster-based industrialization, with economic zones being its linchpin.

In the early 1980s, the Eastern Seaboard Development Program was proposed, focusing on heavy industry plants to manufacture soda ash, fertilizers, and petrochemicals. The number of industrial estates started proliferating, particularly in the Eastern Seaboard area, which became a hub of automobile and petrochemical industries. Industrial estates greatly benefited from the G5 Plaza Accord of 1985. The FDI from Japan and Taipei,China played an important role in economic growth over this period. Thailand abolished protection and regulation measures step by step to stimulate trade and investment in industrial estates. Soon it shifted to a high-growth trajectory and came to be dubbed as the fifth Asian Tiger after Singapore, Malaysia, Indonesia, and the Philippines (Hussey 1993).

During the post-Asian financial crisis, the government shifted the focus to industrial competitiveness to enter the third phase of development. It was during this period that high-tech parks began to be established. However, two major initiatives that would have far-reaching implications for the economy have been launched in post-2014 period. First, the Eastern Economic Corridor (EEC) has been designated as an SEZ to target Industry 4.0[6] to help Thailand become a high-value economy. Second, a strong emphasis on the development of border areas has been supported by setting up the SBEZs (officially named SEZs) to relocate agriculture and labor-intensive industries from the center to border areas to utilize cheap labor and resources of the neighboring countries and promote cross-border supply chains with neighboring countries. Thailand was relatively a latecomer in the active industrial development process, but various economic zones strongly aligned with the national development agenda facilitated the country in the catch-up process.

---

[6]   Thailand 4.0 targets 10 industries equally divided into two segments: 5 S-curved and 5 new S-curved industries. The five S-curved industries include new-generation automotive; smart electronics; affluent, medical, and wellness tourism; agriculture and biotechnology; and food. The new S-curved industries are nascent high-tech industries, which include manufacturing robotics, medical hub, aviation and logistics, biofuels and biochemicals, and digital industries.

General Economic Zones

- **Industrial parks or zones.** Industrial parks are entirely established and managed by private developers. These private industrial parks (or zones) are not allowed to be named industrial estates because industrial parks do not enjoy the special rules and management benefits of industrial estates. Businesses in these parks do not have access to the single solution center facility offered in industrial estates. They need to negotiate with the park or zone operators, who are private sector entities, for services and benefits.

- **Thailand Science Park.** The development of STPs was proposed in the Sixth National Economic and Social Development Plan 1987–1991 (Government of Thailand 1987). But the country's first science park was established in 2002 by the National Science and Technology Development Agency (NSTDA) on 32.37 hectares of land in Pathum Thani province in the northern outskirts of Bangkok. Managed by the Technology Management Center of the NSTDA under the Ministry of Higher Education, Science, Research and Innovation, Thailand Science Park (TSP) has been created to support the development of technology-intensive businesses, and R&D and innovation in the private sector. Phase 1 of TSP, with 14 hectares of built-up space, is fully occupied by the NSTDA and its four national research centers: National Center for Genetic Engineering and Biotechnology, National Metal and Materials Technology Center, National Electronics and Computer Technology Center, and National Nanotechnology Center. Phase 2 adds 12.7 hectares of space for private companies.[7] It is inhabited by over 100 corporate tenants, of which 30% are international companies. The proximity between research institutions and commercial companies provides an opportunity for corporate tenants to gain access to highly skilled personnel, including over 2,000 full-time NSTDA researchers, of whom some 700 are doctor of philosophy (PhD) scientists. Almost half of TSP firms belong to the food and agriculture, electronics, robotics, and automation industries.

- **Regional science parks.** After TSP's success, there have been initiatives to establish science parks in other parts of the country. In 2004, the government approved the Science and Technology Strategic Plan (2004–2013), which proposed the regional science parks (RSP) project and designated it to be executed in three main regions of the country (northern, northeastern, and southern) to enhance science, technology, and innovation capability in agriculture and industrial manufacturing sectors (Phasukavanich 2003). However, it was not until 2013 that they could be officially organized in full scale. In 2013, the government endorsed the involvement of the Science Park Promotion Agency to make the parks fully functional. Unlike TSP, RSPs are primarily led by a network of regional universities. The Northern Science Park (started in 2004) is managed by Thailand Institute of Scientific and Technological Research, headquartered at Chiangmai University. Several local universities operate the northeastern and southern science parks. Initially, they provided only "soft" services to local firms through technology business incubation facilities, technological consultancy, training and contract, and collaborative research projects. There were no physical infrastructure or "hard" facilities such as rental space and laboratories. However, since 2013, business incubation and infrastructure development have been the key elements of their implementation strategy. RSPs generated a $16 million regional economic impact between 2013 and 2016 (Tridech 2016). During this period, they managed to get 37 patents to their credit. Under planning is Amata Science City, the first privately owned STP in Thailand (Tantanasiriwong 2016).

---

[7]   Thailand Science Park. About TSP. https://www.sciencepark.or.th/index.php/en/about-tsp/ last.

■ **Food innopolis.** These areas aim to develop Thailand into an R&D hub for the food industry. A food innopolis involves an innovation area well-equipped with sound infrastructure and human resources in fields related to food science, technology, and innovation through a collaborative effort among academic institutions, research institutions, and the private sector. Innovation-based businesses can enjoy attractive investment privileges and incentive packages for their operation in these areas. So far, 13 sites have been given the status of food innopolis; all of them are in universities, except for one within the TSP. The Ministry of Higher Education, Science, Research and Innovation is the key implementing agency of all types of science parks.

Special Economic Zones

■ **Industrial estates.** Since 1979, the IEAT has been instrumental in developing Thailand's industrial estates. There are two types of industrial estates: (i) those with general and free zones, and (ii) those with general zones only. A general industrial zone is defined as "a tract of land designated for the carrying out of industry, service or any undertaking which is beneficial to, or connected with, industry or service," while free zones are "tracts of land designated for the carrying out of industry, commerce or any undertaking in connection with industry or commerce for economic benefit, security of State, public welfare, environmental management or other necessary reasons as determined by the Board" (IEAT Act 1979, Section 4). Free zones are entitled to exemptions from import and export duties, excise, and value-added tax. The industrial estates with free zones also offer separate custom areas. However, irrespective of their constitution, all industrial estates enjoy the special legal regime to target large foreign and domestic investment and provide a range of industrial infrastructure and, in some cases, social infrastructure (as informed during country consultations). They are essentially second-generation EPZs.

Industrial estates are developed by the IEAT solely or in partnership with one or more private developers who may provide maintenance services and/or build public utilities and infrastructure for business operations. All these sites must be situated on a minimum of 81 hectares, with 60%–70% of the total area set aside for factory usage. As of July 2019, there were 57 industrial estates in Thailand, with a total area of 23,173 hectares, and 5,742 tenants and 479,784 workers (as informed during the country consultations in July 2019). The eastern region housed 75% of the total. Of the total area, only 13% (3,111 hectares) was vacant as per the IEAT. In the second half of 2019, the establishment of four more industrial estates was announced, all in the eastern region (IEAT 2019).

■ **Eco-industrial towns.** Following a court order in 2009 to suspend 76 industrial projects in Map Ta Phut industrial region due to the rising levels of water and air pollution, adversely affecting people's health and the environment (Excell and Moses 2012), the Ministry of Industry launched the program "Eco-Industrial Town (EIT) Development" in 2010 to develop environmentally and socially sustainable industrial communities. It was piloted in five regions to establish industrial estates that maintain equilibrium between physical, economic, social, and environmental elements using integrated solutions. The IEAT adopted an EIT development master plan covering 10 years (2010–2020), divided into two phases. In Phase 1, EIT standards and master plans were prepared and implemented in 15 pilot industrial estates. In Phase 2, the efficiency criteria were enhanced, stakeholders' participation was encouraged, and new projects were initiated to cover the remaining provinces. In 2016, 19 industrial estates were certified as "eco champions." The IEAT has set the long-term goal of upgrading all existing industrial estates into EITs (IEAT 2017).

■ **Special economic zones (special border economic zones).** In 2015, Thailand commenced establishing SEZs in 10 provinces: Tak, Sa Kaeo, Trat, Mukdahan, Songkhla, Chiang Rai, Nong Khai, Nakorn Phanom, Kanchanaburi, and Narathiwat. These SEZs are in border areas and match the description of SBEZs. The government provides highly attractive incentives for businesses operating in 13 industries in SEZs. Each SEZ has its own target industries, which are decided and categorized by the SEZ area. The 13 industries are agriculture, fishery, and related businesses; ceramics; garments, textiles, and leather; home furniture; jewelry and fashion accessories; medical equipment; automobiles, engines, and parts; electrical appliances and electronics; plastics; medical products; logistics; industrial estates; and activities that support tourism. Most of the target industries are labor-intensive. The objective is to connect the selected areas with the neighboring countries in terms of trade, economy, and investment to benefit from the large labor pool in the cross-border areas. The Government of Thailand has relaxed rules on foreign labor to support the SEZs. According to the National Economic and Social Development Council (NESDC), as of July 2020, 82 projects in 10 SEZ provinces were approved, with a total investment amount of $17.6 billion. Tak SEZ leads the pack, with 33 projects in textile and garments, plastics, automotive, machinery and parts, etc., followed by Songkhla, Sa Keao, and Kanchanaburi SEZs (NESDC 2020). Songkhla, which has attracted 15 projects, accounts for most (51%) of SEZs' total investment.

■ **Eastern special development zone.** The EEC covering three provinces—Chonburi, Rayong, and Chachoengsao—has recently been designated as an eastern special development zone (ESDZ) with a special legal regime, spanning 1,328,500 hectares of land. It is around seven times as large as Shenzhen. It is the next level SEZ for economic activities and urban development and modernization of cities. The region has already attracted many industrial development projects in automotive, oil and gas, and petrochemicals. In 2008, it accounted for about 8% of Thailand's GDP, 40% of all chemical products, and 44% of all basic metal products (Board of Investment 2008). Promoted as a hybrid zone, it hosts 14 industrial estates, 12 private industrial parks, and two deepwater ports of Laem Chabang and Map Ta Phut (Board of Investment 2008). The designation of the corridor as a special development zone (SDZ) is in the direction of leveraging the region's competitive advantage to implement Industry 4.0. Besides, a new variety of zones has been introduced within the ESDZ—special economic promotional zones, which prioritize the development of target industries directly or indirectly. A clear distinction has been made between the services and manufacturing promotional zones.

  ● **Special services promotional zones.** These zones include the Eastern Aviation City, the EEC Innovation Zone, and the EEC Digital Innovation Zone. Under the EEC Innovation Zone, the National Innovation Agency, a part of the Ministry of Higher Education, Science, Research and Innovation, plans to promote science parks, Space Krenovation Park, and the Sriracha Innovation District in Chonburi province. Digital Park Thailand (the digital innovation zone) targets global digital players with high-speed broadband infrastructure, data center, and satellite earth station.

  ● **Industrial promotional zones.** These zones will include industrial estates, smart parks, and industrial estates with targeted industries.

The ESDZ is one of Thailand's most ambitious agglomeration programs, which is expected to emerge as the primary growth pole of the country and boost its GDP growth to 5% a year, creating more than 100,000 jobs and generating income exceeding B450 billion annually.

■ **Southern Economic Corridor.** The government has launched an initiative to developing another growth pole, the Southern Economic Corridor (SEC), to spur economic growth in the southern provinces, which have a comparative advantage in local raw materials such as rubber and palm. While the ESDZ aims at achieving a high value-added economy, the SEC seeks to develop Thailand's upper southern region to be the main port of the country's western side, and supporting the Thai economy on bio-based industry and coastal tourism. The SEC covering the four provinces of Chumphon, Ranong, Surat Thani, and Nakhon Si Thammarat is proposed to be connected to the ESDZ (or EEC) to create a trade hub. The plan includes a high-speed rail network, a double-track rail system, road construction, and Ranong port upgrade. In addition, there is a proposal for the development of model cities in southern border provinces under the "Triangle of Stability, Prosperity, and Sustainability" project to promote investment in Southern provinces.

■ **Other economic corridors.** There are proposals to develop a bio-economy corridor in the northeastern and central regions, and a Lanna creative development corridor in the north. While the bio-economy corridor is expected to create immense opportunities in Thailand, the Lanna creative corridor of crafts and folk art will promote skills in crafts and folk art, innovation, and creativity; generate employment; and strengthen international recognition of Lanna crafts and art in new markets.

Mapping of General Economic Zones and Special Economic Zones in Indonesia, Malaysia, and Thailand

As discussed in Chapter 3, economic zones have been the centerpiece of the development strategy in all three IMT-GT countries. As the countries' development agendas evolved, changes were introduced in the economic zones to support them. As a result, several functional and spatial variants of the economic zones have spawned over the years, with their objectives evolved from industrial diversification to balanced regional development to industrial upgrading to urban development. While new types of zones are emerging, the traditional ones are still in operation in all three countries.

Table 6 maps the economic zones of Indonesia, Malaysia, and Thailand using the typological framework presented in Figure 2. It provides the generic category, the name used, the year of initiation, and the number of these zones. The number of industrial estates reported for Malaysia is based on the MIDA's list of 247 industrial estates promoted by the state. Information on other economic zones in the country is compiled from relevant official sources. It must also be noted that the EEC in Thailand is essentially a hybrid zone (Figure 2). However, it is included in the second-generation SEZs, as the entire area is given the SEZ status.

Based on the data in Table 6, two major observations can be made. First, there has been a proliferation of both the number and types of economic zones in the three IMT-GT countries, which have been continuously expanding their economic zones in newer directions. The three countries have 2,092 cluster-based economic zones (excluding the hybrid and single enterprise zones), of which 497 (24%) are general zones and the rest are cluster-based SEZs (1,595) of different varieties. Second, Indonesia has the largest number of SEZs (1,482), followed by Thailand

Table 6. Economic Zones in IMT-GT

		Indonesia	Malaysia	Thailand	Total
		General Economic Zones			
Industrial estates/parks/ business parks	Name used	Industrial estates/ parks	Industrial estates/ parks/ business parks	Industrial parks/ zones	
	Number	87	210	21	318
	Year of initiation	1970	1955	1960	
Technology parks (first generation)	Name used	Techno parks	High-tech/science parks	Science parks	
	Number	4	17	2	23
	Year of initiation	2002	1995	2002	
Technology parks (second generation)	Name used	Science and technology parks	MSC cyber cities/ centers	RSP and Food Innopolis	
	Number	45	61	16	122
	Year of initiation	2015	1996	2013	
Specialized industrial parks	Name	Halal parks	Halal parks	–	
	Number	Under construction	21	–	21
	Year of initiation	2020	2004	–	
Enterprise zone	Name	KAPETs	–	–	
	Number	13	–	–	13
	Year of initiation	1996	–	–	
Eco-industrial parks	Type	Pilot projects	Halal eco-industrial parks, voluntary efforts	Eco-Industrial towns projects	
	Year of initiation	2004	Not known	2010	
		Special Economic Zones			
FTZs: First generation	Name used	Bonded logistic centers	Free commercial zones	–	
	Number	91	21		112
	Year of initiation	2015	1990		
FTZ: Second generation	Name used	–	Digital free trade zone	–	
	Number	–	1	–	1
	Year of initiation	–		–	
EPZs (cluster based); Traditional	Name used	Bonded zones	Free industrial zones	–	
	Number	1,372	22	–	1394
	Year of initiation	1973	1971	–	

continued on next page

Table 6 *continued*

		Indonesia	Malaysia	Thailand	Total
	Special Economic Zones				
Second-generation EPZs	Name used	Special economic zones for manufacturing	–	Industrial estates	
	Number	9	–	57	66
	Year of initiation	2012	–	1979	
Enterprise specific EPZs	Name used	Export-oriented production entrepôts	LMWs	–	
	Number	Not known	2096	–	–
	Year of initiation	1992	1975	–	
Border economic zones	Name used	–	SBEZ	SEZs	
	Number	–	1	10	11
	Year of initiation	–	2019	2015	
SEZ: Traditional	Name used	Free trade zones	–		
	Number	4	–		4
	Year of initiation	2007	–		
SEZs: Second generation	Name used	Special economic zones for tourism	–	Eastern economic corridor	
	Number	6	–	1	7
	Year of initiation	2012	–	2018	
Hybrid zones*	Name used	Regional corridors	Regional economic corridors	–	
	Number	6	5	–	
	Year of initiation	2009	2006	2018	

– = not applicable, EPZ = export processing zone, FTZ = free trade zone, IMT-GT = Indonesia–Malaysia–Thailand Growth Triangle, KAPET = Kawasan Pengembangan Ekonomi Terpadu (Integrated Economic Development Zone), LMW = licensed manufacturing warehouse, MSC = Multimedia Super Corridor, RSP = regional science park, SBEZ = special border economic zone, SEZ = special economic zone.

* The hybrid zones are not strictly comparable.

Source: Compiled by the author from various sources.

(68) and Malaysia (45). Malaysia leads in GEZs (309), followed by Indonesia (149) and Thailand (39). Around 91% of total zones in Indonesia are SEZs, 72% in Thailand, and 13% in Malaysia.

SEZs are essentially a safety valve in development. They allow the government to adopt a special legal and institutional regime to fast-track economic growth without changing the institutional setup in the wider economy. At lower levels of development, the wider the distance between the institutional regime of the wider economy and that of the SEZs, the more attractive the SEZs are. However, institutional transformations occur with economic development, reducing the institutional distance between existing SEZs and the wider economy (Aggarwal 2017). At the same time, policy makers set more ambitious goals, which, in turn, may pose new institutional challenges to be addressed in SEZs. To address these dynamics, SEZs must evolve to remain relevant and attractive. Once the economy reaches a threshold level of economic development, SEZs become less relevant. Thus, while Malaysia—the most developed of the three countries and well on its way to cross the threshold into high-income country status—continues to host traditional EPZs, it increasingly relies on GEZs. In contrast, with the lowest GDP per capita in the group, Indonesia has been focusing on creating SEZs to give a major thrust to economic growth and promoting new growth poles. Thailand has also adopted a vigorous two-pronged SEZ strategy on its way to catch up. On the one hand, it has adopted the SEZ route to upgrade the most successful industrial hub in the country by targeting Industry 4.0. On the other hand, it plans to promote new growth poles through SEZs in hitherto underdeveloped areas and has set up SEZs in border areas to shift low value-added activities in these areas and leverage cross-border synergies. In sum, explosive growth in the use of SEZs is underway in the three subregional countries, with new types of SEZ models emerging in all of them.

Structural Features of Economic Zones

The evolutionary changes in the objectives and types of economic zones have been accompanied by changes in their characteristics, both structural and institutional. In what follows, the structural features are summarized using the framework provided in Figure 3. The latter, comprising of governance structures and legal regulations, are explored in Chapter 4.

Size. Economic zones are growing larger, more diverse, and more complex. While the traditional export processing type zones are still operating in all three countries, they are complemented by more complex varieties. Further, new hybrid zones spread across some states, and provinces are emerging with multiple growth poles formed by the clusters of GEZs and SEZs located within them.

Composition. Economic zones in the region are essentially dominated by manufacturing. However, services zones have also started emerging. A successful example of a services zone is the MSC in Malaysia. Indonesia has set up tourism zones, while Thailand has introduced special services zones within the EEC. Further, the economic zones are increasingly becoming specialized. Early zones were multi-activity zones. However, in recent years, SEZs are being set up to target priority industries with the expectations of accelerating the catch-up process through agglomeration economies.

Level of development. In the early stages of their evolution, SEZs in all three countries were dominated by labor-intensive assembly-type production activity in textile and electrical and electronics industries, while industrial estates hosted import-substituting light and heavy industries. Over time, SEZs also upgraded and attracted skill-intensive activities in various industries such as electronics and electricals, automotive, rubber, food products, textiles and garments, and chemical and petrochemical. The third-generation economic zones have currently emerged, catering to high value-added and relatively more technologically sophisticated manufacturing. In parallel with this, efforts have been made to promote the fourth generation STPs to contribute to technology generation and spillovers. There is an increasing awareness of environmental concerns as well. However, these concerns have not yet been translated into the creation of eco-industrial parks as defined in Table 1.

Figure 3. Structural Features of Economic Zones: A Framework

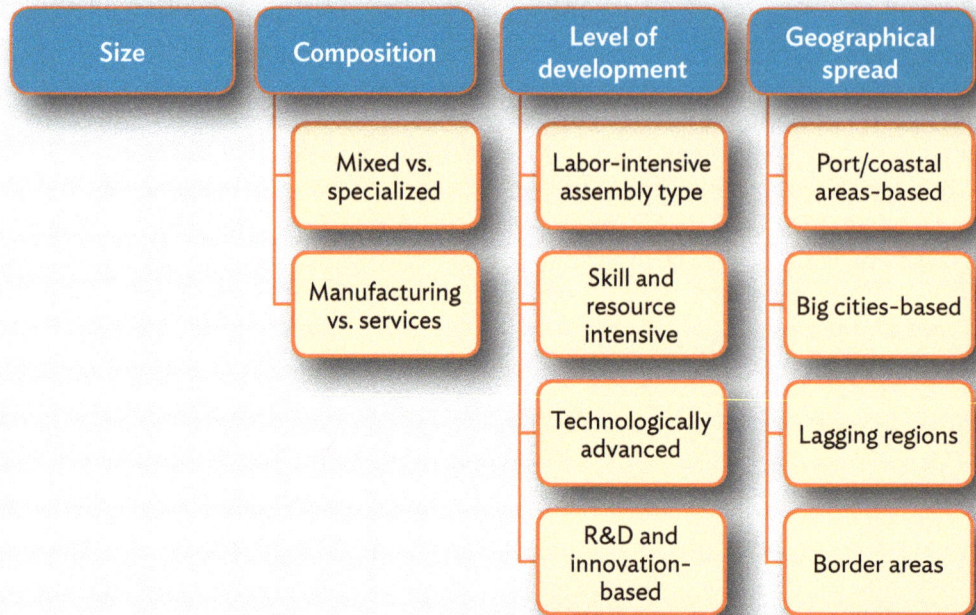

Size	Composition	Level of development	Geographical spread
	Mixed vs. specialized	Labor-intensive assembly type	Port/coastal areas-based
	Manufacturing vs. services	Skill and resource intensive	Big cities-based
		Technologically advanced	Lagging regions
		R&D and innovation-based	Border areas

R&D = research and development.
Source: Author based on Aggarwal, A. 2012a. *Social and Economic Impact of SEZs in India.* Delhi: Oxford University Press.

Location. Originally, economic zones were set up in the most strategic locations, essentially in coastal areas: Penang, Selangor, and Melaka in Malaysia; Java in Indonesia; and Bangkok and surrounding regions in Thailand. In recent years, economic zones are increasingly being located in lagging interior and border regions. The SBEZ in Malaysia, SEZs in Thailand, and KEKs in Indonesia essentially target border or lagging regions with some potential.

To sum up, economic zones have evolved into larger spatial dimensions, complex structures, more comprehensive high-tech orientation, and flexible locations irrespective of whether they are SEZs or GEZs. This evolution reflects a strong commitment, pragmatic approach, and dynamic learning toward economic zones adopted by all three countries, which are critical components of a strategic zones policy (Aggarwal 2012b).

Chapter 4

Legal and Institutional Framework of General Economic Zones and Special Economic Zones

Legal and Institutional Framework

This section presents the legal and institutional framework of economic zones in the three IMT-GT countries to enhance our understanding of their operations. The framework comprises three components as shown in Figure 4: (i) a legal framework, which defines a broad set of rules, governing and regulating the zones; (ii) the institutional structure created for law enforcement; and (iii) the rules and norms that determine the substance of the legal framework in the zones. The legal framework's effectiveness depends on its enforcement (institutional structure) and substance (rules and norms).

Figure 4. Legal and Institutional Framework

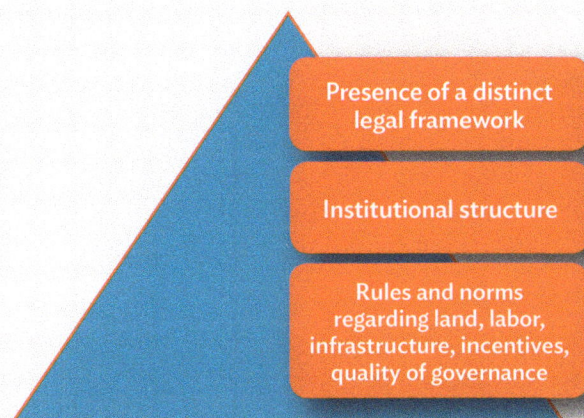

Source: Author.

Legal Framework

The economic zone policy is explicitly cross-cutting, in that it does not fit within one ministerial portfolio or government level, and there is often disagreement among different government organs over the policy provisions. Further, it asymmetrically affects different interest groups, including private businesses and individuals. Successfully addressing the conflicting interests calls for a well-developed and comprehensive legal framework that governs the establishment, development, management, and termination of economic zones with stable and transparent rules established for all stakeholders. While it is not necessary, it may lay a critical foundation for any successful economic zone program. A sound legal framework is particularly important for the SEZ program because it offers a legal regime different from the rest of the economy. Evidence suggests that most countries with successful zone programs put in place a distinct legal framework when they launched the SEZ program to signal strong and long-term government commitment, policy continuity (despite the change in government), and the adequate provision of various public goods such as infrastructures and services (Farole 2011; Zeng 2016).

Table 7 shows that the SEZs in all three countries are being governed by their respective legal frameworks. However, the practice with regard to GEZs varies across countries. Malaysia does not have a distinguished legal framework governing GEZs. It may be partly attributed to the country's common law system. In contrast to Malaysia, Indonesia and Thailand are civil law countries where GEZs are also governed by their respective legislations, albeit with a few exceptions. It may be noted that industrial zones in Thailand, the establishment of which is governed by Section 30 of the Factory Act B.E. 2535 (1992), have no dedicated legal framework to govern them.

In Indonesia, there is an official hierarchy of legislation. The 1945 Constitution of Indonesia is the country's highest legal authority, followed by Resolutions of the People's Representative Council, acts, government regulations, presidential regulations, and regional regulations (provincial and cities or regencies), in that order. In practice, there are also ministerial regulations, but they are surrounded by legal uncertainty and may be conflicting with higher regulations (Aji et al. 2020). According to this hierarchy, the SEZs (KEKs), which are supported by a distinct SEZ act, have been accorded the highest importance of all zone programs. On the other side of the spectrum is the STPs program, which is not yet supported by any distinct regulation.[8] Regulations of different levels of hierarchy govern the rest of the zones. It may also be noted that post-2005, all-new zone programs have been supported either by an act (KEKs) or government regulations (just below acts), indicating increasing importance attached to economic zones.

Institutional Structure

Ownership

The spectrum of possible institutional models extends from those almost entirely developed and managed by the private sector, at one end, to those almost entirely controlled by the public sector, at the other. Between the two are various models involving public–private partnerships (PPPs). According to a World Bank study (Akinci and Crittle 2008), the number of private zones has been growing rapidly across the globe. In 2008, 62% of the 2,301 SEZs in the developing countries were privately developed and managed, in contrast with less than 25% in the 1980s. However, in the IMT-GT member states, SEZs are normally publicly owned and managed (Table 8). Bonded zones and bonded logistics centers in Indonesia are an exception, which private operators can set up. Further, even though the traditional SEZs are publicly owned, the newer generation ones are increasingly based on PPPs. In Malaysia, the upcoming SBEZ on Malaysia–Thailand border is being

---

[8] A legal framework for Science and Techno Parks is planned to be in place in the ongoing RPJMN 2020-2024.

Table 7. Legal Framework of Economic Zones in IMT-GT

Indonesia		Malaysia		Thailand	
General Economic Zones					
Industrial estates	Government Regulation 24/2009 as amended by Government Regulation 142/2015	Industrial parks	–	Industrial parks/zones	Section 30 of the Factory Act, B.E. 2535 (1992)
Science and techno parks	–	High-tech parks	–	Thailand Science Park	Regulations of the Office of the Prime Minister on Science Park Promotion Agency B.E. 2554 (2011)
KAPETs	Presidential decree No. 89/1996	MSC	–	Regional science parks	
Halal parks		Halal parks	–		
Special Economic Zones					
Bonded	The Minister of Finance Regulation No. 147/PMK.04/2011 as last amended through 131/PMK.04/2018	FIZs/FCZs	Free Zones Act 1990	Industrial estates	IEAT Act (1979) as amended in 2007
Bonded logistics	Government Regulation No. 85 of 2015	SBEZ	Given the status of LMW to be governed by section 65/65A of the Customs Act 1967	SEZs	Regulations of the Office of the Prime Minister on Special Economic Zones Development, B.E. 2556 (2013) and Regulations of the Office of the Prime Minister on Administration on Special Economic Zones Development B.E. 2558 (2015)*
Free trade and port zone	Government Regulation No. 36 of 2000 amended in 2007	DFTZ	–	Eastern economic corridor	Eastern Special Development Zone Act B.E. 2561 (2018)
KEKs	SEZ act, SEZ rules, 2020				

– = not applicable, DFTZ = digital free trade zone, FCZ = free commercial zone, FIZ = free industrial zone, IEAT = Industrial Estate Authority of Thailand, IMT-GT = Indonesia–Malaysia–Thailand Growth Triangle, KAPET = Kawasan Pengembangan Ekonomi Terpadu (Integrated Economic Development Zone), KEK = Kawasan Ekonomi Khusus (Special Economic Zone), LMW = licensed manufacturing warehouse, MSC = Multimedia Super Corridor, SBEZ = special border economic zone, SEZ = special economic zone.

* These regulations will be replaced by the draft of new regulations soon. The new regulations will integrate SEZs with other economic corridor programs.

Source: Author.

Table 8. Institutional Framework of Economic Zones in IMT-GT

Indonesia		Malaysia		Thailand	
General Economic Zones					
Industrial estates	All types of ownership	**Industrial Parks**	All types of ownership	**Industrial parks/zones**	Private
Science and techno parks	Public	**High-tech parks**	Public/private	**Thailand Science Park**	Public
KAPETs	Public	**MSC**	Mixed	**Regional science parks**	Public
		Halal parks	Public/private		
Special Economic Zones					
Bonded/ bonded logistics	Private	**FIZs/FCZs**	Public	**Industrial estates**	Public (PPP mainly for utilities)
Free trade and port zone	Public	**SBEZ**	Public (PPP in development)	**SEZs**	Public
KEKs	Public (with PPP in development)	**DFTZ**	Private	**Eastern economic corridor**	Public

DFTZ = digital free trade zone, FCZ = free commercial zone, FIZ = free industrial zone, IMT-GT = Indonesia–Malaysia–Thailand Growth Triangle, KAPET = Kawasan Pengembangan Ekonomi Terpadu (Integrated Economic Development Zone), KEK = Kawasan Ekonomi Khusus (Special Economic Zone), MSC = Multimedia Super Corridor, PPP = public–private partnership, SBEZ = special border economic zone, SEZ = special economic zone.

Source: Author.

developed in a PPP mode.[9] The DFTZ is being developed by Ali Baba, a multinational company from the PRC in collaboration with domestic private companies. In Indonesia, private entities can propose KEKs and participate in their development through PPP mode. However, in Thailand's industrial estates, private participation is limited to managing utilities and other infrastructural developments.

The GEZs may be developed and managed by the private sector in all three countries. In Thailand, the first private industrial zone (GEZ) was set up in the early 1970s, while Indonesia and Malaysia allowed the private sector (both domestic and foreign) to own and develop designated land for industrial estates in the late 1980s. In Indonesia, the industrial estate business has become overwhelmingly dominated by the private sector. Currently, 94% of Indonesia's industrial estates are managed by the private sector, in stark contrast to its regional counterparts: Malaysia (78%) and Thailand (48%) (Tijaja and Faisal 2014). Thus, on one side of the spectrum is Thailand giving a rather limited role to the private sector in establishing economic zones, and on the other side is Indonesia giving an extensive role to the private sector in setting up both SEZs and GEZs.

[9] See the 2020 Budget Speech by YB Tuan Lim Guan Eng. https://www.bnm.gov.my/documents/budget/bs2020.pdf.

In the middle is Malaysia, where traditional SEZs are publicly owned, but the role of private participation is increasingly recognized in the newer ones.

Further, all three countries are open to foreign participation in developing GEZs. Some collaborations with foreign governments for building GEZs include Malaysia–PRC Kuantan Park and PRC–Indonesia Julong Agricultural Industry Cooperation Zone. Foreign and national companies can also collaborate to set up GEZs. For instance, G3 Global Berhad collaborates with two Chinese companies to establish the first artificial intelligence park in Malaysia. Indonesia's Morowali Industrial Park is developed by Shanghai Decent Investment (Group) Co. Ltd. and Bintang Delapan Group. Similarly, Rayong Industrial Zone is a Thai-Chinese park developed by Holley (the PRC) and Amata (Thailand) groups.

Regulatory Approach: Centralized vs. Decentralized

The government may adopt a centralized or decentralized approach in regulating economic zones. A decentralized approach to economic zones is one in which the provincial and state governments own and regulate the zones. Such an approach contrasts with the centralized approach wherein the central government entity is responsible for regulation. In general, relying on a centralized zone regime is considered a good practice because it provides a strong centralized framework and uniformity throughout the country. Yet, because the regional officials are better equipped with the knowledge of regional economic opportunities and challenges (Aggarwal 2012a), the centralized regulatory approach may be complemented by models that involve administrative and fiscal decentralization, ensuring greater local autonomy to provincial and state governments. The centralized approach places only implementation responsibilities in the hands of the local governments, while the decentralized approach accords substantial administrative and financial autonomy also to them (World Bank 2013).

From this perspective, Thailand, a unitary state, is at one extreme of the spectrum where regulatory, administrative, and fiscal powers are concentrated at the center. This system is highly efficient, less costly, and quick. However, it may or may not include significant representation from the local governments. At the other extreme of the spectrum is Indonesia, which has been following the system of decentralized governance and development planning with substantial authority and financial resources assigned directly to regencies and municipalities, bypassing even the provincial governments in the hope of better service delivery. Thus, in addition to administrative decentralization, there is the decentralization of fiscal powers. However, there is evidence that the local governments do not have adequate capacity for economic planning or to take initiatives to promote economic growth or exercise fiscal powers in their jurisdictions (Nasution 2016). This makes the decision-making and implementation process more difficult and slower. In the middle of the two is Malaysia, where regulatory (or political) centralization is combined with administrative decentralization. But the administrative decentralization is not supported by fiscal decentralization, which severely curbs the local governments' financial powers and makes them dependent on the federal government for funding their development projects and leaves immense scope for political favoritism (Wilson 1996).

While all three countries have adopted centralized regulatory regimes for their zone programs, which is considered a good practice, the lack of institutional distribution of administrative and fiscal powers to lower levels of government or lack of their capacity constrain the success of the zone programs. The Chinese experience, where the local governments have played a critical role in the success of

SEZs, shows that the local governments should have certain administrative and financial autonomy and capacity to create an open and conducive policy environment for the SEZs (Zeng 2016).

Regulatory Body

The regulatory body may be fully anchored to a single ministry (the Republic of Korea and Taipei,China), be a cross-ministerial government body (Pakistan), or an autonomous board or body with a board of directors that has cross-ministerial and private sector membership (Bangladesh, Costa Rica, the Dominican Republic, and Jordan). In many countries, the autonomous regulator of SEZs is anchored to the highest possible level of government (Bangladesh, the Dominican Republic, Mauritius, the PRC, and Viet Nam)—a signal to officials that the economic zone program is a central instrument in the government's industrial development strategy and to foreign investors that the government is committed to the program, lowering their perception of risk. It also empowers the regulator to effectively coordinate actions with other ministries. The IMT-GT countries follow diverse practices with regard to the regulatory body.

- **Malaysia.** Most industrial area programs (including SEZs) are directly run by the relevant federal ministries as their programs; the two exceptions are halal parks and the multimedia corridor, which have autonomous regulatory bodies (Table 9). Regional corridor authorities have been set up to oversee the economic corridors program, but they have little regulatory role. They are created as an administrative layer between the central and state governments to support the state governments in planning and negotiating development projects' funding with the central government. While many consider this practice suboptimal, it has its own pros; it provides greater flexibility to the zone programs. But each time a new government takes office, there is a possibility that it reverses whatever decisions predecessors took.

- **Indonesia.** In Indonesia, the regulatory powers are anchored to the relevant ministries for all economic zones except KEKs (Table 9). KEKs are regulated by an autonomous interministerial body named National Council, chaired by the minister in charge of economic affairs, substantiating its importance in the country.

- **Thailand.** All SEZs and science parks have been governed by their respective autonomous bodies. While the IEAT anchored in the Ministry of Industry manages the industrial estates, other SEZs are governed by their respective autonomous bodies chaired by the prime minister. Further, each authority has representation from the private sector. While the IEAT Board has independent directors, the other regulatory bodies (Table 9) are represented by the Confederation of Industries and other experts appointed by the prime minister. To give a major boost to other regional corridor programs, the SEZ program will be integrated with the economic corridor programs and be placed under a single governance unit as per the new regulation approved in principle by the Cabinet Resolution on 9 June 2020 (Theparat 2020).

Rules and Regulations

Rules and regulations pertain to the type of permissible activities, fiscal and non-fiscal incentives, labor, land, governance, administration, and infrastructural requirements. They cover various aspects of economic zones' development, management, operations, and monitoring. Some of the major rules and regulations in the economic zones of the three countries are reviewed as under.

Table 9. Regulatory Bodies of Economic Zones in IMT-GT

Indonesia		Malaysia		Thailand	
General Economic Zones					
Industrial estates	Directorate general for the development of industry in the Ministry of Industry	Industrial parks	Ministry of International Trade and Industry	Industrial parks/zones	Ministry of Industry
Science and techno parks	Ministry of Research and Technology	High-tech parks	Ministry of Energy, Science, Technology, Environment and Climate Change	Thailand Science Park	Science park promotion agency anchored in the Ministry of Higher Education Science Research and Innovation
KAPETs	Ministry of Economic Affairs	MSC	Multimedia Development Corporation	Regional science parks	
Halal parks	Directorate general for the development of industry in the Ministry of Industry	Halal parks	Halal Industry Development Corporation	–	–
Special Economic Zones					
Bonded zones	The Head of Customs Regional Office	FIZs/FCZs	Ministry of Finance	Industrial estates	IEAT
Bonded logistics zones	Ministry of Finance	SBEZ	Ministry of Finance	SEZs	NC-Committee (interministerial body chaired by the Prime Minister and comprised of relevant government bodies and private sector

continued on next page

Table 9 *continued*

Indonesia		Malaysia		Thailand	
Special Economic Zones					
Free trade and port zones	Transportation Ministry	DFTZ	Multimedia Development Corporation	EEC	Eastern Special Development Zone (Inter-ministerial) Policy Committee chaired by the Prime Minister and assisted by the Office of the Eastern Special Development Zone Policy Committee as the secretariat unit of the committee[a]
KEKs	National Zone Council anchored in the Ministry of Economic Affairs	Regional corridors	Regional corridor authorities	Other regional corridors	NC-Committee on SEZ

– = not applicable, DFTZ = digital free trade zone, EEC = Eastern Economic Corridor, FCZ = free commercial zone, FIZ = free industrial zone, IMT-GT = Indonesia–Malaysia–Thailand Growth Triangle, KAPET = Kawasan Pengembangan Ekonomi Terpadu (Integrated Economic Development Zone), KEK = Kawasan Ekonomi Khusus (Special Economic Zone), MSC = Multimedia Super Corridor, SBEZ = special border economic zone, SEZ = special economic zone.

[a] Eastern Special Development Zone Act B.E. 2561 (2018).

Source: Author.

One-Stop Shop

■ **Indonesia.** In July 2018, Indonesia introduced an online single submission service. It is a web-based business licensing system that integrates all business licensing services for all economic zones across the board. However, the KPBPB of Batam has its own single-window services provided by the Batam Free Trade Zone Authority (BP Batam). Recently, in a progressive move, it has been merged with the city administration to debottleneck the licensing system. In KEKs, zone councils administer the one-stop integrated services. To promote investment in the economic zones, Indonesia introduced a 3-hour investment express service (I23J) on 11 January 2016 for investors looking to invest a minimum of Rp100 billion ($8 million) and/or to employ no less than 1,000 local workers at a designated economic zone. Under the scheme, eight documents and a letter of land availability are issued within 3 hours to the investor to start a business in the country (Indonesia Investment Coordinating Board 2016).

■ **Malaysia.** Malaysia does not have a distinct concept of a one-stop shop for industrial areas. MIDA provides comprehensive information on investment opportunities in the country and facilitates investors by working in conjunction with state investment boards that act as the one-stop agencies at the state level. The zone management authorities provide additional assistance to investors.

■ **Thailand.** Thailand provides one-stop shop facilities in all types of SEZs through their respective regulatory bodies. The IEAT offers a single window for visas and work permits as well. Other facilities include the following:

- **IEAT Operation Center.** The headquarters monitors industrial estates and the factories inside them to efficiently manage environmental and safety issues and integrate all information. It also provides a centralized command in case of emergency and disaster.

- **e-Paperless and e-Permission.** Tax privilege application service is provided through the e-Paperless system streamlining the customs clearance procedures for imported and exported goods. An on-site training program is organized for business operators to use this service.

Foreign Investment

■ **Indonesia.** Indonesia has a negative list for foreign investment. It is applicable in all types of zones except KEKs. In KPBPB (FTZs), the master list is decided by the one-stop service of the Indonesian Investment Coordinating Board. There are also relaxations on foreign equity holding in SEZs and FTZs, where foreign nationals can build their plant and own 100% of their businesses, subject to certain conditions.

■ **Malaysia.** Malaysia has been following a liberal policy toward FDI since June 2003. Under the law, foreign investors can hold 100% of the equity in all manufacturing investments in new projects, as well as investments in expansion and diversification projects by existing companies, irrespective of the level of exports and without excluding any product or activity. However, certain services are subject to limits on foreign equity.

■ **Thailand.** Although foreign investors have no general restrictions, foreign ownership in most services is limited to 49%. Further, the Foreign Business Act of 1999 has three annexes that list specific restrictions on foreign investment in selected activities. Annex 1 contains activities where foreign investment is prohibited, while Annexes 2 and 3 impose restrictions on foreign investment in specified activities. However, up to 100% foreign ownership is allowed for the BOI- and IEAT-promoted investments in activities listed in Annexes 2 and 3.

Infrastructure

■ **Indonesia.** The legal framework for industrial estates in Indonesia requires companies to set aside 30% of land for green spaces and infrastructure. The estates must also adhere to specific infrastructure requirements with criminal and financial penalties applicable to violations. The responsibility of developing industrial infrastructure (energy and electricity, telecommunications, water, sanitation, and transportation networks) and supporting infrastructure (housing, education and training, R&D, health, fire stations, and waste disposal) lies with the government, while the basic infrastructure (roads, sanitation, water treatment, etc.) is to be developed by the industrial estate companies (Octavia 2016). In KEKs, the National Council may set its own policies in cooperation with the central, provincial, and local governments and private parties to construct and maintain the infrastructure in the zone. Finally, bonded zone operators are encouraged to set up bonded logistics centers within the boundaries of bonded zones to improve logistics efficiency.

■ **Malaysia.** Industrial areas are normally developed as traditional industrial zones with on-site industrial and supporting infrastructure. There are also instances of township development within economic zones, such as Kulim Hi-Tech Park (KHTP), which is equipped with urban infrastructure. The upcoming SBEZ will also have urban infrastructure such as factories; a shopping complex; housing; hotels; recreation parks; and a new Immigration, Customs, Quarantine and Security (ICQS) facility. However, there are no statutory requirements for infrastructure development in the zones.

- **Thailand.** Industrial estates in Thailand provide the infrastructure necessary for all industrial operations as wide-ranging as electricity, water supply, flood protection, wastewater treatment plant (size approved by the IEAT), solid waste disposal, communication facilities, and security systems. They also have commercial banks and post offices to facilitate business operations further. Most estates have customs offices, schools, hospitals, shopping centers, and other social infrastructure. To provide the necessary infrastructure, all industrial estates must set aside 30%–40% of the area for infrastructure development. Industrial estates larger than 161 hectares can allocate up to 25% of land area for infrastructure.

Foreign Labor Employment

- **Indonesia.** Indonesia prioritizes local employment in all types of economic zones, including KEKs. No relaxation is given to foreign employees. There are restrictions on the types of businesses that can employ foreign workers. The law sets requirements to obtain health insurance for expatriate employees, requires companies to appoint local "companion" employees for the transfer of technology and skill development, and requires employers to facilitate Indonesian language training for foreign workers (US Department of State 2019a). The processes for immigration and resident permit for foreigners have been relaxed only for tourism zones.

- **Malaysia.** As per the national labor code, foreign workers can be employed subject to certain restrictions. Malaysia's 1.78 million documented and 2 million–4 million undocumented foreign workers make up over 20% of the country's workforce, even though the government has been trying to reduce reliance on them (US Department of State 2019b). The employer must first obtain approval from the Ministry of Home Affairs to hire foreign workers. For this, the Foreign Worker One-Stop Approval Centre has been set up. In addition, special services are offered in the MSC through the eXpats Service Center within the Malaysia Digital Economy Corporation as a one-stop shop for foreign knowledge workers.

- **Thailand.** Thailand allows foreign experts and technical staff with their spouses and dependents in promoted projects including industrial estates and other SEZs. BOI permits the employment of unskilled foreign workers in SBEZs (officially named SEZs). Thailand has also unrolled the "Smart Visa" to attract qualified foreign experts, executives, new entrepreneurs (start-up), and investors who wish to work or invest in the country's targeted industries regardless of location; they are even given personal income tax exemptions under the Eastern Special Development Zone Act.

Labor Laws

- **Indonesia.** The law allows independent labor unions, legal strikes, and collective bargaining in all zones. However, two specialized labor institutions have been set up in KEKs as derogations: (i) Special Tripartite Cooperation Councils for labor administration and dispute prevention and resolution, and (ii) Remuneration Council for wage-related issues. Further, companies with more than one labor union may establish an employee or labor union forum, the establishment of which is governed by the minister in charge of the workforce.

- **Malaysia.** Labor relations in Malaysia are generally nonconfrontational. Despite a system of government controls that discourages strikes and restricts the formation of unions to the enterprise level, territorial federations of unions have emerged. The government protects the electronics and textile sectors, which dominate Malaysia's SEZs, from territorial federations. The electronics sector is limited to forming four regional federations of unions, while the textile sector is limited to state-based federations of unions in the states where this industry exists.

- **Thailand.** While labor unions are not discouraged, there are restrictions on trade unions' right to establish branches, federations, and confederations or to affiliate with national and international organizations. There are restrictions on trade unions' right to organize their administration, strikes, and collective bargaining in all types of SEZs.

Land

- **Indonesia.** Foreigners cannot own freehold land in Indonesia. Leasehold titles (right to build) are granted for 25 years and, under the 2016 law, can be renewed for a maximum period of 80 years. Prior to 2016, the maximum extension period was only 20 years. KEKs already have the provision of 80 years' lease. However, the rules for property ownership by foreign nationals in Batam fall under Decree No 068/KPTS/KA/III/1999, allowing foreign nationals or companies to 100% own residential or commercial property in the Barelang area (Batam, Rempang, and Galang).

- **Malaysia.** The National Land Code recognizes two types of landownership: freehold and leasehold. Foreigners can legally own freehold land, condominiums, and houses and can get a residency permit for 10 years for a fee.

- **Thailand.** Like Indonesia, Thailand does not allow foreign individuals or corporations to hold title to land; they can only obtain leasehold interests. However, unlike in Indonesia, foreign companies in all types of SEZs in Thailand can own land for commercial and residential purposes. In ESDZ, foreigners are also exempted from restrictions on the ownership of condominiums.

Direct and Indirect Tax Incentives

- **Indonesia.** Massive investment incentives are being offered to firms on new investment in 18 designated "pioneer industries that have a wide range of connections, provide additional value and high externalities, introduce new technologies, and have strategic value for the national economy" (PwC Indonesia website).[10] In addition to industry and merit, place is also a consideration in determining fiscal incentives. KEKs offer the most comprehensive direct tax benefits on investment in target industries (Table 10). Direct tax benefits in KEKs can be extended up to 25 years. In addition, there are indirect tax benefits as well. Economic activities other than in target industries enjoy standard tax benefits.

- **Malaysia.** Tax incentives are essentially industry- and merit-based. Special incentives offered to activities in backward regions are independent of the industrial unit's location within or

---

[10] PwC. Indonesia: Corporate - Tax Credits and Incentives. https://taxsummaries.pwc.com/indonesia/corporate/tax-credits-and-incentives.

Table 10. Direct and Indirect Tax Incentives in Indonesia

Direct Tax Incentives							
Standard tax exemptions applicable to 18 industries			IEs*	Additional tax incentives KEKs for primary activities			Bonded Zone/Logistics KAPET FTZ
Investment (Rp)	Exemption (%)	Years		Investment (Rp)	Exemption (%)	Years	
100 billion–500 billion	50+25	5+2	Y*	100 billion–500 billion	Discretionary	5–15	No additional direct tax benefits
500 billion–1 trillion	100+50	5+2	Y*	500 billion–1 trillion	20–100	5–15	
1 trillion–5 trillion	100+50	7+2	Y*	1 trillion and above	20–100	10–25	
5 trillion–15 trillion	100+50	10+2	Y*				
15 trillion–30 trillion	100+50	15+2	Y*				
30 trillion and above	100+50	20+2	Y*				
Tax allowance for 145 business fields: 30% of investment value reduction of corporate net income tax for 6 years, 5% each year				TA for non-primary activities of KEKs			
Indirect Tax Incentives							

Non-collection of VAT and local sales tax on certain imports

Exemption or postponement of import duties on capital goods, components, and raw materials

- Non-collection of VAT and LST on the domestic purchases of certain goods
- Non-collection (Article 22) of income tax on importation of certain goods
- Non-collection of excise duties on certain imported goods
- Exemption of VAT on transactions of intangible goods and taxable services

FTZ = free trade zone, IE = industrial estate, KAPET = Kawasan Pengembangan Ekonomi Terpadu (Integrated Economic Development Zone), KEK = Kawasan Ekonomi Khusus (Special Economic Zone), LST = luxury goods sales tax, TA = technical assistance, VAT = value-added tax.

Note: Y* = All tax incentives are applicable, but the provinces have been divided into four categories for tax incentives: developed industrial development estates (WPI) in Java; developing WPIs in Southern Sulawesi, Eastern Kalimantan, Northern Sumatera (other than Batam, Bintan, and Karimun) and Southern Sumatera; potential WPIs in Northern Sulawesi, Western Kalimantan, Bali, and Nusa Tenggara; and potential WPIs in Papua and West Papua (Amin 2016). Tax and regional incentives for both industrial zone operators and industrial tenants vary depending on the zone category.

Sources: Author; and Amin, K. 2016. New Regulation Aims to Attract Investment to Industrial Zones. *The Jakarta Post*. 7 January. https://www.thejakartapost.com/news/2016/01/07/new-regulation-aims-attract-investment-industrial-zones.html.

outside the zones. Companies are eligible for either pioneering status or income tax allowance. The direct tax incentives may be given for up to 10 years, subject to the project's merit (Table 11).

- **Thailand.** Thailand offers wide-ranging tax benefits, which are classified as category and merit based. A project's merit is based not only on competitiveness enhancement and decentralization but also on its location in the industrial zone. Thus, companies in all types of SEZs enjoy additional benefits, unlike in Malaysia (Table 12).

Table 11. Direct and Indirect Tax Incentives in Malaysia

Direct Tax Incentives				
	Pioneering Status		Investment Tax Allowance	
Qualifying Industry	Benefit	Year	Benefit	Year
Standard deduction for companies	70% of increased SI	5	60% new QCE against 70% of SI	5
Projects of national and strategic importance involving heavy capital investment and high technology including halal parks, and those in Sabah	100% of SI	10	100% QCE -against 100% of SI	10
High-technology companies in areas of new and emerging technologies	100% of SI	5	60% QCE against 100% of SI	5
Companies manufacturing specialized machinery and equipment	100% of SI	10	100% QCE against 100% of SI	10
Existing locally owned companies reinvesting in production of heavy machinery, specialized machinery, and equipment	70% of increased SI	5	60% new QCE against 70% of SI	5

In addition, there are sector-specific incentives to biotechnology industry, palm oil, halal, and Industry 4.0.

Indirect Tax Benefits
Service and sales tax: Manufactured goods for exports are exempted from sales tax. All imports and exports of services are exempt from service tax.

QCE = qualifying capital expenditure, SI = statutory income.

Source: PricewaterhouseCoopers, Malaysia.

The SEZs and SBEZs and ESDZ enjoy the most attractive tax regimes. In SBEZs, those running businesses in the target industries can avail a maximum of 8 years' exemptions and 50% corporate income tax reduction for 5 years for all activities irrespective of technology sophistication. SEZ companies enjoy exemption from import duty on raw materials and inputs used in the production of products and reduced or waived import duty on machinery irrespective of whether they are producing for export or domestic markets. The SEZ projects in non-targeted industries can avail themselves of additional 3 years' corporate income tax exemption or 50% corporate income tax reduction for 5 years. In addition, 10 years' double deductions are offered from the costs of transportation, electricity, and water supply and 25% deduction from the cost of installation or construction of facilities. The special promotional zones within EEC (EEC Innovation Zone, EEC Digital Innovation Zone, and Eastern Aviation City) offer personal tax relaxation for foreign staff who will be taxed at 17%. Projects for human development in ESDZ attract an additional (to the standard) tax break of 2 years for targeted technologies. The conditional tax benefits can thus be extended up to 13 years in the ESDZ.

Under the standard incentive package, the BOI offers exemption of import duty on machinery as well as import duty on raw materials used for the production of exports (BOI incentives). Free zones can bring supplies or raw materials for production without being subject to import permits, standard and quality controls, or any other control except for those under the Customs Act (Thai Customs

Table 12. Direct and Indirect Tax Incentives in Thailand

	Category	Activity and Technology — Tax Exemption (%)	Standard Years	IEs	Area Based — SEZs	Area Based — EEC
Category based	A1	No cap	8	8	Up to 8 plus 5 years of 50% reduction	Up to 8 plus 5 years of 50% reduction
	A2	100	8	8		
	A3	100	5	6		
	A4	100	3	4		–
	B1	–	–	–		–
	B2	–	–	–		–
	Targeted technology	No cap	10	11		Up to 13 years
Merit based (competitiveness enhancement)	R&D	300% of R&D investment amount	Up to 13 years			
	Indirect Tax	Import duty exemption on machinery (all but B2), import duty on raw material for production on exports, and import duty exemption on goods for R&D				

– = not applicable, EEC = Eastern Economic Corridor, IE = industrial estate, R&D = research and development, SEZ = special economic zone.
Source: Board of Investment of Thailand.

Department's website).[11] The 2007 IEAT Act also provides tax burden relief for goods from the free zones sold to the local market; the raw materials and components are entitled to tax and duty exemptions if they are produced locally (Thai Customs Department).

Summary

The above analysis shows a clear-cut distinction between the SEZs and GEZs in terms of the legal and institutional frameworks. The SEZs are not just about tax benefits; they also address some binding institutional constraints in the wider economy. Further, the economic zones are evolving not only in terms of their structural features such as size, design, location, and economic composition but also in legal and institutional frameworks. Along with the provisions of fiscal incentives, the range of facilities, services, and amenities available within zones has also been extended in new ambitious zone programs, particularly in Indonesia and Thailand. The preferential regulatory contents have been enriched and enlarged as well. Apparently, the SEZs, which have always been the centerpiece of industrial policy of the three IMT-GT countries since the 1970s, have grown in importance with an aggressive drive launched by these countries to build a new variety of zones in recent years and achieve various goals by leveraging their full potential.

[11]   Thai Customs Department online information. http://www.customsclinic.org/ index.php?option= com_content&view=article&id=399&Itemid=367&lang=en (accessed on 10 February 2021). The Thai Customs Department is in the process of moving their database from http://www.customsclinic.org to http://tic.customs.go.th.

Chapter 5

Special Economic Zones and General Economic Zones in IMT-GT Corridors

There are five priority economic corridors designated in the IMT-GT subregion, each with its comparative advantage (CIMT 2017b): (i) Extended Songkhla–Penang–Medan Corridor (Nakhon Si Thammarat–Phatthalung–Songkhla–Yala–Pattani–Penang–Medan) with specialization in agriculture; (ii) Straits of Malacca Corridor (covering the western coastal belt from Trang in Southern Thailand to Melaka in Peninsular Malaysia), with considerable potential to augment production networks particularly in food and halal but also in technologically sophisticated industries; (iii) Banda Aceh–Medan–Pekanbaru–Palembang Economic Corridor (a road corridor running south to north through Sumatera) abundant in natural resources with potential in becoming a processing hub; (iv) Melaka–Dumai Economic Corridor (a maritime corridor linking Sumatera and Peninsular Malaysia); and (v) Ranong–Phuket–Aceh Economic Corridor (primarily a maritime corridor). These corridors (Map 2) ensure internal regional connections between all provinces and states within the subregion to increase transport services; reduce transport and trade costs; and serve as the basis for clustering economic activities through the movement of goods, labor, and raw materials, and access to cross-border markets. This chapter takes stock of the existing economic zones in these corridors and identifies upcoming projects in each of the 32 provinces and states within the IMT-GT subregion based on the data from the relevant agencies during country consultations, which were combined with information from various government reports, academic papers, and newspaper articles to prepare a rich database on the location of economic zones in the subregion. Since the size, age, and occupancy of these zones vary significantly and may not provide a good idea of the concentration of manufacturing activity in these corridors, we also analyze trends in a few selected quantitative manufacturing indicators in the subregion. These indicators include (i) the share of manufacturing in gross regional domestic product (GRDP)[12] of IMT-GT provinces and states, (ii) the share of provincial and state manufacturing in national manufacturing, and (iii) the ratio of the subregion's GRDP to national GDP per capita. The nomenclature used for the IMT-GT subregional areas in Indonesia, Malaysia, and Thailand are Indonesia-GT, Malaysia-GT, and Thailand-GT, respectively, following the standard practice.

Indonesia

The Indonesia-GT covers all 10 provinces of Sumatera in Indonesia: Aceh, Bangka Belitung, Bengkulu, Jambi, Lampung, North Sumatera, Riau, Riau Islands, South Sumatera, and West Sumatera. Sumatera is resource-rich, accounting for almost 70% of Indonesia's oil palm

---

[12] GRDP is a generic term for the subnational equivalent of the national gross domestic product. It represents the total gross value added of all producer units located within the boundaries of a state or province. The nomenclature of GRDP varies across countries. In Thailand, it is termed as gross provincial product (GPP); in Indonesia it is called GRDP while Malaysia uses the term GDP by state. This study has taken care of the context sensitivity of this concept.

Map 2. Indonesia–Malaysia–Thailand Growth Triangle Economic Corridors

Source: Asian Development Bank.

plantations and two-thirds of the rubber latex harvested, followed by Kalimantan, Sulawesi, and Java. Sumatera is also one of the four oil-producing regions and three main gas-producing regions of Indonesia. There has been a drive to promote processing activity by setting up economic zones in the region to leverage the abundance of natural resources. Table 13, which summarizes the spatial distribution of all economic zones in Indonesia-GT, shows that Sumatera hosts around 23 (26%) of 87 industrial estates, which covered 30% of 86,059 hectares of area under industrial estates in 2019. It also comprises 91 (6.7%) of 1,350 bonded zones (Damuri, Christian, and Atje 2015), 5 of 15 SEZs, and all 4 KPBPB (FTZs) created in the country. Overall, the area has 124 economic zones. Besides, out of the 28 national strategic projects on SEZs and industrial zones under Presidential Regulation No. 58 of 2017, eight are in this area. Out of 24 economic zones proposed to be promoted outside Java in RPJMN 2020–2024, 14 are in Sumatera.

Table 13. Cluster-Based Economic Zones and Manufacturing Shares in the Indonesia Growth Triangle

	Riau Island	Riau	North Sumatera	South Sumatera	Banka Belitung	Jambi	Lampung	West Sumatera	Aceh	Bengkulu
Bonded zones	2		42	22				24	1	
Industrial estates	11 12.6%	2 2.3%	5 5.7%	1 1.1%	1 1.1%	1 1.1%	1 1.1%	1 1.1%		
SEZs		1	1	1	1 tourism				1	
FTZ	3								1	
KAPETs	–		–						1	
Total	16	3	48	24	2	1	1	25	4	
Contribution to national manufacturing value added (%)	2.7	5.9	4	2.2	0.8	0.6	1.7	0.7	0.3	0.1
Manufacturing share of GRDP (%)	38.8	27.8	19.8	18.4	23.3	11.4	17.8	11.2	6.9	6.8
GRDP per capita as ratio of national GDP per capita (2018)	1.9	1.7	0.8	0.9	0.9	1	0.7	0.7	0.6	0.5

FTZ = free trade zone, GDP = gross domestic product, GRDP = gross regional domestic product, KAPET = Kawasan Pengembangan Ekonomi Terpadu (Integrated Economic Development Zone), SEZ = special economic zone.

Source: Compiled by the author from various sources; *Statistical Yearbook of Indonesia 2019.*

Sumatera's 10 districts form a development ladder in terms of GRDP per capita, at the top of which are Riau Islands and Riau, two of the major industrial development centers and among the most well-off provinces with their GRDP per capita being above the national average. At the second tier are Bangka Belitung, Jambi, North Sumatera, and South Sumatera, with the GRDP per capita roughly equal to the national average. West Sumatera, Lampung, Bengkulu, and Aceh have been at the third tier and are among the bottom states, falling 30%–50% short of the national income. The spatial distribution of economic zones is also linked with this development ladder. The Riau and Riau Islands form the largest hub of economic zones in the subregion with 13 industrial estates of 23 (57%) and 3 FTZs, contribute 8.6% of the national manufacturing value added, and form Indonesia's second-largest industrial hub after Java. Another hub of economic zones is emerging in North Sumatera with 5 industrial estates, 42 bonded zones, 1 SEZ, and 4% contribution to the national manufacturing value added. It is followed by South Sumatera. The share of bottom tier provinces remains marginal both in economic zones and manufacturing value added (Table 13).

Prominent Economic Zones by Provinces: Proposed and Operational

Aceh. The discovery of natural gas reserves in the early 1970s and a liquefied natural gas (LNG) refinery that became operational in 1977 triggered the development of the petrochemical cluster Lhokseumawe in Aceh, until then the rice barn of Indonesia. However, the industrial area could not bring structural change to the economy, which remained predominantly agrarian. The plantations of oil palm, rubber, coffee, cacao, coconut, and clove helped the growth of the processing industry, which was dominated by low-productivity small firms. Currently, two major industrial sites benefiting from Aceh's strategic location at the entrance to the world's busiest trade route, the Strait of Malacca, are KAPET Bandar Aceh Darussalam and SEZ Arun Lhokseumawe (Table 14).

- **Bandar Aceh Darussalam Integrated Economic Development Zone.** It is one of 13 KAPETs with a total area of 6,356.87 square kilometers or 10.89% of the total area of Aceh Province[13] covering the city of Bandar Aceh, Aceh Besar Regency, and Pidie Regency with the hinterland of the Central Aceh, West Aceh, and South Aceh regions. Its major objectives are to support the (i) development of Sabang Free Port and Malahayati as a port of transportation of goods and services; (ii) development of Aceh Island as a center of distribution services; and (iii) promotion of industrial estates to develop five targeted sectors: agriculture and plantation, fisheries, energy, animal husbandry, and tourism. A joint initiative between India and Indonesia is underway to develop a deep-sea port in Sabang in Aceh to enhance maritime connectivity and push logistics activities in the province (Roy Chaudhury 2019).

- **Special economic zone: Arun Lhokseumawe.** It is located 250 km away from the capital Bandar Aceh and is spread over 2,600 hectares of land, focusing on the oil and gas industry, petrochemical, agro-industry, logistics, and paper industry. Around half of the area was the Arun LNG facility, formally decommissioned in 2014 due to falling natural gas reserves. It is established as an SEZ in February 2017 to accelerate economic development. There are plans to develop social infrastructure in the area, which is expected to create 40,000 jobs. Recently launched RPJMN 2020–2024 has proposed to develop an industrial estate in Ladong.

Bangka Belitung Islands. The province has tremendous tourism potential along with the mining sector, especially tin, which is still a major investment attraction despite a decline in importance. Other industries of interest in the province are fisheries and palm oil. Some of the major (proposed or under development) projects are as follows.

---

[13] Author's research.

Table 14. Prominent Projects by IMT-GT Provinces in the Indonesia Growth Triangle

Province	Existing (Operational Fully/Partially)	Under Development/Proposed
Aceh	KAPET Bandar Aceh Darussalam SEZ Arun Lhokseumawe	Sabang Free Trade Zone and Free Port Ladong Industrial Estate
Bangka		Tanjung Kelayang SEZ (Belitung Tourism Zone) Sadai Industrial Estate Tanjung Gunung KEK Sungailiat KEK
Riau Islands	Galang Batang SEZ Nongsa Digital Park	Bintan Aerospace Park
Bengkulu		Baai Island Port to become a Special Economic Zone (KEK)
Jambi	Jambi Agro Industrial Park	Kemingking in Muaro Jambi: Jambi Integrated City
Lampung	Tanggamus Industrial Park	Pesawaran Integrated Industrial Park Way Pisang in Way Pisang The Sebalang Integrated Energy Industrial Zone Katibung Industrial Estate
Riau	Tanjung Buton Industrial Estate Dumai Industrial Park	Tenayan Industrial Estate
North Sumatera	KEK Medan Sei Mangkei Kawasan Industri Medan	Kuala Tanjung Industrial Estate
South Sumatera	Tanjung Api-Api SEZ	Tanjung Enim
West Sumatera	Padang Industrial Park	

KAPET = Kawasan Pengembangan Ekonomi Terpadu (Integrated Economic Development Zone), KEK = Kawasan Ekonomi Khusu (Special Economic Zone), SEZ = special economic zone.

Source: Compiled by the author from various sources.

- **Tanjung Kelayang Special Economic Zone.** Located in Sijuk District, Belitung Regency, it has 324.4 hectares dedicated mainly to tourism sector activities. It is expected to employ around 23,645 people (Government of Indonesia 2019). This SEZ is one of the 10 national priority tourism destinations called Bali Baru[14] and will transform the tin mining-based economy of Bangka Belitung province into one based on international tourism.

- **Sadai Industrial Estate.** This project in Bangka Selatan is one of the nine priority industrial projects to be developed outside Java from 2020 to 2024. Apart from the potential in natural resources, its major advantage lies in its strategic geographical position. Bangka Selatan is near the Indonesian Archipelago Sea Channel 1, which is a route to international shipping lines and offers an immense opportunity to promote trade, logistics, and investment (Noer et al. 2019).

---

[14] Bali Baru is a program that has set the target of promoting 10 new destinations as icons of Indonesian tourism: Lake Toba, Belitung, Tanjung Lesung, Pulau Seribu, Borobudur Temple, Mandalika, Mount Bromo Tengger, Wakatobi, Labuan Bajo, and Morotai.

■ **Tanjung Gunung and Sungailiat special economic zones.** The proposal for two more Kawasan Ekonomi Khusus (KEKs)[15] in the province is under review. This will increase the number of KEKs to three. The Tanjung Gunung KEK will span 385 hectares of land, while Sungailiat will be spread over 600 hectares of land that includes Rambak Beach and Rebo Beach. Tanjung Gunung has been earmarked for meetings, conferences, and exhibitions-based tourism. Sungailiat has been designated to promote sports-based tourism, particularly a golfing hub. These projects are not yet included in the national strategic plan. However, the Tanjung Gunung SEZ is already approved as an SEZ site.

Riau Islands. Riau Islands—strategically located on the Indian Ocean and Pacific Ocean only 19 km from Singapore—represent one of the most attractive industrial, manufacturing, and logistical platforms in the subregion. Its three main islands are Karimun, Batam, and Bintan. Batam has numerous industrial parks dealing with electronics, biotech, semiconductors and other technology applications, oil services, shipbuilding, and a wide range of other industrial and consumer products. Bintan is known primarily for tourism and smaller industrial parks. Karimun, the least developed of the three FTZs, attracts space-intensive industries such as shipbuilding and agriculture along with oil and gas exploration. Some major projects are in the pipeline to uplift Bintan.

■ **Galang Batang Special Economic Zone.** Operational since August 2018 in Bintan, it is an integrated bauxite downstream center. It is also expected to boost the regional economy and generate 23,200 jobs.

■ **Nongsa Digital Park.** Opened in 2019 in Batam for digital start-ups and companies, it was first proposed by a Singapore-based integrated media entertainment and creative services company Infinite Studios. It has 50 companies, mostly from Singapore (Ng 2019). It is being developed by a joint venture between Sinar Mas Land and Citramas Group (the parent company of Infinite Studios), which appointed Surbana Jurong, an Asia-based urban and infrastructure consultancy group, as master planner. It aims to be a digital bridge between Indonesia and Singapore and is under review for the SEZ status.

■ **Aerospace Park (maintenance, repair, and overhaul) on Bintan Island.**[16] It will be a part of Bintan Industrial Estate adjacent to Bintan Airport's runway and spread over 177 hectares. There will also be a dedicated township, including employee compound houses, dormitory, health center, sports center, convenience stores, to cater to the management and staff of the park. Bintan Industrial Estate is one of the nine priority industrial estates proposed to be developed in RPJMN 2020–2024.

In addition, the RPJMN 2020–2024 proposes to develop Tenayan industrial estate to give a thrust to the development of Tenayan Raya district, which remains constrained due to poor infrastructure development (Harakan 2017).

Bengkulu. With several active volcanos, Bengkulu is prone to natural calamities. Coal mining is a major economic activity other than agriculture. Agriculture accounts for around 40% of the GRDP. There are initiatives to brand Robusta and Sintaro coffee produced in the province as also local batik: Kain Besure and Bumpak woven. The population is centralized only around the central and

---

15   KEKs is the Indonesian name for SEZs.
16   The other two are Kendal SEZs (Central Java) and Likupang SEZs (North Sulawesi).

western coast, while the hinterland people live in small groups and are dispersed. Bengkulu City and Rejang Lebong are the two most inhabited centers with other regions supporting them (Tatiana et al. 2015). To revitalize the province's economy, the provincial government is pushing for Baai Island Port to become an SEZ (KEK) as a future investment destination. It is argued that the port directly faces the high seas and can drive economic development, especially in Sumatera's central and western coast.

Jambi. Jambi in the Strait of Malacca is a center of rubber, palm, and coconut plantations. It has a strategic location facing Malaysia and Singapore, but its poor infrastructure, topography, and human capital remain major constraints on promoting its manufacturing potential. The major projects are the following:

- **Jambi Integrated City.** It is the first integrated industrial estate developed by PT Jambi Kemingking Ecopark as a modern city with industrial and logistics (bonded logistics center) parks, a techno park, and residential and commercial infrastructure. It targets light consumer industries, rubber, and biodiesel over 2,020 hectares.

- **Jambi Agro Industrial Park.** It is an area of over 100 hectares, currently being promoted by the Jambi provincial government to develop agriculture and industry. It is on the east coast of Sumatera, in the East Tanjung Jabung Regency in a lowland and tidal area. It is known for several plantation commodities such as corn, soybean, and coconut.

Lampung. Lampung is Indonesia's center of pepper and coffee production. It is among Indonesia's top exporting provinces for animal and vegetable oil and fats, coffee, tea, spices, and mineral fuels. Other prominent export crops are banana, cassava, sugarcane, and coconut. The availability of a wide range of agricultural products provides a good setting for the growth of processing industries with numerous industrial areas and industrial zones in the province. Currently, the focus is on the maritime and logistics industry with the following major projects.

- **Tanggamus Industrial Park.** Being developed on 800 hectares for maritime industry and logistics, it will be Indonesia's fourth major shipbuilding area after Surabaya, Cilegon, and Batam. The integrated park will be built in stages, eventually covering over 1,000 hectares owned by the state oil and gas company PT Pertamina (H.N. 2013). It is expected to generate 10,400 jobs and is one of the 245 national strategic projects.

- **Pesawaran Integrated Industrial Park.** It is proposed to be a priority project to be spread over 1,200 hectares, focusing on various industries. Located near Trans-Sumatera Toll Road, it seeks to be an environment-friendly and sustainable industrial park.

- **Way Pisang Industrial Estate.** It will accommodate agriproducts, plantations, and livestock from the Southern Lampung Province. The 3,500 hectares of land will be developed in three phases and is proposed to be a priority project along with Pesawaran Industrial Park.

- **Sebalang Integrated Energy Industrial Zone.** The government is reviewing a proposal from the provincial government to accelerate the development of the Sebalang Integrated Energy Industrial Zone.

Riau. Riau Province is rich in agriproducts, palm oil, rubber, sago, and minerals, particularly oil and gas. It has two industrial parks being set up in Dumai and Siak areas, both of which are included in the acceleration program of national strategic projects.

■ **Dumai Industrial Park.** Spread over 1,000 hectares of land in Riau Province, Dumai Industrial Park has been declared as Palm Oil Industrial Cluster and Palm Oil Green Economic Zone by the Government of Indonesia. Strategically located with a private jetty alongside Rupat Strait opposite the Strait of Malacca, it is being developed in two phases: Phase 1 (400 hectares) and Phase II (600 hectares).

■ **Tanjung Buton Industrial Estate.** It started in 2004 and was given priority status in 2017. The development plan is divided into three stages, with 3,500 hectares earmarked for industry and 1,500 hectares for the support and basic infrastructure.[17] It is supported by the Port of Tanjung Buton and is considered central to the development of trade, the shipping industry, and various other investment activities. It is targeted to be developed into an integrated industrial town in the RPJMN 2020–2024.

South Sumatera. It holds the largest rubber plantation area of 812,570 hectares (22.85% of the total), followed by North Sumatera (472,140 hectares), Jambi (384,780 hectares), Riau (356,240 hectares), and West Kalimantan (350,750 hectares). It is found to be suitable for a rubber city site. Launched in 2014, Tanjung Api-Api SEZ in the province is the site for a rubber city in Indonesia-GT.

■ **Tanjung Api-Api Special Economic Zone (site for a rubber city).** The three IMT-GT countries are the world's leading producers of natural rubber, accounting for around 70% of the global natural rubber production (Rubber Journal Asia 2019). To leverage their production and technological capabilities in rubber production, they are collaborating to develop rubber cities within the IMT-GT subregion. The objective is to promote downstream activities and the manufacture of value-added products through cross-border value chains. Tanjung Api-Api SEZ, the site for a rubber city in South Sumatera complements Sei Mangkei in North Sumatera, Kedah in Malaysia, and Songkhla in Thailand. It is one of the 245 national strategic projects. The zone will focus on three main industries: rubber, oil palm, and petrochemical. It integrates a modern industrial park with the longest deep-sea port called Tanjung Carat. With a total area of 2,030 hectares, Tanjung Api-Api SEZ is funded and managed by the government of South Sumatera Province. It will be divided into four zones: EPZ, logistics zone, industrial zone, and energy zone.

■ **Tanjung Enim.** It is an important oil and coal-producing sedimentary basin in Indonesia. RPJMN 2020–24 proposes to develop an integrated industrial zone in this area to leverage the availability of energy.

North Sumatera. Among the industrial projects to be developed in the area are plants for the regasification of LNG, an LNG trading hub, an LNG plant, a petrochemical cluster, and an agro-industry and its related products. Three major industrial estates in the province are as follows.

■ **Medan Sei Mangkei.** A national strategic project, the Sei Mangkei Special Economic Zone (SEZ or KEK), was established on 27 February 2012 and was the first SEZ in Indonesia that was officially inaugurated in January 2015 to target investment in palm oil, rubber industry, fertilizer industry, logistics, and tourism (already operational in January 2015). As part of the rubber cities project, it focuses on the rubber industry (along with palm oil). It is expected to become a center for developing large-scale, international-quality downstream palm and

---

17   Forum Investasi Lampung. Investment Project. https://investlampung.id/desinvestasi.

rubber industries. Sei Mangkei KEK also has supporting businesses in logistics and tourism due to its proximity to the Strait of Malacca. With a total land area of 2,003 hectares, it is open to the potential of other industries, especially in the high value-added downstream sector. It is supported by a dry port and a railway line that connects it to the Port of Belawan. According to the official sources, the Sei Mangkei KEK, when fully operational in 2025, will make a significant contribution to the national economy.

- **Kuala Tanjung Industrial Estate.** Kuala Tanjung international hub port and Kuala Tanjung Industrial Estate are two national strategic projects to be developed in an integrated manner. Kuala Tanjung is near Malacca Strait, one of the busiest commercial shipping routes in the world. Its water depth is sufficient to accommodate large international vessels and makes Kuala Tanjung Port fit to be positioned as an international port. Belawan, a domestic port, will serve as a spoke terminal for Kuala Tanjung Industrial Estate (Sinaga, Humang and Kurniawan 2018).

- **Kawasan Industri Medan.** The Medan industrial estate developed by a state-owned enterprise was established on 7 October 1988, comprising shares of the Government of Indonesia (60%), North Sumatera Province (30%), and Medan City government (10%). The developers continue to extend the land area, which currently covers 780 hectares (HKI 2019a). It is strategically located near the Belmera Toll Gate and Port of Belawan. It is developed in two phases: I and II. Phase I is located on the western highway, while Phase II is on the eastern highway and is called circuitry Medan Industrial Estate. Phase II, in particular, is well planned with modern infrastructure water pipes, wastewater, hydrants, gas pipes, electricity, and telephone cables. The estate has not only the basic and supporting infrastructure but also a commercial area comprising a post office, ATM, and gas station. It has social infrastructure such as a food court and polyclinic. The estate has 335 enterprises operating in diverse sectors like palm oil and its derivatives, rubber, chocolate, coffee, tea, other agricultural products, forest products, furniture, rattan furniture, building materials (steel), and others.[18]

West Sumatera. West Sumatera is rich in cocoa processing, fisheries processing, and the snacks industry. The government is targeting West Sumatera as the center of cacao in Western Indonesia. Initiatives have been taken to provide training to cacao farmers in cacao learning centers. The province is also rich in tuna and is strategically located for landing and exporting (HKI 2019b). However, it has only one industrial estate, Padang Industrial Park, spread over 616 hectares. It is one of the bottom provinces in terms of GDP per capita, with the share of manufacturing in its GRDP being as low as 11.8% against 28% in Riau Islands.

Malaysia

The Malaysia-GT covers eight states of Northern Peninsular Malaysia: Melaka, Kedah, Kelantan, Negeri Sembilan, Penang (Pulau Pinang), Perak, Perlis, and Selangor, which form IMT-GT Economic Corridor 2 and parts of Corridor 3. These states, which account for 42.6% of national GDP and 19% of the total area, host 119 (48%) of 247 major economic zones identified by MIDA in the country and 55% of 216 zones in Peninsular Malaysia. They contribute 60.5% of the national manufacturing

---

18 Kawasan Industri Medan. Industrial Partner. https://kim.co.id/new/en/business-enterprise/industrial-partner/.

value added. Map 2 presents the economic zones' map of Peninsular Malaysia. It shows that Penang (with parts of Kedah and Perak) and Selangor (with N. Sembilan and Melaka) form two major manufacturing and logistics hubs comprising 45 (38% of 119) and 57 (48%) economic zones, respectively. In addition to publicly developed zones, they also have a sizable number of privately developed zones, albeit the number is unknown. The SEZs such as free industrial zones (FIZs), LMWs, and FCZs and specialized parks such as halal parks are also concentrated in these areas. Of 22 FIZs, 16 are located within these hubs. Similarly, of the 16 FCZs for which we have information, all but two are in these hubs, along with 7 of 13 HALMAS parks (accredited halal parks) and 56 of 61 cybercities and centers.

Selangor has been historically the most developed state with GDP per capita 63% higher than the average of Peninsular Malaysia in 1971, due to its strategic geographic position with Klang Valley at its center and the easy availability of skilled labor. Penang took off when a free industrial zone (FIZ) was set up near Bayan Lepas airport of Penang in 1971 to attract foreign investment in labor-intensive industries. The FIZ changed the manufacturing landscape of Penang. As the two poles of Penang and Selangor expanded and the demand for land increased, the peripheral states also benefited due to relocation of assembly-type activity: Negeri Sembilan and Melaka in the proximity of Selangor, and Kedah and Perak on the borders of Penang. Currently, Selangor, Melaka, and Negeri Sembilan are among the top five states in terms of GDP per capita and account for 38% of manufacturing value added. Penang, along with Perak and Kedah, contributes another 22% of manufacturing value added. Even though Perak and Kedah are among the four lowest GDP per capita states (along with Perlis and Kelantan), they contribute 8.5% of national manufacturing value added.[19] However, Perlis and Kelantan remain marginalized in terms of industrial growth. Table 15 presents the distribution of economic zones by type and location. The numbers of industrial parks and high-tech parks are extracted from the MIDA statistics of 247 industrial locations; the rest are based on their distinct sources. It shows 354 economic zones in Malaysia, out of which 201 are in Malaysia-GT, with 145 being in manufacturing and logistics and 56 in cybercities and centers. Selangor, Penang, and Melaka are at the top, followed by Kedah, Negeri Sembilan, Perak, and Kelantan. Perlis remains at the bottom.

Prominent Economic Zones by State: Proposed and Operational

In addition to the existing parks, there are several economic zones in the pipeline. Some of the prominent economic zones, both operational and proposed, are presented in Table 16.

Penang. Penang hosts the oldest and most successful FIZs in Bayan Lepas and Prai. Penang's electrical and electronics (E&E) ecosystem—especially in the area of semiconductor, solar energy, light-emitting diodes (LED), storage technologies, and electronic manufacturing services—has been a major driver of industrialization in the state, the emergence and growth of which owes much to the establishment of SEZs in the state. In 2018, the industry accounted for around 34% of the total exports with a trade surplus (Workman 2019). Semiconductor Equipment and Materials International (SEMI), an international organization in the semiconductor field, attributes approximately 8% of the global back-end semiconductor output to Penang, making it among the

---

[19] Perak is at the top of the bottom five states, with its GDP per capita being 30% short of the national GDP per capita, while Kelantan is the poorest, with its income per capita being only 30% of the national average.

Table 15. Cluster-Based Economic Zones and Manufacturing Shares in the Malaysia Growth Triangle

	Selangor	Penang	Melaka	Negeri Sembilan	Perak	Kedah	Perlis	Kelantan
Industrial parks	18	7	16	12	9	13	5	10
High-tech parks	1	4	2	1	1	2	0	0
Halal parks	2	2	1	2	1	1	2	2
FCZs (including SBEZ)	6	4	0	0	0	3	0	2
FIZs	4	5	5	0	2	0	0	0
Cybercities/centers	47	6	1	0	1	1	0	0
Total	78	28	25	15	14	20	7	14
Contribution to national manufacturing value added 2015 (%)	28.9	13.3	4.6	4.5	3.9	4.5	0.3	0.3
Manufacturing share as ratio of state GDP (%)	29	45	41	40	18	29	8	5
GDP per capita by state as ratio to national GDP per capita	1.1	1.2	1.1	1.0	0.7	0.5	0.6	0.3

FCZ = free commercial zone, FIZ = free industrial zone, GDP = gross domestic product, SBEZ = special border economic zone.
Source: Author, based on various sources.

world's top locations for microelectronics assembly, packaging, and testing (InvestPenang).[20] Penang also has a strong presence in the automotive, precision engineering, plastics, software, and packaging industries. The Penang state government has taken initiatives to transform the Batu Kawan Industrial Park into an innovation district as the "Silicon Valley of the East."

■ **Batu Kawan Innovation District.** It is envisioned to be a site offering mixed-use housing, office, and retail, which can serve as a test bed for nascent technologies and where leading-edge anchor institutions and industry clusters can interact with start-ups, business incubators, and accelerators, leveraging Penang's strength in the semiconductor industry and associated sectors (Choy 2018).

Melaka. It has as many as 21 industrial zones attracting investment mainly in seven sectors: medical, food, electronics, petroleum, transportation, metal manufacturing, and nonmetallic mineral. Recently, Melaka state government has announced that it plans to develop a new maritime-oriented economic corridor officially named as Melaka Waterfront Economic Zone with areas dedicated to tourism products, duty-free zones, shopping malls, offices, hotels, residences, and Industrial Revolution 4.0 (IR4.0) industries to revamp the economy of the state.

Selangor. Selangor is dotted with industrial parks, FIZs, and FCZs forming industrial hubs in five major sectors: E&E, life sciences, food (halal), transport, and machinery. Halal is the fifth-largest industry in Selangor. The main driver for the halal-certified food sector is the halal hub in Pulau

[20]   InvestPenang. Electrical & Electronics (E&E). https://investpenang.gov.my/electrical-electronics/.

Table 16. Prominent Projects in the Malaysia Growth Triangle

IMT-GT State	Prominent Projects Operational (Fully/Partially)	Under Development/Proposed
Selangor	• Klang Valley • Cyberjaya • Pulau Indah Halal hub	• Halal hub in Pulau Indah (Expansion) • An aerospace and high-tech park within the Subang Aerotech Park
Penang	• Bayan Lepas • Prai • Penang Science Park • Batu Kawan industrial park	• Batu Kawan innovation district
Negeri Sembilan	• Nilai Industrial Estate • Enstek Sci-Tech City • Pedas Halal Park (MIEL)	• Malaysia Vision Valley 2.0
Melaka	• Melaka Technology Park • Composite Technology City • Elkay Industrial Park • Serkam (halal food hub)	
Perak	• Parit Lumut Port • Seri Manjung • Kampung Aceh Technology Park	• A Proton City automotive hub in Tanjung Malim • Green Asia Aerospace Technology Park • Batu Gajah Locomotive Hub • Ipoh Aerospace Park • Perak Eco-Industrial Hub • Perak Free Commercial Zone
Kedah	• Kulim Hi-Tech Park Phase 1 • Automotive hub	• Bukit Hitam SBEZ • Rubber city • Manufacturing and logistics industrial hub, Sidam near Kulim • Science and Technology Park • Kulim Hi-Tech Park Master Plan 2
Perlis	• Kuala Perlis Industrial Park • Pauh Putra Technology Park • Perlis Halal Park	• Chuping Valley • Kuala Perlis Mixed Development project
Kelantan	• IMT-GT Plaza • Pasir Mas Halal Park • Tok Bali Supply Base	• Tok Bali Industrial Park • Tok Bali Integrated Fisheries Park

IMT-GT = Indonesia–Malaysia–Thailand Growth Triangle, SBEZ = special border economic zone.

Source: Compiled by the author from various sources.

Indah. Set up in 2003, Phase I was the first halal park in Malaysia, with an area of 121.40 hectares. Phase 2, with an area of 161.87 hectares, is being developed. Phase 3, with 121.40 hectares, will be developed later. Further, Malaysia Airports Holdings Berhad and Singapore-listed Boustead Projects Limited propose developing an aerospace and high-tech park within the Subang Aerotech Park in Selangor over 14.03 hectares within the proximity of the Sultan Abdul Aziz Shah Airport.

Negeri Sembilan. Negeri Sembilan is one of Malaysia's most industrialized states, with 39.7% of GDP contributed by manufacturing. According to the state government's website, it hosts 50 industrial parks forming seven industrial clusters: biotechnology, automotive, ancillary, food, aerospace, advanced electronics, and medical devices. It has an ambitious project in the pipeline: Malaysia Vision Valley 2.0.

■ **Malaysia Vision Valley 2.0.** According to MIDA (2018a), Malaysia Vision Valley 2.0 is a state-led private sector-driven development initiative covering over 153,411 hectares of land in Nilai, Seremban, and Port Dickson—an area twice the size of Singapore. It will focus on four types of activities: high-tech industry; services and tourism; education and research; and logistics, aviation, and maritime. Sime Darby Property Bhd will be the master developer. The first phase of the project spans over 30 years, covering 10,927 hectares of land. Six projects have been identified in this phase: a hi-tech industrial park (1,135 hectares), an integrated transportation terminal and downtown transit-oriented development (3,518 hectares), specialized and integrated logistics services (1,240 hectares), World Knowledge City (2,000 hectares), Biopolis and Wellness City (2,000 hectares), and a tourism district (920 hectares).

Kelantan. Kelantan specializes in food and beverages, including halal food-based products, herbs, agriculture-based products, and meat-based products. It is proposed to be branded as the country's main halal hub by further enhancing the existing halal parks and creating new ones in each district, focusing on the production and marketing of local halal products. The plans are to strengthen the agricultural poultry and biotechnology industries. It is also a center of hospitality services and distribution. Some important projects it hosts are the following:

■ **IMT-GT Plaza.** The IMT-GT Plaza in Bukit Bunga is strategically located along the border area of Rantau Panjang-Sungai Golok and Pengkalan Kubor-Tak Bai. It is an organized platform for traders from the IMT-GT countries to introduce, showcase, and market their products. It can provide space for close to 100 entrepreneurs and create 150 jobs. It is expected to boost cross-border trade, tourism, and commercial industrial development in the area. Its commercial areas are almost all tenanted. Prior to shifting to the IMT-GT Plaza, most of these entrepreneurs were operating from makeshift stalls.

■ **Pasir Mas Halal Park.** The State Economic Development Council is developing this park over 43.7 hectares in two stages. Phase 1 (20.23 hectares) is already developed and operating, comprising a business complex, a warehouse, and industrial plots. Phase 2 (23.47 hectares) is under construction and will comprise a logistics hub; a commercial zone; a collection, processing, and packaging center; and industrial plots. According to MIDA (2018b), the park is expected to attract RM611 million in private investments by 854 units and create more than 4,200 job opportunities by 2020.

■ **Tok Bali Integrated Fisheries Park.** This park in Pasir Puteh, along with a collection, processing, and packaging center in Pengkalan Kubor, is key in developing Kelantan into a hub for fish and marine-based activities.

■ **Tok Bali Pasir Puteh.** Spread over 101.17 hectares, Tok Bali Supply Base, an offshore oil and gas supply, has been given the status of an LMW. Developed by Matrix Reservoir Sdn. Bhd., it commenced operations in July 2015. It is strategically located and ensures providing integrated support services and facilities, including all-weather 473 meters of berthing facilities with fuel bunker, potable water, liquid mud, and dry bulk off-take points, which can accommodate five supply vessels and three crew boats at a time (TB Supply Base Sdn. Bhd.).

Perlis. It has the largest proportion of agriculture and the lowest of manufacturing among the four states of the Northern Corridor Economic Region. The Northern Corridor Implementing Authority has approved the Chuping Valley project to diversify the state's economy.

- **Chuping Valley.** The Chuping Valley Industrial Area is northeast of Perlis in Padang Besar, bordering the south of Thailand. Padang Besar serves as a major stopover along the rail routes that stretch from Singapore to Thailand. It is also linked with Thailand through a highway with low value-added shopping tourism as the main activity. It is littered with business complexes and duty-free complexes. The plan is to transform it into a hub of high value-added activity. According to a presentation by Northern Corridor Implementation Authority during country consultations, the Chuping Valley Industrial Area, spread over 1,214 hectares of land, is projected to leverage the existing road and rail infrastructure to enhance cross-border trade, increase logistics activities, and boost the area's development. Three clusters are planned with renewable energy, halal pharmaceutical, and green industries (automotive, E&E, and building materials) as the target industries and are proposed to be equipped with modern facilities, including an international school, Green Manufacturing Integrated Business Center, Perlis Inland Port, a solar farm, and a knowledge center.

- **Kuala Perlis Mixed Development Project.** It is a partnership project between State Economic Development Corporation and TH Properties. It is a mega project to develop a maritime commercial center hosting offices, residential apartments, hotels, and malls. Other projects are Kangar City Center and K-Parc in Seriab, Integrated Public Transport Terminal (Kangar Sentral), and Sanglang Jetty development stretching toward the Strait of Malacca and from Sungai Padang to Simpang Ampat.

Perak. It is the second-largest state in Peninsular Malaysia and, according to the website of InvestPerak,[21] hosts around 70 industrial parks, of which 14 are listed by MIDA as prominent (Table 15). It specializes in agriculture, agro-food, agrochemical, and pharmaceuticals. It also hosts a cyber center that houses MSC corridor status companies. The government plans to push industrialization in the state by promoting 4.0 industries through ambitious projects, some of which are listed below.

- **Perak Hi-Tech Industrial Park.** The park will be revived by attracting high-tech and high value-added industries as a Global Business Services center.[22] It is seen as a catalyst project for adopting and developing Industry 4.0 in Perak.

- **Perak Eco-Industrial Hub.** Spread over 1,376 hectares of reclaimed land at Mukim Rungkup, it will have an iron and steel integrated industry and other supporting industries as part of the development of Batang Padang and Hilir Perak districts.

- **Other high-technology projects.** Other proposed high-tech projects in the state include Kampung Aceh Free Commercial Zone near the Lumut Maritime Terminal to facilitate import–export of cargo, Proton City Automotive Hub in Tanjung Malim, Batu Gajah Locomotive Hub for locomotive components and maintenance-related services, an aerospace park near Sultan Azlan Shah Airport, and an 81-hectare Green Asia Aerospace Technology Park in Seri Iskandar.

---

21   InvestPerak. Overview. https://www.investperak.gov.my/key-figures/.

22   Global Business Services is a business model that provides services beyond transactional functions to deliver higher-value functions such as consulting and business analytics.

Kedah. Kedah State has a similar structure of the GDP's industrial composition as Perak, but its manufacturing share is larger than Perak's. Even though it has a large agriculture sector ("Rice Bowl of Malaysia"), manufacturing contributes 29% to its GDP. Notwithstanding, it still is among the bottom states in terms of GDP per capita. Several projects in the pipeline are expected to transform the state into a thriving industrial power. The thrust is on creating two major growth nodes: Kulim and Bukit Hitam.

- **Kulim Hi-Tech Park (KHTP).** Since its opening as Malaysia's first high-tech science park in 1996, it has attracted several hi-tech multinational companies. On the border of Penang, KHTP is just about 40 minutes from Penang International Airport. However, considering the limited capacity of Penang International Airport, the state of Kedah has proposed a new international airport to be built near the park. More than 1,760 hectares of land at KHTP has been developed, with a further 2,000 hectares set to be developed in the KHTP Master Plan 2. It is envisioned to be the "Science City of the Future."

- **Manufacturing and Logistics Industrial Hub, Sidam near Kulim.** It will reinforce the existing cluster in Kulim by promoting high-volume manufacturing of E&E, precision machinery, bio-medicine, and logistics Industries (air express logistics, aviation logistics, international distribution center, and e-commerce).

- **Bukit Kayu Hitam Kota Perdana Special Border Economic Zone.** Bukit Kayu Hitam–Sadao is the busiest border crossing between Malaysia and Thailand. According to the UN COMTRADE database, Thailand is currently Malaysia's fifth-largest trading partner, with a total trade value of $25.36 billion in 2019. Approximately 70% of this value is attributed to trade across the land border with Bukit Kayu Hitam–Sadao crossing alone. To leverage this benefit, the government is developing Kota Perdana SBEZ over 1,780 hectares of land in Bukit Hitam by Northern Gateway Sdn Bhd, a company fully owned by the government. It will be an integrated zone comprising a logistics hub and commercial area, inland port, and a free industrial park, with the Songkhla deep port as the gateway. The project will be developed in seven phases and is expected to be completed in 20 years. The Kedah Bukit Kayu Hitam ICQS complex project, which commenced on 14 June 2014, was completed on 25 June 2019 and has been fully operational since August 2019. In the next phase, Bukit Kayu Hitam Inland Container Depot (ICD), over 20.2 hectares of land will be developed and managed by a joint venture company, Bukit Kayu Hitam ICD Sdn Bhd, a 60:40 partnership between PKT Logistics Group Sdn Bhd (private company) and Northern Gateway Sdn Bhd. The ICD, linked to the Bukit Kayu Hitam ICQS complex, would be the integrated logistics hub to cater to the annual throughput of 200,000 containers along the warehouses and cross-dock facilities (Bernama 2019). The ICD will contain a petrol station and multistory tower providing office space, a logistics institute, and recreational facilities to cater to the needs of truckers. The logistics hub will catalyze cross-border trade by improving efficiency in the cross-border mobility of goods. This zone sets an example of the benefits emanating from regional integration. It will provide Southern Thailand's traders access to Malaysian ports in the Strait of Malacca and Malaysian traders easy access to the Port of Songkhla for trade with East Asia, reducing transport costs. It will be a win–win situation for both Thailand and Malaysia.

- **Kedah Science and Technology Park.** Located in Bukit Kayu Hitam Industrial Area (north part of Kedah), 2 km bordering Thailand, Kedah Science and Technology Park will focus on research and science-based manufacturing and leverage Bukit Kayu Hitam SBEZ to reinforce the cluster.

- **Rubber City.** The IMT-GT rubber city will cover 505.86 hectares in Ladang Bukit Ketapang, Kedah. It is expected to be catalytic in attracting well-recognized leading manufacturers of various rubber products, including innovative, high value-added, and specialized products for niche customer segments, e.g., specialty and surgical gloves, catheters, latex mattresses, adhesives, "intelligent" rubber, precision-engineered rubber products, and "green" rubber products.[23] The Kedah Rubber City is to be developed in three phases, with the first phase spread over 203.96 hectares. WZ Satu Bhd, a private company, has been given the responsibility for Phase 1 infrastructure development.

Thailand

The IMT-GT subregion consists of all 14 provinces of Southern Thailand: Nakhon Si Thammarat, Narathiwat, Pattani, Phatthalung, Satun, Songkhla, Trang, Yala, Chumphon, Krabi, Phangnga, Phuket, Ranong, and Surat Thani. These provinces are among the most backward provinces of the country. The region's gross provincial product (GPP)[24] per capita is less than one-third of that of Eastern Thailand, with the average share of manufacturing in GPP being 11%, compared with 50% of Eastern Thailand (Table 17). Agriculture, trade, and tourism are the major sectors accounting for almost 55% of the GPP. Four major tourist provinces in the region—Phuket, Krabi, Surat Thani, and Phangnga— have a GPP per capita income close to the national GDP per capita; in the rest of the provinces, it is 70% to 30% short of the national average. The region's contribution to the national manufacturing value added remains less than 4%. Songkhla is the most industrialized province with 20% of GPP constituted by manufacturing, followed by Trang (14.9%), Surat Thani (14.7%), Nakhon (12.8%), and Pattani (12%). In the rest of the provinces, it is marginal (Table 17).

Map 3 presents the map of industrial estates in Thailand. It shows a large hub of industrial estates in the central region covering Bangkok and Eastern Seaboard areas. The rest of the country has a small share in industrial estates. New industrial areas, named SEZs, have been developed in border areas to address the regional imbalance and leverage the availability of cheap cross-border labor. Following such development, industrial zones have also emerged in the southern region.

Songkhla. Despite being a backward province with manufacturing GPP contributing only 1.2% to national manufacturing value added and GPP per capita falling 28% short of the national average, Songkhla is one of the most industrialized provinces in Southern Thailand. Manufacturing in the province is propelled mainly by rubber, para wood and furniture, and seafood and halal food. Agriculture, which accounts for 15% of GPP, provides abundant raw materials and the basis for agro-industries. The service sector is dominated by low value-added services, which absorbed 61% of the workforce, contributing 46% of the GPP in 2011.[25] Songkhla has three districts adjacent to Malaysia and four custom check posts (Padang Besar, Sadao, Hat Yai, and Songkhla), accounting for most border trade, as stated above. Padang Besar and Sadao check posts account for as high as 97% of total border trade (Krainara and Routray 2015). Most trade is in rubber and rubber products,

---

[23] Green rubber products are produced using environment-friendly processes such as Ekoprena tires, or reclaimed rubber products such as rubberized bitumen, or products with a lower carbon footprint.

[24] GPP is the term used in Thailand for GRDP (as in Indonesia) and GDP by state (as in Malaysia).

[25] This information is provided in a Microsoft PowerPoint presentation during a field visit to Songkhla.

Table 17. Cluster-Based Economic Zones and Manufacturing Shares in the Thailand Growth Triangle

	Phuket	Surat Thani	Ranong	Phangnga	Krabi	Chumphon	Nakhon	Songkhla	Satun	Yala	Trang	Narathiwat	Phatthalung	Pattani
IE	0	0	0	0	0	0	0	1	0	0	0	0	0	0
SEZ	0	0	0	0	0	0	0	1	0	0	0	1	0	0
Total								2				1		
Share in national manufacturing (%)	0.01	0.7	0.05	0.05	0.1	0.2	0.5	1.2	0.1	0.1	0.3	0.1	0.1	0.2
Share of manufacturing in GPP (%)	1.7	14.7	7.8	3.9	4.4	11.4	12.8	19.9	8.3	8.3	14.9	6.3	10.3	12.0
Ratio of GPP per capita to national GDP per capita	1.5	0.9	0.5	1.0	1.1	0.7	0.5	0.7	0.6	0.5	0.5	0.3	0.3	0.4

GDP = gross domestic product, GPP = gross provincial product, IE = industrial estate, SEZ = special economic zone.

Source: Compiled by the author from various sources, including the National Statistical Office.

E&E appliances, fertilizer, and automotive parts. The province's economic zone profile is not very elaborate, even though it has an operational industrial estate since 1984.

- **Southern Region Industrial Estate.** It was established in Hat Yai District in 1984. Spanning over 363 hectares, it is 47 km from Songkhla deep-sea port and 82 km from the Malaysian border. Phase 1 of the industrial estate was developed over 140 hectares, with a general industrial zone and IEAT Free Zone. Phases 2 and 3 are currently being developed.

- **Rubber City Industrial Estate.** The Rubber City is located in Phases 2 and 3 of the Southern Industrial Estate. Spanning over 197 hectares of land, it aims "to serve as the hub or cluster for rubber products, from midstream to downstream industries, such as rubber innovations, concentrated latex, compound rubbers, and other related downstream industries" (IEAT). Of the total area, 71 hectares is developed as a premium zone for the clean general industries. To support the rubber industry, the government has set up the "Centre of Excellence in Natural Rubber Technology" at the Prince of Songkhla University. Moreover, a memorandum of understanding has been signed with Qingdao University of Science and Technology and the Rubber Valley Group from the PRC for technological development and to introduce joint and/or double degree programs focusing on learning about rubber products. The rubber city project is complete, but it is yet to take off.

- **Songkhla Special Economic Zone.** The Songkhla SEZ is coming up in Sadao District covering 552.3 square kilometers spread over four *tambons* (subdistricts). Phase I covers an area of 179.44 hectares. IEAT has completed the construction of an industrial estate in phase I in March 2021. It is the first industrial estate in Songkhla SEZ. It is divided into seven sections: general industry, FTZ, logistics services area, commercial area, electric station, public utilities

Map 3. Spatial Distribution of Industrial Estates in Thailand

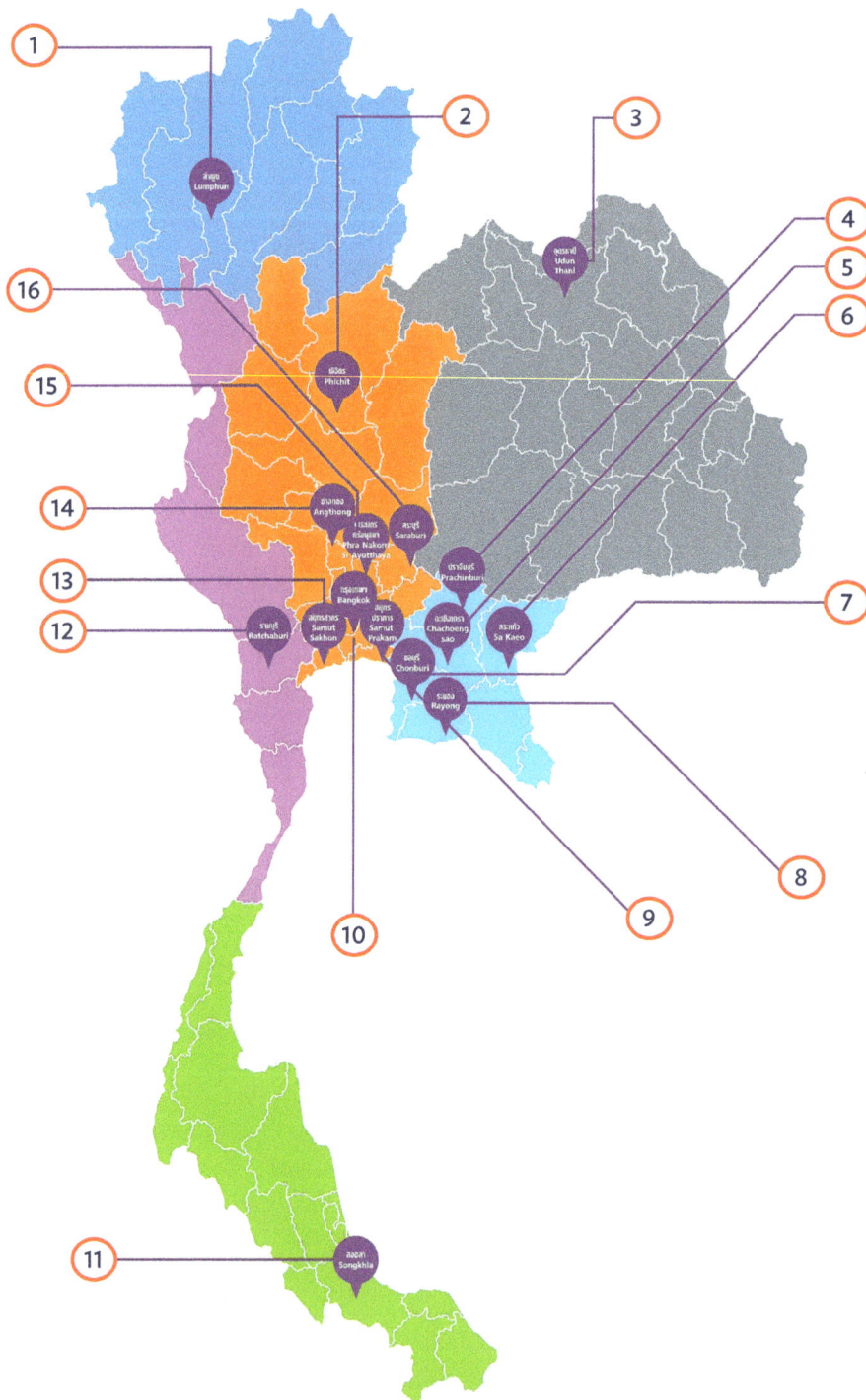

1. **Lumphun**
   - Northern Region Industrial Estate (Lumphun)
   - World Lumphun Industrial Estate

2. **Phichit**
   - Phichit Industrial Estate

3. **Udon Thani**
   - Udon Thani Industrial Estate

4. **Prachinburi**
   - Hi-Tech Kabin Industrial Estate
   - Borthong 33 Industrial Estate

5. **Chachoeng sao**
   - Well Grow Industrial Estate
   - Gate Way City Industrial Estate
   - TFD Industrial Estate
   - TFD Industrial Estate (Project 2)

6. **Sa Kaeo**
   - Sa Kaeo Industrial Estate, Special Economic Zone, Sa Kaeo Province

7. **Chonburi**
   - Laem Chabang Industrial Estate
   - Amata City Chonburi Industrial Estate
   - Amata City Chonburi Industrial Estate Project 2
   - WHA Chonburi Industrial Estate 1
   - WHA Chonburi Industrial Estate 2
   - Pin Thong Industrial Estate
   - Pin Thong Industrial Estate (Leam Chabang)
   - Pin Thong Industrial Estate (Project 3)
   - Pin Thong Industrial Estate (Project 4)
   - Pin Thong Industrial Estate (Project 5)
   - WHA Eastern Seaboard Industrial Estate 2
   - WHA Eastern Seaboard Industrial Estate 3
   - Yamato Industries Industrial Estate
   - Banbung Industrial Estate
   - Rojana Laem Chabang Industrial Estate
   - Asia Clean Chonburi Industrial Estate
   - Rojana Chonburi 2 (Khaokhansong) Industrial Estate
   - Rojana Nongyai Industrial Estate

8. **Rayong**
   - WHA Eastern Seaboard Industrial Estate 4
   - WHA Rayong 36 Industrial Estate
   - RIL Industrial Estate
   - WHA Industrial Estate Rayong
   - Luckchai Rubber Industrial Estate
   - Amata City Rayong Industrial Estate
   - CPGC Industrial Estate
   - Smart Park Industrial Estate
   - Pin Thong Industrial Estate (Project 6)
   - Egco Rayong Industrial Estate
   - WHA Eastern Seaboard Industrial Estate 1
   - WHA Eastern Industrial Estate (Map Ta Phut)
   - Eastern Seaboard Industrial Estate (Rayong)
   - Asia Industrial Estate
   - Map Ta Phut Industrial Estate
   - Map Ta Phut Industrial Port
   - Padaeng Industrial Estate

9. **Samut Prakarn**
   - Bangpoo Industrial Estate
   - Bang Plee Industrial Estate
   - Asia Industrial Estate (Suvarnabhumi)
   - Bangpoo Industrial Estate (North)
   - Bhakasa Industrial Estate

10. **Bangkok**
    - Bang Chan Industrial Estate
    - Lad Krabang Industrial Estate
    - Gemopolis Industrial Estate

11. **Songkhla**
    - Southern Region Industrial Estate (Songkhla)
    - Rubber City in Southern Region Industrial Estate, Songkhla Province
    - Songkhla Industrial Estate, Special Economic Zone, Songkhla Province

12. **Ratchaburi**
    - Ratchaburi Industrial Estate

13. **Samut Sakhon**
    - Samut Sakhon Industrial Estate
    - Sinsakhon Industrial Estate
    - Maharaj Nakorn Industrial Estate

14. **Angthong**
    - World Food Valley Thailand Industrial Estate

15. **Phra Nakorn Si Ayutthaya**
    - Ban Wa Industrial Estate
    - Bang Pa-in Industrial Estate
    - Nakhon Luang Industrial Estate

16. **Saraburi**
    - Kaeng Khoi Industrial Estate
    - Nong Khae Industrial Estate

Note: **Eastern Economic Corridor Development (EEC)** in red text.

area, industrial support unit, and land reserved for green and buffer area. In addition to typical industrial infrastructure (roads, electricity, water, etc.), the SEZ will also host a school and hospital for community members within the zone. The target investments for the Songkhla SEZ are processed agricultural products, logistics, halal, textiles, and light industries. It is expected to increase border trade on the southern border.

- **Chana Southern province model city.** In January 2020, the government designated Chana District in Songkhla as a model city under the Triangle of Stability, Prosperity, and Sustainability Project. In January 2020, the cabinet approved developing five projects in the zone, comprising new town planning in three tambons: water transport and a second deep-sea port in Songkhla; land transport linked to the main highway and local roads; electricity plants from natural gas; solar cell or renewable energy; and an industrial estate (Econ 2020). The project covering 2,680 hectares of land will have areas allocated for light industries, heavy industries, energy complex, related industries for export and import, logistics and goods distribution, and recreation and accommodation. The development projects are expected to create 100,000 new jobs.

Narathiwat. Most of the area in the province consists of primary rainforest jungles and overgrown mountains. It is an agrarian province with agriculture accounting for over 32% of GPP and the industry's share being less than 5%. The province is being developed as a center for halal food production. There is a large potential for Thailand to expand this industry through collaboration projects with Malaysia and Indonesia, as well as Brunei Darussalam. The province has three custom checkpoints: Sungai Kolok, Tak Bai, and Buketa. While there is an increase in border trade over time, it is relatively small. To give an impetus to industrial development, the government has proposed to develop an SEZ.

- **Narathiwat special economic zone.** In January 2020, the Southern Border Provinces Administrative Center was assigned to purchase 270 hectares of land from the private company that owns a rubber plantation with a budget of B390 million. IEAT will develop about 96 hectares of land as an industrial estate, with 160 hectares set aside for rent to the private sector and the remaining land for the offices of state agencies. The target industries are the labor-intensive industries: textiles and clothing, furniture, agro-processing, halal, rubber processing.
- **Sungai Kolok model city.** Sungai Kolok District in Narathiwat Province has been designated as one of the model cities. It is to be developed as an international border trade city.

Development of the other model cities under the Triangle of Stability, Prosperity, and Sustainability Project. In addition to Chana and Sungai Kolok cities, two more model cities are proposed in Nong Chik and Betong districts of Pattani and Yala provinces. The plan is to elevate Nong Chik into an agricultural industry city with emphasis on the processing of agricultural products, and Betong into a tourism city (Table 18).

However, the progress has been slow due to the challenges of extremism that the provinces of Narathiwat, Pattani, and Yala have been facing along with parts of Songkhla.

Southern Seaboard Development Plan. The Southern Seaboard Development Plan was originally proposed in 1975. The Hunting Technical Service did the first study in 1975. In 1989, the National

Table 18. Prominent Projects in the Thailand Growth Triangle

	Operational	Under Implementation
Songkhla	• Southern Industrial estate • Rubber city	• Songkhla SEZ • Chana district model city
Narathiwat		• Narathiwat SEZ • Sungai Kolok model city
Yala		• Betong district model city
Pattani		• Nong Chik district model city

SEZ = special economic zone.

Source: Compiled by the author from various sources.

Economic and Social Development Council (NESDC) proposed the southern region's strategic development plan to the cabinet. The cabinet approved only the Land Bridge project, which connects the Andaman Sea and the Gulf of Thailand. This project, which consists of a multimodal transport linkage to combine road, railway, and pipeline in the corridor, is regarded as the beginning of the Southern Seaboard Development Plan. NESDC was assigned to conduct the master plan of the Southern Seaboard Development Project. The plan was completed in 1992 and was, in principle, approved by the cabinet in 1993. Of late, the government has accelerated efforts to implement the project.

Subregional Economic Zones from Economic Corridors' Perspective

The above analysis indicates that the IMT-GT corridors host various economic zones at different stages of operation. There are 355 zones of various types in the IMT-GT region for which there is specific information available. Malaysia accounts for 57% of the total subregional zones, followed by Indonesia (36%) and Thailand (7%). The pipeline of zone projects in the subregion is rather long, with several ambitious and large projects in all three countries. However, the density and stage of development of economic zones vary across the priority corridors.

- **Economic Corridor 2 (Malaysia).** This comprises the northern states of Peninsular Malaysia along the Strait of Malacca and is most densely populated with economic zones. It hosts the most technologically sophisticated economic zones attracting high- to medium-tech industries in E&E, digital technologies, automotive products, pharmaceuticals, and halal products. In the northern states of Kedah, Perlis, and Perak, processed food and other resource-based products also dominate the zones along with E&E and automotive sectors.

- **Economic Corridor 3 (Indonesia).** This covers the whole of Sumatera in Indonesia and follows Economic Corridor 2 in terms of the number of zones. It is largely dominated by resource-based zones (rubber, palm oil, and minerals) and light- and medium-tech activities in E&E and shipbuilding.

- **Economic Corridor 1 (Indonesia–Malaysia–Thailand).** Economic Corridor 1 is dotted with diverse economic activities and connects Medan, the industrial center of Sumatera, with industrially advanced states of Penang and agriculturally dominated Kedah and Songkhla.

- **Economic Corridor 4 (Indonesia–Malaysia) and Economic Corridor 5 (Indonesia–Thailand).** These corridors are essentially connectivity corridors and resonate with transport and trade corridors.

A crucial implication is that IMT-GT economic zones also form a development ladder in terms of the type, composition, and development levels across the corridors to ensure factor complementarity, which is one of the critical conditions for the subregion's success. Indonesia, Malaysia, and Thailand can benefit from considerable economic synergies in economic zones if economic corridors are effectively implemented, ensuring the mobility of capital, people, and goods and through coordinated and concerted efforts.

Chapter 6

Assessing the Alignment of Broader National Policies and Strategies with the IMT-GT Approaches

The outcome of a transborder economic corridor hinges on its success in strengthening industrial agglomerations and driving cross-border and regional value chains (RVCs) to facilitate shared prosperity through regional cooperation along and beyond the corridor. In line with this, the spatial approach of IMT-GT Vision 2036 seeks to promote cross-border production networks through collaborative efforts and maximize the economic network externalities of the five priority economic corridors in the subregion. The economic zones and other production sites are the key drivers of this collaborative approach. However, economic zones, particularly SEZs, are typically set up as part of the competitive strategy to attract investment, which is not quite consistent with the principles of the collaborative (regional cooperation) approach.

This chapter assesses whether the approach toward the subregional economic zones is aligned with the IMT-GT vision agenda or is competitive. While doing so, it addresses two pertinent questions. First, is the subregional agenda integrated into national plans and priorities? Second, are the subregional economic zones aligned with the collaborative approach of the subregional agenda? It begins by explaining the term "collaborative approach" in the context of economic zones and the relevance of its mainstreaming into the national plan agenda.

Linkages between Subregional Economic Corridors, Economic Zones, and National Development: The Collaborative Approach

In this globalized world where GVCs or RVCs increasingly dominate trade and investment, place-based competencies have assumed a critical role in driving economic dynamism (Ascani, Crescenzi, and Iammarino 2012). However, these competencies are generally heavily biased toward one or two core areas at the expense of other peripheral development axes, exacerbating regional inequality and weakening economic growth by pulling down the average economic productivity. The policy of setting up economic zones with attractive fiscal incentives in the lagging regions may not achieve the intended outcomes because fiscal incentives alone cannot compensate for other local disadvantages. Rothenberg et al. (2017), for instance, reveal that the substantial tax breaks offered to KAPET districts in Indonesia could not ensure the intended development outcome in these lagging districts. The centripetal forces such as proximity to harbor, river, or central location; market size; availability of resources; and knowledge-generating institutions tend to attract investment to the national cores (Krugman 1992).

The subregional program aims to turn the national peripheries into cross-border growth centers through economic corridors, which promote regional development and economic growth by strengthening local specificities, empowering local actors, creating connectivity among them, and facilitating the creation of cross-border production networks through regional integration (Ortiz-Guerrero 2013). These economic corridors can be instrumental in initiating the subregional flying geese paradigm of regional cooperation (Aggarwal 2019). In this paradigm, firms in the lead region relocate the less complex, lower value-added activities to the following less developed ones in accordance with their comparative advantage to form cross-border value chains (Kasahara 2013). Driven by economic zones, this process leads to simultaneous upgrading of the subregional economies at three levels: intra-industry upgrading from low to high value-added activities; inter-industry upgrading from low to high value-added industries; and interregional structural upgrading, pushing up productivity and, in turn, economic growth.

The cross-border value chains in the region can enhance the capacity of the clusters through the infusion of innovations and conserve the environment and natural resources through cross-border aggregation of resources. Further, economic zones along the corridors benefit from expanded market access and economies of scale. The subregional economic zones, particularly SBEZs, have easy access to new cross-border markets, thus creating new opportunities for companies to expand their activities beyond their national borders, as well as providing consumers with a wider range of products and services. Finally, economic cross-border cooperation may spill over into political cooperation, leading to peace and stability in these areas, which is conducive to growth. As industrial development occurs, economic dynamism further spurs growth and expansion of the clusters, expanding spin-offs and suppliers of both the clustered industry and related industries to

Figure 5. Links between the IMT-GT Subregion, Economic Corridors, and Production Hubs

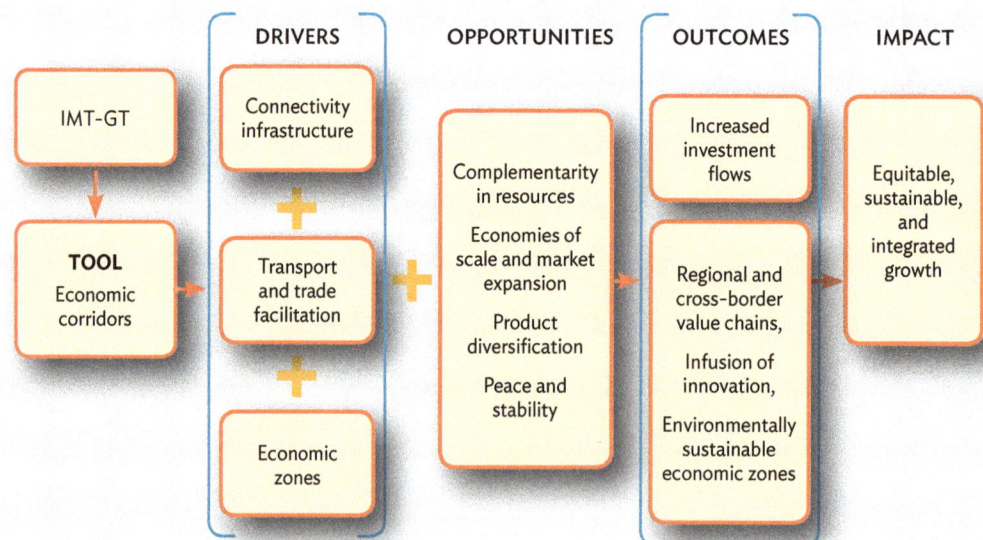

IMT-GT = Indonesia–Malaysia–Thailand Growth Triangle.
Source: Author.

catapult the regional economies to a higher growth trajectory (Myrdal 1957). Figure 5 summarizes these channels.

COVID-19 global pandemic and economic zones. The coronavirus disease 2019 (COVID-19) pandemic has further underscored the need for a collaborative approach in economic zone development. The measures designed to contain the pandemic have disrupted the GVCs by curbing economic activity; restricting the mobility of people, goods, and services; dampening global demand; and deteriorating the financial environment. Since 70% of the world trade involves GVCs, world trade and investment fell substantially due to these measures (WTO 2020). In its press release in March 2020, the International Monetary Fund reported that capital outflows from emerging markets had amounted to $83 billion since the beginning of the COVID-19 crisis (International Monetary Fund 2020). According to UNCTAD (2021), global FDI flows plummeted by 42% in 2020, and this effect will linger with investors who may adopt a cautious approach in the future in committing resources in overseas locations.

The major brunt of the drastic fall in trade and investment is borne by SEZs, which are heavily reliant on exports (Barbieri et al. 2020). Some assert that the new normal would be renationalizing GVCs to insulate countries from the pandemic's economic consequences. Others dismiss this argument as uncompetitive and infeasible because it would require an economic restructuring of the home countries of multinational corporations (MNCs). They argue that the companies may diversify their supplier base by establishing shorter RVCs (Javorcik 2020). This opportunity may be leveraged to promote subregional economies by adopting a collaborative approach in SEZs to overcome the regional disadvantages. The regional cooperation in economic zones may also contribute to better management of external shocks such as COVID-19. For instance, this pandemic gave a major thrust to two critical industries: (i) food, and (ii) pharmaceutical including medical equipment. The IMT-GT subregion, which has a competitive advantage in food, palm oil, and rubber (raw material for medical equipment) industries, can leverage these advantages through RVCs and become a prominent global supplier.

The Need for Mainstreaming the IMT-GT Subregional Agenda in National Development Agendas for the Collaborative Approach

The world economy's internationalization has placed the regional collaborative approach to development at center stage. The subregional programs, along with economic corridors and zones, are building blocks in this approach. However, in principle, subregional programs are informal because they are not supported by international law or agreements. They are not binding and cannot be enforced. Their success depends on a long-term vision, strong political will, and collective ownership, all of which should be backed by generous financial resources. This, in turn, requires the integration of subregional agendas into national development planning. It means that the objectives, targets, and strategic approaches (including economic zones) of the subregional program should be mainstreamed into national development plans and priorities. In the absence of coordination between the subregional programs and the national plan agenda, the program may deviate from optimal development outcomes because, normally, development strategies are locked in structural interdependencies in terms of shared resources, workforce, and organizational and bureaucratic capacities.

Thus, unless the subregional initiatives are integrated into national development agendas, they may lose out to other plan priorities and may not receive wide governmental support beyond specific line ministries and resource commitments for the program. This issue is particularly important for the development of economic zones, which are explicitly cross-cutting. The alignment of the subregional economic zone program with the national strategy can help leverage synergies across different programs and development agencies.

There is yet another important reason for mainstreaming the IMT-GT agenda into national planning. Typically, the economic zones are set up as a competitive tool to attract foreign investment and technologies. The subregional agenda of regional integration needs to be incorporated into development planning to recognize the regional aspect of the economic zones and the linkages between subregional economic corridors, economic zones, and national development.

Forms and Approaches of Mainstreaming IMT-GT Agenda into National Development Agendas

This section explores the linkages between the IMT-GT subregional and national development agendas using both qualitative and quantitative approaches.

Qualitative approach. For qualitative analysis, the study identifies four forms of linkages between the two agendas according to depth and scope. At one end of the spectrum is the broad alignment between the long-term vision and objectives of the two agendas but nothing beyond; at the other end of the spectrum is the mainstreaming of the IMT-GT strategic framework into national development strategies. In the middle of the spectrum, two forms of linkages are identified: (i) mainstreaming of IMT-GT projects, and (ii) alignment of economic zones with the IMT-GT regional agenda (Figure 6). Each form of these linkages is assessed using information collected from the national development plan documents (Figure 6).

National development planning has been a guiding force in the process of economic development in IMT-GT countries. Each of these countries' development agendas has been set out in a series of long-term, medium-term, and annual plans. Further, all three countries follow an "indicative planning framework," which sets out broad directions operationalized through legislative, fiscal, and other policy measures. It signals the government's investment priorities and opportunities for the private sector. Whether at the center or state levels, all other supporting plans and policies are framed within the broad framework of the national plan document. Therefore, the qualitative analysis focuses on the national long- and medium-term plans. An overview of development plans in the three countries is presented below.

- **Indonesia.** In accordance with Law Number 25 of 2004 on the National Development Planning System, Indonesia draws up two interrelated development plans at the national level: National Long-Term Development Plan (RPJPN) and National Medium-Term Development Plan (RPJMN). Corresponding to these plans are long- and medium-term regional plans. The RPJPN, which spans over 20 years, is hierarchically the most important and is implemented through four medium-term plans of 5 years each. These two plans serve as the reference document for all long- and medium-term regional development plans. The current

Figure 6. Linkages between National Plans, Economic Corridors, and Economic Zones: The Conceptual Framework

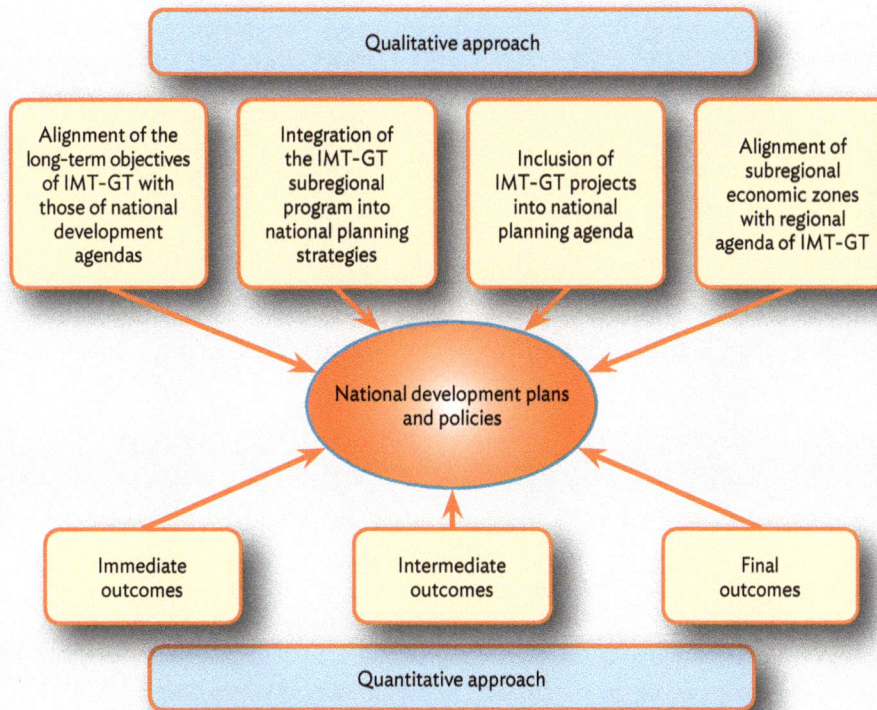

IMT-GT = Indonesia–Malaysia–Thailand Growth Triangle.
Source: Author.

long-term plan spans from 2005 to 2025. Under this, the third national medium-term plan RPJMN 2015–2019 is recently completed, and the final plan 2020–2024 has just started.

- **Malaysia.** Since 1971, Malaysia has been following long-term plans of various durations, with five yearly medium-term plans published regularly. The long-term plans such as the New Economic Policy (1971–1990), Vision 2020 (1991–2020), National Development Policy (1991–2000), National Vision Policy (2001–2010), and National Transformation Policy (2011–2020) form the long-term vision and benchmark for medium-term plans and policies to follow. The latest medium-term plan is the 11th plan (2016–2020), which is set under the 10 years' strategic objective of national transformation and represents the final medium-term plan toward Vision 2020.

- **Thailand.** Thailand follows the practice of 5-year strategic plans. However, the current 12th National Economic and Social Development Plan (2017–2021) is guided by the 20-year National Strategy (2018–2037).

Quantitative analysis. The purpose of the quantitative assessment is to measure the program's impact using a set of performance indicators of the subregion to gauge if the program is considered a national priority. The analysis is based on the premise that a program's success is directly linked with the importance attached to the program at the national level. The performance indicators of the subregion used in the analysis are organized into three broad categories: immediate, intermediate, and final. The analysis required national income accounts data both at the national, and provincial and state levels. For Malaysia, the data were acquired from the Department of Statistics for 2010–2018, on request. For Indonesia, we relied on the statistical yearbooks of 2019 and 2016 provided by BPS-Statistics Indonesia with detailed provincial statistics. Thailand's provincial data were downloaded from the website of the National Economic and Social Development Council. The national accounts data of three countries were supplemented by other databases from national and international sources.

Mapping of the IMT-GT Cooperation Program with the National Plans: A Qualitative Approach

Linkages between the Long-Term Objectives of IMT-GT and National Development Agendas

The IMT-GT vision is to create an integrated, innovative, inclusive, and sustainable subregion by 2036. Typically, there are no contradictions between the IMT-GT vision 2036 and the long- and medium-term development objectives of the member states (Table 19). These countries have long emphasized the objectives of economic growth, regional (subnational) equity, and competitiveness, which are in line with the IMT-GT vision of innovative and inclusive growth. In recent years, sustainable development has also been mainstreamed into national planning. The recently launched RPJMN for 2020–2024 in Indonesia has mainstreamed the Sustainable Development Goals (SDGs) with the targets and indicators of the 17 goals accommodated in all seven development agendas, which were conceptualized with the SDGs in mind (Halimatussadiah 2020).

Notwithstanding the above, there is a crucial missing link between the IMT-GT vision and the development objectives of the member countries. Even though the regional cooperation frameworks are booming in the region, with subregional programs also gathering momentum alongside the ASEAN Economic Community (AEC), the goal of regionally integrated development is not yet mainstreamed into the national plan vision, objectives, or targets (Table 19). Thailand has addressed this gap by specifying regional integration as a goal of national importance in the 12th National Social and Economic Development Plan (2017–2021) (Table 19). Further, while elaborating its vision statement in its long-term national strategy, it implicitly underscores the importance of regional integration as an economic development tool when it expresses the aspiration to be a key hub for the region's transportation, manufacturing, trade, investment, and business operations to attain robust development (National Strategy 2018–2037). Indonesia and Malaysia are yet to address this gap.

Mainstreaming of IMT-GT Spatial Approach as a Strategic Pillar

Indonesia. The just-completed medium-term plan RPJMN (2015–2019) highlighted the importance of strengthening the role of global, regional, and subregional cooperation in achieving the objective of balanced regional development (Chapter 6.3, Government of Indonesia 2015). The plan document expressed its commitment to the subregional program by highlighting the need to build capacity of the local governments and business community to ensure that the program was implemented in a mutually beneficial way. The recently launched RPJMN 2020–2024 adopts

Table 19. Mapping of Long- and Medium-Term Objectives of National Plans with Those of IMT-GT

	IMT-GT	Indonesia	Malaysia	Thailand
Vision	Developed sustainable, inclusive, integrated, and innovative subregion	**RPJPN (2005–2025)** Developed and self-reliant, just and democratic, and peaceful and united society	**Vision 2020 (1991–2020)** Modernize and develop the nation economically, politically, socially, spiritually, psychologically, and culturally	**National Strategy B.E. 2561–2580 (2018–2037)** A developed country with security, prosperity, and sustainability in accordance with the Sufficiency Economy Philosophy A key hub for the region's transportation, manufacturing, trade, investment, and business operations to attain robust development
Medium-term plans objectives		**RPJMN 2020-2024** Creating a developed Indonesia that is sovereign, independent, and with characteristics based on gotong royong or mutual cooperation (inclusive development with increased local involvement and participation of all community members in the development process)	**Mid-Term Eleventh Plan Review (2018–2021)** Inclusive and sustainable development Greater emphasis on the less developed states to ensure a more balanced regional growth	**National Development Plan 2017–2021** To promote an economy that is strong, competitive, stable, and sustainable Objective 1.7: Strengthen connectivity between Thailand and other countries at the subregional levels. Promote Thailand as a leading actor in trade, services, and investment within subregional frameworks. Target 2.5: Thailand becomes a vital partner in subregional cooperation. Transportation, logistics, and value chains should be interconnected. The rate of investment and exports from Thailand to subregional countries should increase.

IMT-GT = Indonesia–Malaysia–Thailand Growth Triangle, RPJMN = Rencana Pembangunan Jangka Menengah Nasional (National Medium-Term Development Plan), RPJPN= Rencana Pembangunan Jangka Panjang Nasional (National Long-Term Development Plan).

Source: Compiled by the author from various plan documents.

two main strategic approaches for regional development: the growth corridor approach and the island-based equity corridor approach. While the former prioritizes the development of growth centers in particular industrial estates, KEKs, and KPBPBs, the latter focuses on the development of buffer zones (hinterland) around centers of growth, as well as disadvantaged areas and regions. The role of the subregional program is not appreciated in achieving regional development. The plan document makes a fleeting reference to various regional and subregional programs in achieving the objective of export upgrading and diversification of markets (p. II.32-33, Government of Indonesia 2020). Likewise, it is recognized in the subnational development strategies of Sumatera that the subregional program along with other regional cooperation programs will expand trade and diversify export markets, but there is nothing beyond that.

Malaysia. Until the 10th Malaysia Plan 2011–2015 (Government of Malaysia 2011), there had been little mention of the IMT-GT subregion in Malaysia's plan documents. As part of the strategic focus on accelerating regional growth for better geographic balance, the 11th Malaysia Plan 2016–2020 (Government of Malaysia 2016) proposed the Border Economic Transformation Program to bring about inclusive development and prosperity to Malaysia's border regions. The strategy outlined was to "start [the Border Economic Transformation Program] with the Malaysia-Thailand border with the aim of attracting investment, creating jobs and increasing incomes for the local communities in and around border areas" (11th Malaysia Plan 2016, p. 3-31). Notwithstanding, there was no direct reference made to the IMT-GT subregional program, undermining the role of the subregional program in the border transformation program.

The Mid-Term Review of the Eleventh Malaysia Plan in 2018 (Government of Malaysia 2018), which embarked on new priorities taking into consideration the new government's aspirations and outlined revised socioeconomic targets for 2018–2020, saw a link between the border area transformation and IMT-GT agenda. It recognized that the subregional cooperation platforms had not been utilized to accelerate and facilitate economic development, particularly in border areas, and explicitly committed to intensifying the ASEAN subregional programs to stimulate economic activities in bordering areas. Toward that goal, enhancing the IMT-GT subregional cooperation was set out as a strategic pillar for achieving balanced regional development. Two major objectives in that pillar were improving connectivity and accelerating the development of SEZs in Malaysia-GT. The subregion's role was thus recognized by incorporating it as a strategic component in addressing regional imbalances. This was a major step toward integrating the IMT-GT cooperation program into the national development agenda.

Thailand. In Thailand, the long-term vision of security, prosperity, and sustainability under the National Strategy, 2018–2037 is to be achieved through six key strategies: national security, growth with competitiveness enhancement, development of human capital, equality, environment-friendly development and growth, and improvement in government administration (Government of Thailand 2018). Although regionally integrated development is not an explicit pillar of the long-term strategies, there are references to regional connectivity and trade facilitation in the strategic directions for competitiveness enhancement. Further, the 12th National Economic and Social Development Plan (Government of Thailand 2017) sets regional integration as an objective of national importance in line with the vision statement of IMT-GT Vision 2036 (Table 19) and translates the objective into proposed actions by integrating the IMT-GT cooperation program as one of the pillars of development strategies. More specifically, the plan is built on 10 strategic pillars, with the Strategy for International Cooperation for Development being the 10th pillar supported by selected targets and their indicators. The IMT-GT strategic approach is mainstreamed into this strategic pillar. It sets the targets to

- revise laws and regulations to support Thailand as a production, investment, and services hub to increase the intraregional and subregional volume of transport in goods and services, cross-border trade value, and investment;
- promote subregional and ASEAN value chains; and
- increase trade and investment value between Thailand and countries in the region.

The 11th National Economic and Social Development Plan (2012–2016) had also emphasized the need for mutually beneficial cooperation with ASEAN countries and other neighbors with respect to labor, energy, natural resources, production bases, supply chains, goods processing, and logistics systems. However, the focus was on ASEAN rather than the subregional programs. The plan document acknowledged the subregion's importance and identified it as the most crucial element in Thailand's foreign policy and a key mechanism that served as the foundation for cooperation within ASEAN (Government of Thailand 2012). Against this background, the 12th national plan constitutes a major step toward institutionalizing and internalizing the subregional programs in Thailand's development agenda.

Mainstreaming of IMT-GT Projects in National Planning Documents

The IMT-GT Vision 2036 has adopted a project-centric approach for ensuring regionwide physical integration and regulatory reforms. The target is to implement 400 cross-border projects by 2036 (20 projects per year) with direct participation of micro, small, and medium-sized enterprises (MSMEs) and social enterprises (CIMT 2017a). The projects encompass constructing and upgrading roads, bridges, seaports, airports, customs, immigration, and quarantine (CIQ) facilities, and ICT infrastructure; technical administrative and regulatory reforms to improve mobility of resources, persons, goods, and services; and technical and administrative cooperation. The objective is to facilitate investment in agriculture, tourism, and food sectors on the one hand, and human resource development on the other. These projects must be integrated into the national development agendas to ensure that they are linked with the budget cycle and that they receive annual budgetary allocations to fund their implementation.

Typically, the IMT-GT projects are national projects with regional implications and are normally automatically included in the national plans. This paper focuses on whether the regional dimension of these projects has been recognized in the plan documents. A project's regional dimension is defined by its role in regional integration through physical connectivity among regional economies and/or cross-border trade, mobility, and investment facilitation. The study explores for each member country whether the regional integration elements of the IMT-GT projects included in the national development plan are highlighted, marking political ownership of the IMT-GT agenda.

Indonesia. It has 28 economic zone projects of national strategic importance, of which three overlap with the IMT-GT projects. The trans-Sumatra Toll Road connecting Aceh and Lampung provinces is an example of a project that is included in the project pipelines for both the national development plan and IMT-GT Implementation Blueprint. However, there is little mention of the strategic importance of these projects from the perspective of subregional connectivity or facilitation of cross-border trade, transport, and investment. The connectivity projects envisage only the long-term plan vision of "internally united Indonesia;" their regional dimension is not fully recognized. It is also noted that the IMT-GT flagship project of rubber cities finds no mention in the RPJMN 2020-2024, although the country has two sites of rubber cities in the subregion.

Malaysia. Until the 11th Malaysia Plan 2016–2020, there was little mention of the subregional projects in Malaysian development plan documents. The plan included a range of large-scale economic growth projects to be developed in the border areas, including the Chuping Valley, Perlis Inland Port in Perlis, Rubber City in Kedah, IMT-GT Plaza, as well as the redevelopment of Kampung Laut in Tumpat, Kelantan. However, there was no direct reference made to the

IMT-GT subregional program. The Mid-Term Review of the 11th Malaysia Plan 2018 changed that by explicitly referring to all nine IMT-GT connectivity projects. These projects include the new Immigration, Custom, Quarantine and Security Complex in Bukit Kayu Hitam, Kedah, as well as two new bridges: (i) between Rantau Panjang, Kelantan and Sungai Golok, Narathiwat; and (ii) between Pengkalan Kubor, Kelantan and Tak Bai, Narathiwat. However, the focus is only on connectivity projects; other projects have received little attention. For instance, the plan document proposes to develop an SBEZ in Bukit Kayu Hitam and the Rubber City in Kedah with little reference to the IMT-GT agenda. Even while it is acknowledged that these initiatives aim to enhance border trade activities, improve local businesses, and create employment in border areas of Perlis, Kedah, Perak, and Kelantan, there is no reference to cross-border cooperation.[26]

Thailand. In contrast to Indonesia and Malaysia, Thailand has integrated into the 12th National Economic and Social Development Plan IMT-GT projects for all seven pillars as provided in the IMT-GT Implementation Blueprint with an explicit reference to cross-border cooperation and the IMT-GT agenda (Table 20).

Alignment between the Economic Zones Policies and the Spatial Approach of IMT-GT

Economic zones are a critical tool in the IMT-GT spatial approach of subregional cooperation. In conformity with this approach, as seen in Chapter 5, the subregion is awash with various operational and proposed economic zones. Does that mean a convergence of the national policy of creating economic zones in the subregion and the spatial approach of IMT-GT? Not necessarily because the underlying principles of both could be different. The spatial approach proposed in the IMT-GT Vision 2036 is founded on the principle of the collaborative approach, i.e., stimulating cross-border integration to augment the resources and opportunities and foster cross-border supply chains or RVCs with economic zones as a tool. In contrast, in national development planning and policies, the subregional economic zones may be treated at par with other national economic zones, which are internally connected with domestic factors and product markets and are competing regionally.

A review of the evolution of economic zones in the three IMT-GT countries in Chapter 3 reveals that the economic zones have been profoundly linked with the evolution in national development goals and policies in these countries. Economic zones were introduced to kick start industrial diversification in all these countries, with Malaysia taking the lead, followed by Indonesia and Thailand in that order. While the GEZs were created to provide subsidized industrial infrastructure to domestic investors and promote import-substituting industries, SEZs aimed at attracting export-oriented FDI by offering relaxed regulatory regimes along with a host of financial incentives. Over time, as regional equity became a development concern, economic zones were spread out spatially to generate economic activity and employment in the backward regions.

In the 1990s and early 2000s, industrial upgrading became a development objective. Accordingly, economic zones were also upgraded to promote high-tech industries and new high-tech parks were launched. During post-Asian financial crisis, all three countries have moved to a cluster

---

[26] The Northern Council of Economic Region, which has initiated the Super fruits project on 25 hectares of land in the Chuping Valley with FigDirect Sdn. Bhd. as the anchor company, misses out on mentioning on its website that it is IMT-GT supported.

Table 20. List of Projects Included as Part of the IMT-GT Subregional Program in the 12th Development Plan of Thailand

IMT-GT Pillars	Projects Covered
Transport and ICT connectivity	• Construction of the new Sadao Customs, Immigration, and Quarantine (CIQ) in Songkhla and Border Post facilities in Songkhla (arrival) • Upgrading of Padang Besar customs house in Songkhla • Betong Customs House in Yala and Upgrading of Buketa Customs House in Narathiwat • Expansion of Wang Prachan CIQ in Satun • Construction of the new Tak Bai CIQ in Narathiwat • Construction of the second bridge over the Golok River connecting Sungai Golok, Narathiwat with Rantau Panjang, Kelantan
Trade and investment facilitation	• Sadao–Kedah and Sadao–Perlis, and Narathiwat–Kelantan SEZs • Thailand–Malaysia Rubber City Project • Cross-border Trade and Transport Facilitation • IMT-GT Database of Trade, Investment, and Tourism
Tourism	• Improvement of dive sites over 5 years • Improvement of diving routes over 4 years
Halal products and services	• IQRAH System (H-numbers) between Thailand and Malaysia (2016–2017) • Harmonization and Standardization of Halal Standards • Halal Education and Research, Halal Logistics and Supply Chain, and Laboratory Program • Halal SMEs Competitiveness • Halal Verification System for Entrepreneurs
Human resource development, education, and culture	• Increase labor competitiveness to accommodate an expanded labor market under the IMT-GT • Joint Labor Skill Certification • Labor Skill Standard and Certification, in accordance with the ASEAN Qualification Reference Framework • IMT-GT Labor Database
Agriculture and agro-based industry	• Agriculture and agro-based technology exchange through research and development of public agencies, the private sector, and the academia • Development of the Surath Red Goat Breed to strengthen the subregional food production base
Environment	• Green Cities Initiatives in Songkhla (Hat Yai and Songkhla)

ASEAN = Association of Southeast Asian Nations, ICT = information and communication technology, IMT-GT = Indonesia–Malaysia–Thailand Growth Triangle, SEZ = special economic zone, SMEs = small and medium-sized enterprises.

Source: The 12th National Economic and Social Development Plan (2017–2021).

approach to accelerate the growth process and move up the value chains. Indonesia primarily focuses on leveraging its abundant natural resources by promoting processing activities to achieve regionally balanced growth. Malaysia has adopted the concept of high-density cluster development with economic zones at the center to promote the growth of cities, which are seen as the locus of the forces that promote growth, innovative firms, skilled workers, supportive public and private institutions, and modern infrastructure. Thailand followed Malaysia and introduced the Eastern Special Development Zone (ESDZ) initiative, by far the most ambitious SEZ program in the subregion to transform three Thai provinces into smart cities to drive Thailand 4.0.

Thus, the objectives of the economic zones evolved with the evolution of the national development agenda. The contribution of cross-border value chains to economic and regional development and the role of economic zones in promoting them are yet to be recognized in the development agendas of these countries.

Notwithstanding, Thailand announced the formation of 10 SEZs and SBEZs in border areas to leverage the cross-border availability of cheap labor, prevent the influx of unskilled labor, bring prosperity to border areas, and solve security problems. Although the SEZ program is not from the IMT-GT subregional agenda but rather an outcome of the domestic challenges, it is in line with the spatial approach of IMT-GT. Two SEZs have been set up in Thailand-GT, one each in Songkhla and Narathiwat under the program to promote the development of the border areas by leveraging regional integration. The SEZ development policy envisions them as "economic gateways connecting with the neighboring countries for the people to have better quality of life" (NESDC 2020, 3). The Songkhla SEZ is a successful SEZ and, as of July 2020, has attracted B9 billion ($300 million) investment (51% of total SEZ investment) in 15 projects (NESDC 2020). Narathiwat has secured B218 million ($7.3 million) investment in four projects. Thus, Thailand sets an example of leveraging regional cooperation to promote economic transformation using economic zones. Further, as Table 21 shows, Thailand has recognized the regional dimension of the three IMT-GT cross-border SEZ projects that it is promoting in the 12th National Economic and Social Development Plan (Government of Thailand 2017): Sadao–Kedah, Sadao–Perlis, and Narathiwat–Kelantan SEZs. It has also set the target of promoting cross-border trade and investment. Malaysia is also committed to developing an SBEZ in Bukit Kayu Hitam, albeit with a focus on logistics services to leverage border trade and not manufacturing.

To sum up, there is a growing recognition of the importance of the IMT-GT subregional program in national strategic plans, documents, and agendas. Malaysia and Thailand have explicitly or implicitly incorporated the IMT-GT subregional agenda into their national development agenda, albeit in varying degrees. Thailand has taken the lead, followed by Malaysia, while Indonesia lags behind. Overall, the role of the IMT-GT spatial approach, particularly that of economic zones, in unlocking subregional potential is yet to be fully recognized.

Assessing the Achievements: A Quantitative Approach

The plan documents are not an end in themselves in the indicative planning framework that the three countries follow. The objective of indicative planning is to communicate the preferred strategic directions and represent policy intent (Chimhowu, Hulme, and Munro 2019). Actual implementation of the development projects proposed in the plan documents depends on the availability of finance, national priorities, and other political economy factors. Thus, a pertinent question is: how effectively is the growing recognition of the subregional program as a strategic element in national planning translated into actions to accomplish strategic objectives and targets set by IMT-GT Vision 2036? The mapping of IMT-GT goals and targets with the actual performance is crucial to understand if the IMT-GT integration into planning is rhetoric or matches the reality. The relevant literature yields a large set of indicators of the performance of the subregional corridors. For a structured analysis, we organize the selected ones into a three-layered system: immediate, intermediate, and final.

Immediate Performance Indicators

■ **Projects completed.** One of the approaches of the IMT-GT Vision 2036 is project centric. The countries have committed to implementing $47 billion worth of 38 projects to enhance physical connectivity across the IMT-GT subregion. Six of these projects worth less than $1.3 billion could be implemented over time—(i) four projects of $75 million in Thailand (Thungsong distribution center phase 1; Songkhla Rubber City; the Customs, Immigration and Quarantine in Wang Prachan; and the Customs, Immigration, and Quarantine in Padang Besar); and (ii) two projects of $1.3 billion in Indonesia (South Sumatera Light Rail Transit in Palembang, and Port of Kuala Tanjung). Even though, the IMT-GT projects are typically mainstreamed in national development agendas with or without explicit reference to the program, progress in regional connectivity projects has been rather slow.

Intermediate Performance Indicators

■ **Intra-regional trade.** According to the data provided by ADB's Asian Regional Integration Center, intra-subregional trade share, i.e., the percentage of intra-IMT-GT trade to total trade of the three member countries, grew by 5 percentage points from 3.3% to 8.3% between 1990 and 2003. Thereafter, the growth slowed down. In the next 10 years, the increase was 2 percentage points to 10.2% (Figure 7). It reached a peak in 2012 and has been slowly sliding down since then. Intra-IMT-GT trade intensity, as measured by the intra-IMT-GT trade share as a ratio to the share of the three member countries in world trade, has been moving downward since 2006. It means that the trade share of IMT-GT countries with the world has been growing faster than the intra-subregional trade share. A similar trend can be observed in cross-border trade between Malaysia and Thailand in recent years. It grew rapidly between 2007 and 2015 from B180 billion to B500 billion per year ($6 billion to $17 billion), accounting for more than half of all Thailand's border trade that also includes Cambodia, the Lao People's Democratic Republic, and Myanmar (Parpart 2016). Since then,

Figure 7. Trends in Intra IMT-GT Trade, 1990–2017

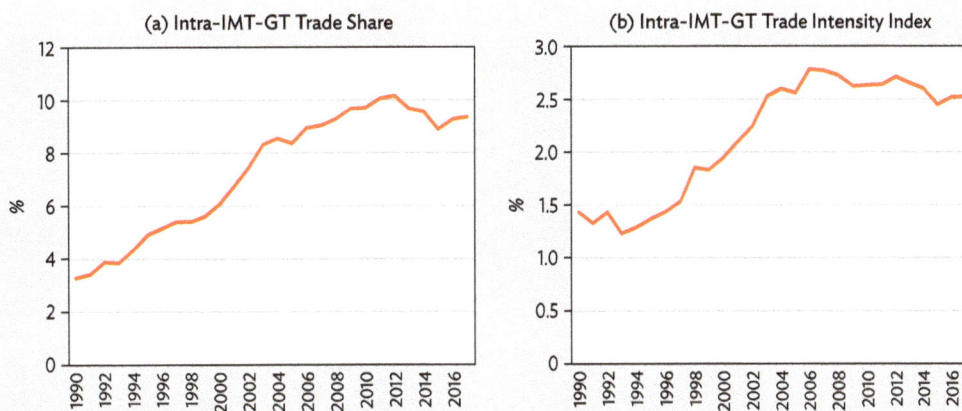

IMT-GT = Indonesia–Malaysia–Thailand Growth Triangle.
Source: Asian Development Bank, Asia Regional Integration Center.

it has not shown any increase. In 2019, it declined due to the fall in exports of rubber products and computers (Econ 2019). In contrast, border trade between Thailand and south PRC is growing rapidly. The most favorable products are fresh fruits and vegetables, computer parts, and dried longan. Thailand and Malaysia share a border that stretches along 647 km, and their bilateral trade is already the largest in ASEAN in terms of value. To promote it further, Malaysia and Thailand have agreed to build new bridges at the checkpoints between Rantau Panjang (Kelantan, Malaysia) and Sungai Kolok (Narathiwat, Thailand), and between Tak Bai (Narathiwat, Thailand) and Pengkalan Kubor (Kelantan, Malaysia). The objective is to reduce congestion. However, nontariff barriers (NTBs) remain a major obstacle to the cross-border mobility of trade in goods and services between the two countries (as discussed below).

■ **Foreign direct investment.** Intra-ASEAN FDI accounted for 17% of total FDI attracted by the region during 2014–2018. The year-wise breakup shows little variation. IMT-GT countries constituted 29% of the total intra-ASEAN FDI. The ASEAN statistics on the composition of intra-ASEAN FDI inflows by the three IMT-GT countries shows that most investments are in real estate and financial and insurance services (Figure 8). The mining and quarrying sector is also somewhat prominent. These three sectors formed on average 87% of Indonesia's intra-ASEAN FDI during 2014–2018; and manufacturing inflows were negative. In Malaysia and Thailand, intra-ASEAN inflows were more diversified, with manufacturing featuring among the top four sectors but accounted for less than one-fifth of the total investment.

Figure 8. Sectoral Composition of Intra-Association of Southeast Asian Nations Average Foreign Direct Investment Inflows Attracted by IMT-GT Countries, 2014–2018

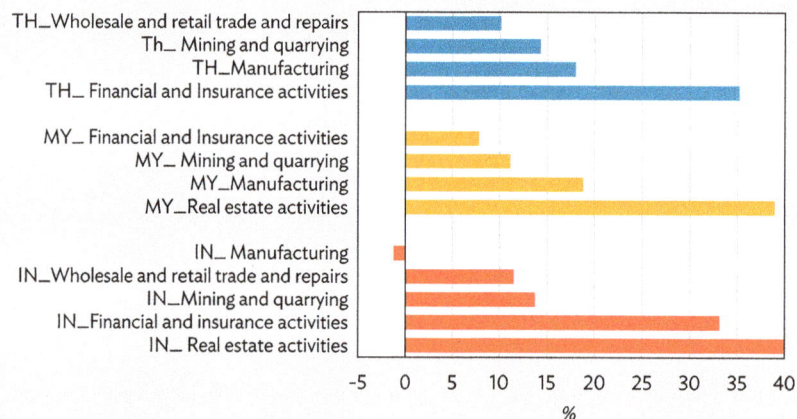

IMT-GT = Indonesia–Malaysia–Thailand Growth Triangle, IN = Indonesia, MY = Malaysia, TH = Thailand.
Source: Association of Southeast Asian Nations (ASEAN). 2019. *ASEAN Statistical Yearbook, 2019*. Jakarta.

Final Performance Indicators

Gross domestic product. Figure 9(a) reveals that the subregion's GRDP as a percentage of the national average has declined between 2012 and 2019 in all member states, except Malaysia, indicating that the IMT-GT has not had an overall catalyzing effect in the region. The share of Malaysia-GT in national GDP has shown some improvement. This can be attributed to the performance of the most developed states of Penang, Selangor, Melaka, and Negeri Sembilan. The bottom four states in the GT have lost their shares in national GDP.

- **Gross domestic product per capita.** One of the targets of IMT-GT is the rise in GDP per capita from $13,844 in 2015 to $32,120 in 2036, at over 6% for 21 years. It means that the GDP per capita in the subregion should grow faster than the national average, which has been 3%–4% since 2015. However, Figure 9b shows that there has been a decline in GDP per capita in the subregional economies relative to the national average. In Malaysia, the bottom four states are relatively worse off in 2019 than in 2012.

Figure 9. Share of Subregional Economies in GDP and Ratio of Subregional GRDP to National Average: 2012 and 2019

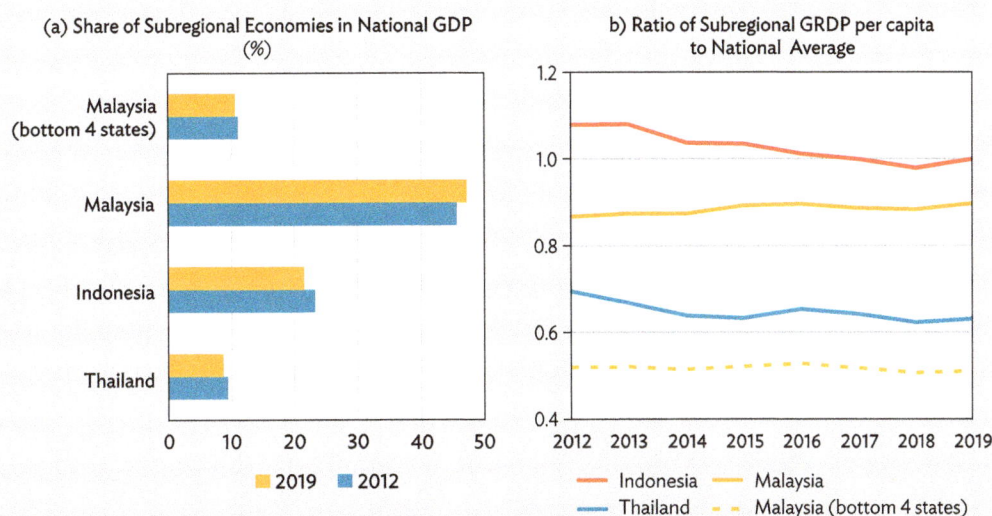

(a) Share of Subregional Economies in National GDP (%)

b) Ratio of Subregional GRDP per capita to National Average

GDP = gross domestic product, GRDP = gross regional domestic product.
Source: National accounts data of the three countries.

Overall, the IMT-GT corridors and the proliferation of economic zones have not made the subregion better-off relative to other regions. One may argue that the simple analysis of trends conducted here is not eligible to make a definitive conclusion and that it would be important to know the counterfactual, i.e., what would have happened in the absence of these initiatives. However, even though the possibility that these regions would have further marginalized in the process of globalization cannot be ruled out, one can conclude that the catching-up process has not set in as envisaged in the IMT-GT Implementation Blueprint (2017–2021).

Chapter 7

Economic Zones as Engine of Subregional Growth: Importance and Challenges

The Role of Economic Zones in Driving Growth in IMT-GT Countries

The industrial estates and export zones have played an important role in the economic transformation of all three IMT-GT countries and catapulted them to a high growth trajectory. As discussed in Chapter 3, FIZs became instrumental in plugging Malaysia into the value chains of the electronics industry, which became the main engine of growth, with FIZs and LMWs accounting for approximately one-third of Malaysia's total exports even in 2018 (Rasiah 2019) and employing 575,000 workers in 2019 (Statista). Penang has over 200 plants of multinational enterprises, which directly employ over 250,000 workers (Athukorala and Narayanan 2018). There have also been spillover effects of industrial clustering in the state. For instance, KHTP, which benefited from the relocation of activities from Penang, created 30,000 high-income jobs by 2015 (Athukorala and Narayanan 2018). The regional economic corridors that have created 1.87 million jobs since inception have been reinforcing these gains (Aziz 2018).

In a similar vein, the bonded zones and industrial estates established Indonesia as a hub for automobile, electronics, oil and gas, and shipbuilding industries. While there are studies that do not find evidence of significant contributions of Indonesian bonded or FTZs to the economy (Rothenberg et al. 2017; Wicaksono, Mangunsong, and Anas 2019), the available statistics indicates that in 2016, the bonded zones and Kemudahan Impor Tujuan Ekspor or the Ease of Import Facility for Export Purposes (KITE) facilities contributed 37.76% of national exports and 3.59% of GDP; attracted investment of Rp168 trillion; absorbed 2.1 million workers equivalent to 13.5 % of the national industrial labor; and increased state revenues significantly (Sulistyawati, Sulistiyono, and Imanullah 2019).

In Thailand, industrial estates have transformed its agriculture-based economy into a hub of automobile, electronics, and petrochemical industries. In 1975, agriculture and live animals constituted over 59% and machinery and transport equipment 1.27% of Thailand's exports (Ajanant 1987). However, in 2019, the share of machinery and transport to total exports leaped to 42%, putting Thailand on the automobile industry's global map. Thailand has come to be known as the "Detroit of the East." Many global companies such as Honda, Nissan, Toyota, GM, BMW, Isuzu, and Ford have set up their assembly operations in these industrial zones (Kuchiki and Tsuji 2011) and contributed significantly to the industrial diversification of Thailand by creating production capabilities in diverse sectors.

As discussed in Chapters 3 and 4, all three economies continue to rely on economic zones and have committed large infrastructure funds to their expansion. However, since the mid-2000s, these countries have been in a synchronized slowdown despite massive investments in building economic zones.

Weakening of the Link between Economic Zones and Growth

Figure 10 presents trends in six key performance indicators of economic growth for the IMT-GT countries, capturing growth in GDP per capita, structural transformation in GDP, export growth, and changes in export structure. Figure 10a, which depicts the 5-year moving averages of growth in GDP per capita in the three countries, reveals four phases in their growth process: early 1970s–mid-1980s (initial growth spurt); mid-1980s–1997(growth acceleration); 1997–mid-2000s (crisis and recovery); and mid-2000s onward (stagnation in growth rates). The initial growth spurt and growth acceleration phases from the 1970s to the late 1990s are directly associated with the proliferation of economic zones. However, this relationship is weakened in the last phase from the mid 2000s onwards. The growth rates in the post-crisis period plateaued despite an aggressive drive to build economic zones with massive incentives. Figure 10b shows the distance of GDP per capita from the global average in all three countries. Malaysia is the only country of the three that surpassed the global average GDP per capita. Thailand has managed to maintain the gap with the global average, while Indonesia finds it growing. Despite impressive growth performance, however, Malaysia missed the goal of crossing the high-income threshold by 2020.

Further, all three countries have witnessed profound economic structural changes in terms of the decline in the share of agriculture (the primary sector) in GDP (Figure 10c). As noted, EPZs and industrial estates have contributed significantly to industrial diversification in these countries by creating production capabilities in diverse sectors. However, in the post mid-2000s, the process started slowing down, with almost one-third of the population in Indonesia and Thailand still in the primary sector (Figure 10d). Finally, the share of the three countries in world trade is almost stagnant, and so is their share of high-technology exports in total exports (Figure 10, panels e and f).

While all three countries have achieved impressive growth, their potential remains locked. In the initial stages, the proliferation of GVCs and the national policies offering a highly favorable investment climate and low-cost production platforms through economic zones worked in tandem to propel their growth. However, over time, the process has slowed down, and the proliferation of economic zones could not spur it. The linkages between the economic zones and growth seem to be weakening in the region. A renewed thrust on zones' programs from the perspective of regional integration can infuse a new dynamism to economic growth. Connecting the economic zones with regional markets and fostering agglomeration economies through cross-border production networks can be a useful tool for debottlenecking these regions' growth potential. It will not only turn the marginalized border areas into growth centers but also upgrade the central cores where diseconomies have kicked in (Gordon and McCann 2000). There are challenges in this experimentation, which need to be identified and addressed through a strategic approach.

Figure 10. Trends in Six Key Performance Indicators of Economic Growth for the IMT-GT Countries

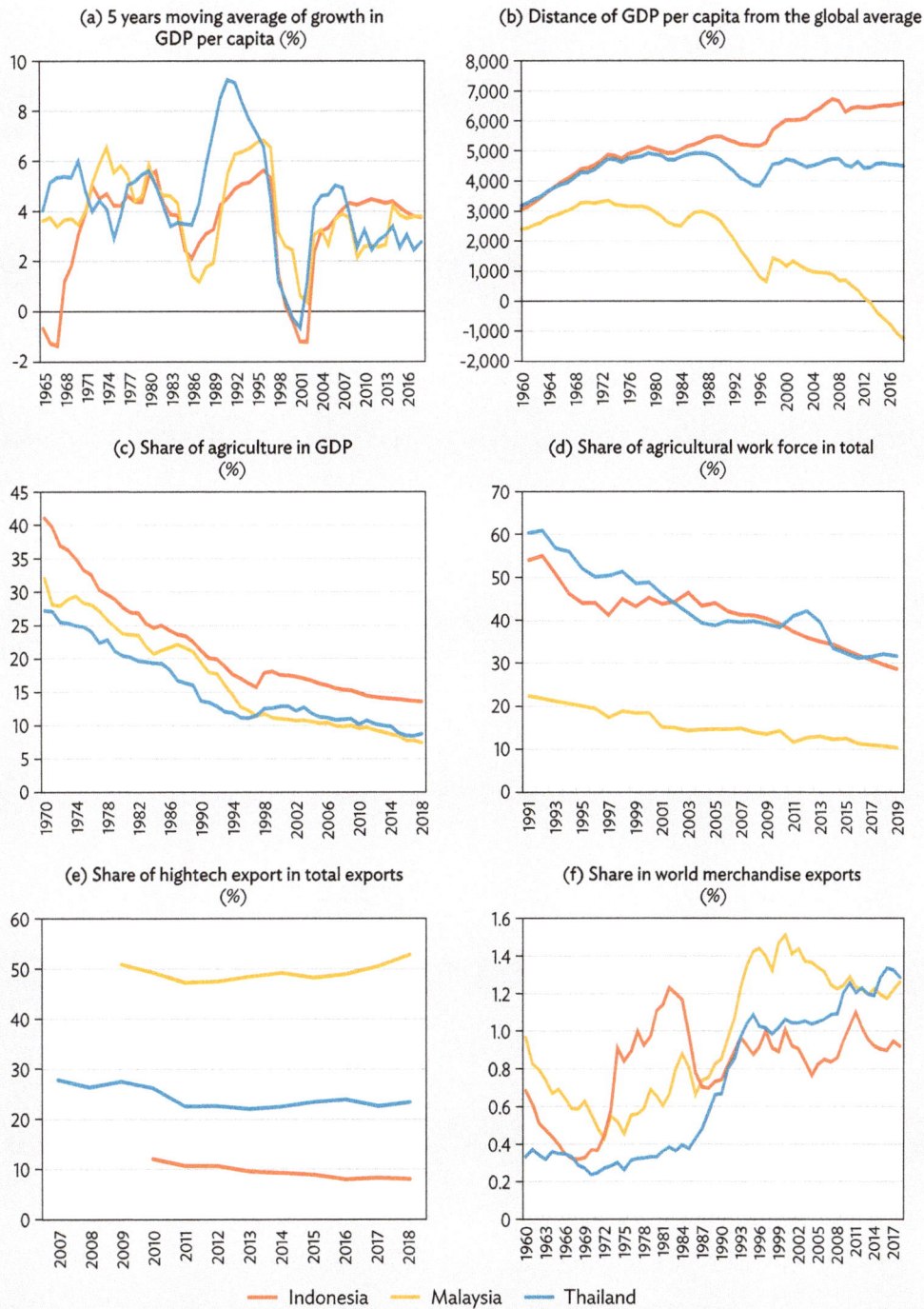

(a) 5 years moving average of growth in GDP per capita (%)

(b) Distance of GDP per capita from the global average (%)

(c) Share of agriculture in GDP (%)

(d) Share of agricultural work force in total (%)

(e) Share of hightech export in total exports (%)

(f) Share in world merchandise exports (%)

Indonesia   Malaysia   Thailand

GDP = gross domestic product, IMT-GT = Indonesia–Malaysia–Thailand Growth Triangle.

Source: Author based on World Development Indicators.

General and Specific Challenges to IMT-GT Corridors and Economic Zones

External Shocks

The economic zones, particularly SEZs, are heavily reliant on export-oriented manufacturing. They are propelled by the GVCs, the expansion of which has been a dominating trend in world trade and investment since the early 1970s. However, over time, entry into GVCs has become increasingly difficult for several reasons:

- intensified competition for GVC-linked FDI with new centers emerging in Africa and Asia;
- Increasing protectionist sentiments across the developed world;
- the PRC–US trade war;
- the rise of digital technologies, which may lead to back-shoring or reshoring of production within the borders of the developed parts of the world (Wijeratne, Plumridge, and Raj 2019); and
- more recently, the COVID-19 pandemic and lockdown measures to contain it.

Evidence suggests that, since 2011, the expansion of GVCs has stopped. Indicators measuring the length of value chains confirm that even before the COVID-19 pandemic, GVCs had become shorter, i.e., for each dollar of output, there had been less trade in intermediate goods and services (Miroudot and Nordström 2019). There is strong evidence of back-shoring of manufacturing activities in the US. Between 2002 and 2018, import penetration had grown from 23% to 31%, but this trend has shown reversal, according to the reshoring index developed by the Coalition for a Prosperous America (CPA).[27] According to the May/June Thomas Report surveying manufacturers on industry trends, "Two in three (69 percent) of manufacturing companies are looking into bringing production to North America."[28] The European Reshoring Monitor reports 253 reshoring cases including back-shoring, near-shoring, and other shoring, as of February 2019 (Eurofound 2019). In 2018, the number of US companies reporting new reshoring was at its highest level in recorded history when a record 1,389 companies announced the return of 145,000 jobs (Moser 2019).

The pandemic and shutdown measures to contain it have exacerbated the situation. A survey conducted by the Kiel Institute for the World Economy in partnership with the World Free Zones Organization showed that 91% of the zones reported limitations to their production due to lockdown restrictions (Gern and Mösle 2020). According to World Bank, the global economy contracted by 4.3% in 2020, with most economies experiencing a decline in GDP per capita (World Bank 2021). The countries with a heavy reliance on global trade, tourism, commodity exports, and external financing are most severely affected. As such, the IMT-GT countries, despite having a moderate incidence of the pandemic, will be among the most vulnerable countries.

---

[27] Coalition for a Prosperous America.
[28] Thomas Industrial Survey 2020 COVID-19's Impact on North American Manufacturing, Report May/June 2020, New York.

Domestic Conditions

Regional disparities. Regional disparities persisting in the IMT-GT countries have also hampered economic zones in economic peripheries. The centripetal forces (as defined in Chapter 6) are attracting investment in the core areas: the West Coast in Malaysia, Java in Indonesia, and Eastern Thailand. But there is a threshold level beyond which growth slows down even in the core, and increasing returns, which are vital for growth, are undermined due to diseconomies of agglomerations. This challenge requires a rise of new growth centers, which means that the marginalized areas must take off.

Limited spillover effects. All three countries aspire to upgrade their industrial structure and have accelerated their efforts to promote economic zones. However, a major challenge is the lack of spillover effects of these zones, particularly SEZs. Indeed, Malaysia has experienced remarkable growth in the E&E industry, with E&E exports accounting for over 34.4% of total exports in 2018. Yet, it could not shift to a high-value trajectory along the lines of its East Asian counterparts. The upgrading success remained limited to Penang. According to Rasiah, Crinis, and Lee (2015), in 2010, the E&E industry contributed 27.0% to the country's manufacturing output, 49.0% to exports, and 32.5% to overall employment, yet almost all of the related investments were foreign. In 2011, a staggering 93.23% (almost $6 billion) of investment in the Malaysian electronics sector was foreign. Similarly, a study by ASEAN-Japan Centre (2019) on automobile value chains in Thailand shows that over the past 2 decades, the share of foreign value added (imported inputs) in the exports of automobiles remains 70%–75% of the total, an indicator of small domestic production facilities and capacities in the industry. Indonesia's involvement in GVCs has increasingly relied on providing primary and raw materials to other economies despite rapid growth in the number and types of economic zones (ADB 2019). These cases imply that (i) the FDI attracted by these countries could not create spillovers that would generate significant multiplier effects in other industries within the local economy, and (ii) there remains huge potential for strengthening linkages among sectors for the benefits of specialization to trickle down.

Proliferation of economic zones and competition. The proliferation of economic zones in the region has intensified regional competition for GVC-linked investment, affecting the performance of these zones (Aggarwal 2019). The establishment of several zones at the same time affects the quality of infrastructure provisions in the new zones. Further, as the number of zones increases, the zones tend to be in suboptimal locations, inflating the cost of setting them up and return.

Subregional Challenges

Gaps in physical connectivity and transport facilitation. One of the key stumbling blocks in promoting cross-border production networks is the lack of mobility of resources, goods, and services within the subregion. As seen in Figure 3, the IMT-GT subregion is geographically fragmented. The necessary condition for the collaborative approach of economic zones within the subregion is to restore the natural economic spatiality between different regions across members. This requires physical integration of the subregion through falling costs of transport and trade, extending economic geography beyond the national borders. However, there are strategic gaps in connectivity in the subregion, and the progress in connectivity projects has been slow (as discussed in Chapter 6). Transport-related laws also vary across countries inhibiting cross-border mobility.

ASEAN-wide agreements for transport facilitation have not yet been implemented due to delays in ratifying key protocols and/or enacting necessary domestic laws and regulations (Umezaki 2019).

Nontariff trade barriers and custom facilitation. Significant progress has been made in reducing tariff barriers within ASEAN. Yet, nontariff impediments to trade increased in the region from 1,634 to 5,975 between 2000 and 2015 (Menon 2018). According to the 2017 data from the UNESCAP-World Bank International Trade Cost Database, the overall cost of trading goods (both transport and regulatory) among ASEAN members is equivalent to 76% average tariff on the value of goods traded, the bulk of which is accounted for by policy-related nontariff trade costs (UNESCAP and ADB 2019). It means that trade facilitation can bring higher trade gains than reduced tariff barriers (e.g., Anderson and van Wincoop 2004, Hoekman and Nicita 2010, Hoekman and Nicita 2011, Arvis et al. 2016, Hummels 2007). Progress has been slow in simplifying customs procedures, removing nontariff barriers (NTBs) to trade, and harmonizing standards and regulations. There is evidence that investors are getting increasingly skeptical about the effects of regional ASEAN integration on their business prospects due to inefficient customs procedures and NTBs. In the EU-ASEAN Business Sentiment Survey 2019, which polls European firms in ASEAN, only 3% of respondents said that economic integration under the ASEAN Economic Community (AEC) is progressing fast enough, compared to 11% in 2018. And when asked whether ASEAN has achieved its aim of creating a single market and production base, only 4% agreed, compared to 12% in 2018 (EU-ASEAN Business Council 2019).

Heterogeneity in cross-border policies, rules, and regulations. Knowledge gaps about economic processes and sales opportunities on the other side of a border, along with different rules and regulations, technical standards, structures, and proceedings, hamper regional companies' initiatives to form cross-border RVCs.

Weak alignment between the national development agendas and IMT-GT economic corridor approach. The IMT-GT is a natural economic territory that forms a development ladder. It has the most developed regions of Selangor, Penang, Negeri Sembilan, and Melaka, on the one hand, and the industrially most backward provinces of Southern Thailand on the other. In the middle of the ladder is Sumatera, which has acquired production capabilities in medium- and low-tech industries. A development ladder creates synergies to immensely benefit the region and trigger the flying geese paradigm if implemented effectively. The benefits may be further reinforced by aggregation of resources, diversification of markets, and infusion of innovations. However, to leverage the regional synergies, there must be alignment between the national development and subregional agendas of deepening regional integration.

Non-differential treatment to economic zones in the subregion. Lagging regions face several structural challenges, including adverse sectoral structures, poor business environment, skill deficits, and absence of support services. Therefore, the development of economic zones in the lagging border areas needs special and differential treatment to overcome the disadvantages of these areas, requiring a customized package of infrastructure, management, and governance, with relaxed immigration rules. However, their treatment is essentially at par with other national zones in the three countries, affecting the incentives to invest in subregional zones when zones are proliferating in core areas as well.

Social and environmental challenges. Border areas often face multiple social and environmental challenges in addition to economic disadvantages. Social challenges pertain to lack of skill development, industrial culture, and basic social amenities including health and education. Any large-scale intervention not organically grown in these areas can shock the local communities, who often feel marginalized in the process and approach such an issue with strong, emotionally laden feelings and opinions. Border areas are also often home to ethnic minorities who face very specific challenges. They may view any transformative process of capitalist development as a threat to their existence and identity. Further, difficult terrain, dense forests, inaccessibility, the lack of roads or rail in these areas may require substantial public investment to create conditions for industrial development. Finally, the construction of economic zones may pose environmental threats by destructing diverse landscapes, flora and fauna, and natural ecosystems.

Border security issues. Borders are frequently associated with a continuous tension that exists between the need to prevent illicit people and goods (such as timber, drugs, humans, wild animals, and arms) from crossing borders and the economic vitality that a country gains through trade and movement of people (Fujimura 2014, Gerstein et al. 2018). This tension may be heightened along subregional economic corridors depending on the perceived risks, threats, and vulnerabilities in the border areas. A dynamic landscape of radicalization and terrorism in Southeast Asia can provoke significant security anxieties in the subregion and need to be addressed through an integrated border management strategy (Henkins, Boyd, and Martin 2020).

The rest of the report sets forth recommendations for enhancing the development role of economic corridors and zones in the subregion. Recommendations are broadly grouped into the remaining three stages of public policy making: (i) strategy and policy development, (ii) policy adoption into planning agenda, and (iii) policy implementation strategy and its adoption.

The next chapter focuses on strategy and policy development, followed by policy adoption in Chapter 9 and implementation in Chapter 10.

Chapter 8

The Proposed Strategic Approach to the Subregional Economic Zones: The Coopetition Strategy

Typically, economic zones (particularly SEZs) are a tool of competitive strategy to attract GVC-linked FDI. But competition between regional partners may constrain the potential of economic zones in attracting investment due to limits posed by domestic comparative advantages, factor endowments, and market size. There is also a possibility of competition leading to a race to the bottom in fiscal incentives that may subsidize large MNCs with little gains to host countries. The subregional agenda views the economic zones in economic corridors as a means of a collaborative approach to counter these challenges. This approach is expected to facilitate regionwide industrialization based on value addition through cross-border chains and RVCs.

The collaborative approach toward economic zones in the subregion involves acquiring access to subregional resources and markets and forming regional and cross-border value chains. It can maximize mutual gains by maximizing the positive externalities generated by industrial complementarity, economies of scale, and large market size. Nonetheless, full cooperation is not without its cons. It may also pose challenges if some member countries are relatively less benefited, a possibility that cannot be ruled out, given that the member countries are at different development levels. Further, there are social, political, and security issues that can hinder full cooperation. Thus, neither of the two alternative approaches to economic zones development: collaborative and competitive, is without cons. It is proposed here to combine the elements of the collaborative approach with those of the competitive approach to synergize the pros of both approaches and address the cons. This proposed action is called the coopetition strategic approach. Coopetition is defined as a situation where economic zones of subregional countries simultaneously cooperate and compete (Figure 11). This is a strategy through which the economic agents jointly create added value while simultaneously competing to capture a part of that value. The central idea is that the coopetition approach enables countries to augment their capabilities by having access to subregional resources and markets to enhance their competitive advantage, which they can use to attract more investment in their SEZs. As Brandenburger and Nalebuff (1996) noted, coopetition is a game where different players increase the business "pie" (markets) by cooperating in making markets and then competing for dividing up the markets. The two pillars, cooperation and competition, reinforce each other despite being contradictory. Indeed, the literature recognizes the paradoxes and tensions of the coexistence of two contradictory forces of competition and cooperation, and the challenges in managing them (Peng, Yen, and Bourne 2017; Fernandez, Le Roy, and Gnyawali 2014; Raza-Ullah, Bengtsson, and Kock 2014; Gnyawali, He, and Madhavan 2008). Yet, coopetition has been widely used as a win–win strategy by economic agents. This study emphasizes that the coopetition strategy toward subregional economic zones can present a sustainable alternative to either full collaboration or competition in the subregion.

Figure 11. Coopetition Strategic Approach

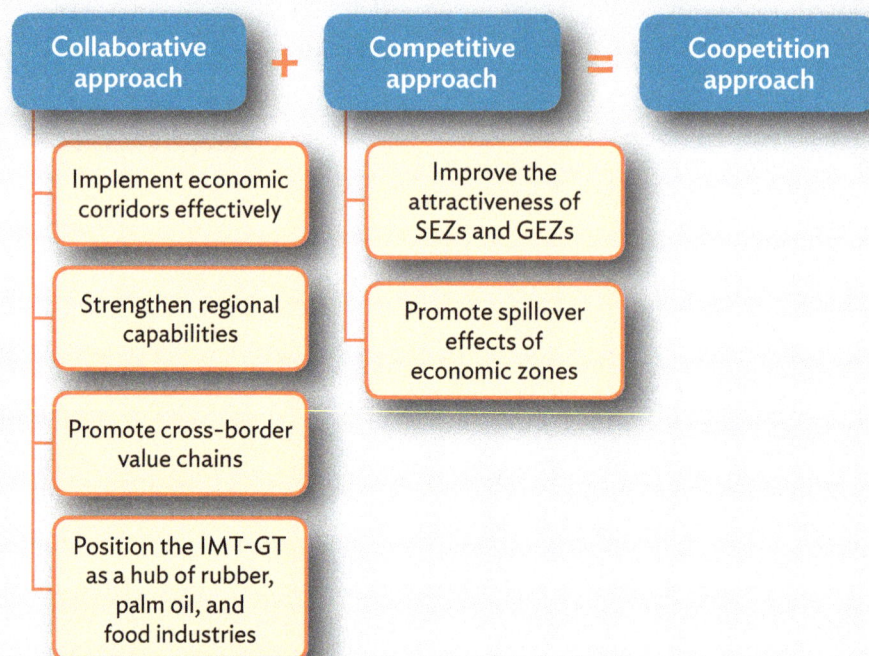

GEZ = general economic zone, IMT-GT = Indonesia–Malaysia–Thailand Growth Triangle, SEZ = special economic zone.
Source: Author.

Below we discuss the strategic elements of the cooperative and competitive approaches as depicted in Figure 11. Each of the two approaches consists of strategies, which are broken down into strategic interventions that are further divided into enabling actions.

Collaborative Approach: Strategies, Strategic Interventions, and Enabling Actions

Strategy: Implement Subregional Economic Corridors Effectively

The imperative of a collaborative approach consists of viewing the subregion as a transborder hybrid zone, the potential of which can be unlocked by establishing a single market and production base in the subregion. The two prerequisites for the single market and production base are (i) seamless connectivity through transport infrastructure; and (ii) transport and trade facilitation for uninhibited mobility of people, goods, materials, and services. Subregional economic corridors serve to meet these prerequisites. They reduce transport cost and journey time; reduce the transaction cost of trade; and influence both the factor and product markets through the mobility of labor, people, capital (location or relocation of firms), and freight (trade), leading finally to the acceleration of cross-border production networks and economic growth as depicted in Figure 12 (see World Bank et al. 2018, Quium 2019, Berg et al. 2017, Regmi and Hanaoka 2012 for a rich literature review).

Figure 12. Synergies between Various Elements of the Economic Corridor

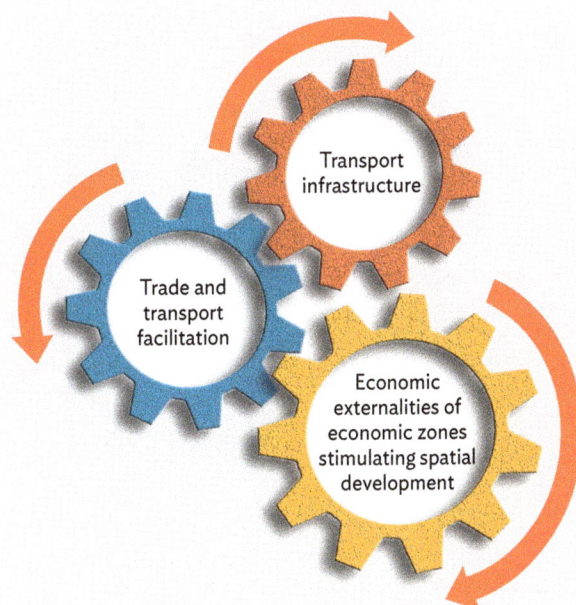

Source: Author.

Thus, one of the most critical elements of the collaborative approach of IMT-GT economic zones is implementing the priority economic corridors, which call for a set of systematic strategic interventions. Strategic interventions and enabling actions are marked by serial numbers, which are used in Tables 27–29.

Strategic Intervention 1: Mainstream the IMT-GT Vision Agenda, Objectives, and Strategic Approaches into National Plans and Programs

1.1 **Mainstream the vision agenda.** In the IMT-GT Vision 2036 (CIMT 2017a) preamble, the leaders of three countries have expressed their commitment to enhancing trade, investment, and connectivity within the subregion and agreed to strengthen and accelerate the economic cooperation to achieve mutual goals. This commitment resonates with the ASEAN Economic Community Vision 2025, which reads, "Our ASEAN Economic Community by 2025 shall be highly integrated and cohesive; competitive, innovative and dynamic; with enhanced connectivity and sectoral cooperation . . . ." (ASEAN 2015, p.15). As a first step, these basic regional cooperation principles need to be integrated into long- and medium-term national development plans to recognize regional integration as an element of national development strategy.

1.2 **Mainstream the subregional objectives and spatial approach.** The success of subregional economic zones requires a long-term vision and collective efforts, backed by generous financial resources. For that purpose, it is important that the IMT-GT spatial approach of promoting cross-border production networks is integrated into national development agendas and that it receives wide governmental support beyond specific line ministries anchoring the program (UNESCAP 2017). This integration means that the long-term objectives of IMT-GT are mainstreamed in the long-term plan and broken down into medium-term targets to be further integrated into medium-term plans.

Strategic Intervention 2: Improve Physical Connectivity through Efficient and Integrated Physical Infrastructure

2.1 **Prioritize the existing IMT-GT projects.** In general, high infrastructure costs are a stumbling block to implementing large infrastructure projects, which require ample financial and technical resources and large tracts of land to prepare projects, plans, and construction. Since the availability of such resources, especially in the public sector, is limited in developing countries, projects with the most favorable economic, social, and environmental impacts at the regional level may be prioritized for implementation.

2.2 **Develop a pipeline of physical connectivity projects.** The subregional countries would need to develop a well-planned pipeline of regional connectivity projects to

- close gaps in physical integration within the region, which can improve transportation efficiency, reduce cargo damage, reduce transportation costs, reduce highway congestion, and promote energy savings and emissions reduction (SteadieSeifi et al. 2014, as quoted in Chen et al. 2019);
- bring the corridors up to the required quality and capacity standards and meet future projections;
- develop the feeder network to spread local socioeconomic benefits of corridors; and
- develop transport nodes and access links.

2.3 **Constitute a project selection committee to strengthen the project selection process.** In principle, project proposals come from the working groups, national secretariats, Chief Ministers and Governors Forum (CMGF), Centre for IMT-GT Subregional Cooperation (CIMT), or Joint Business Council (JBC). Before they are approved and included in the IMT-GT agenda, they pass through various stages of appraisal and assessment of their contribution to IMT-GT goals by working groups and the Project Appraisal Committee (see ADB 2016 for the detailed procedure). In this project cycle, the sector or line ministries involved in the IMT-GT working groups play a critical role. But their human and financial resources and capacity in identifying and formulating sound projects are an area of concern (ADB 2016). Further, the national secretariat (anchored in a line ministry) has little influence over other line ministries to manage their involvement in the working groups (ADB 2016). In view of this, it is proposed to constitute a project selection committee (PSC), which may comprise independent technical and economic experts and private sector representatives, along with working group members and other stakeholders to study the infrastructural and sectoral gaps and build a pipeline of projects.

2.4 **Adopt an ex ante approach in developing a project pipeline.** Notwithstanding the "in principle" project selection process described above, the IMT-GT infrastructure projects typically— though not always—are national projects with regional implications. We recommend developing an independent project pipeline from the perspective of strengthening subregional connectivity by identifying all existing connectivity bottlenecks based on a detailed analysis of corridor features, growth projections, and well-defined costs and benefits criteria. The PSC can lead in coordinating such studies of mapping the bottlenecks along the corridors.

2.5 **Develop techno-analytic criteria for project assessment.** The techno-analytic criteria involve an objective assessment of technological, social, and environmental feasibilities and certainties, and potential economic effects to evaluate the projects. The current approach to project selection is open and subjective. There are few specific guidelines for the assessors and assessment. Besides, it is not clear who the assessors are and how they reach a particular conclusion. An objective set of criteria based on sustainability elements by approved agencies is important, at least for large connectivity projects, to ensure that the projects are technically feasible, economically sound, socially impactful, and environmentally safe. If a detailed assessment is already done at the national level, it should be further assessed by experts in the PSC from the regional perspective.

Strategic Intervention 3: Remove Impediments to Mobility

3.1 **Pilot test ASEAN agreements on transport facilitation in the subregion.** Transport facilitation means removing nonphysical hindrances that make the movement of people, vehicles, and goods across national borders onerous, time-consuming, and expensive to ensure efficient, safe, seamless, and sustainable movement of people and freight (UNESCAP 2018). It requires (i) harmonization of technical and operational standards of the modes of transport across borders; (ii) implementation of uniform commercial and legal framework involving the harmonized regulatory framework, transport documents, safety rules, and inspection procedures; and (iii) streamlining of border crossing procedures to facilitate international traffic. Recognizing the importance of transport facilitation, ASEAN member states have concluded four agreements: (i) ASEAN Framework Agreement on the Facilitation of Goods in Transit (1998), (ii) ASEAN Framework Agreement on Multimodal Transport (2005), (iii) ASEAN Framework Agreement on the Facilitation of Inter-State Transport (2009), and (iv) ASEAN Framework Agreement on the Facilitation of Cross Border Transport of Passengers by Road Vehicles. Of the four agreements, only two, the ASEAN Framework Agreement on Multimodal Transport and the ASEAN Framework Agreement on the Facilitation of Inter-State Transport, have been enforced among a limited number of ASEAN member states who have ratified them; Indonesia and Malaysia are not among them. Ratification is only a first step toward implementing an agreement. Even after ratification, the operationalization of these agreements may be constrained due to conflicting domestic laws, rules, and regulations. To explore the potential of transport facilitation, the subregional countries should pilot test these agreements within the subregion in the short and medium run without initially ratifying them.

3.2 **Pilot test trade facilitation agreements in the subregion.** The ASEAN Single window, launched in 2018 after long delays, has a few member states (Indonesia, Malaysia, Singapore, and Viet Nam) on board. As of 2020, only one functional module is implemented: the electronic exchange of preferential certificates of origin. The rest are yet to be implemented. A recent study shows that in Indonesia, even the limited implementation of the ASEAN Single Window has helped improve efficiency and import–export activities through its service contribution (Arifin, Taufiqulhakim, and Salsabila 2020). Moreover, the ASEAN Customs Transit System has been developed for end-to-end computerization of transit operations with a single electronic customs transit declaration. However, it is not yet ratified by all IMT-GT countries. Indeed, the member states are committed to removing trade barriers and tariffs under the AEC umbrella. But there is a need to expedite the processes given the changing global trade and investment scenario. The subregion can be used as a test lab to move forward.

3.3   **Relax labor mobility.** Cross-border labor mobility—which is likely to offer some advantages to subregional economic zones by allowing a more efficient matching of workers' skills with job requirements—is also challenging. By 2017, mutual recognition agreements had been reached for eight professional qualifications, but these cover only 1.5% of ASEAN's total workforce (Menon and Melendez 2017). Labor mobility needs to be improved by putting favorable policies and rules in the subregion.

3.4   **Ensure seamless mobility within the subregion in the long run.** At the subregional level, the most critical impediments to the mobility of goods and services may be identified and addressed as a way forward to create conditions for the success of economic zones. According to a study by Dosch (2013),[29] it may take some time to implement the common market at the regional level due to the disparity in economic development between member states. However, the IMT-GT subregion provides an ideal setting for pilot testing the existing agreements to be implemented in the wider economies, and going beyond the ASEAN agreements in the long run.

Strategy: Augment Regional Capabilities through Cooperative Strategies

The second critical condition for the collaborative approach of economic zones is to augment subregional capabilities to attract investment. The three IMT-GT countries have had a long experience of building economic zones. However, the most successful economic zones in these countries are geographically concentrated in the strategically most attractive locations: the west coast of Malaysia, the eastern seaboard of Thailand, and Jakarta and Batam in Indonesia, all of which benefited from their proximity to the capital city and/or international shipping routes. The subregional zones in the lagging regions have locational disadvantages, which need to be compensated by additional benefits. Evidence suggests that SEZs are successful only if sufficient extant industrial capacity and organizational skills in the area exist in terms of networks of specialized firms, service providers, human skills, start-ups, and industry consortia that create an ecosystem for the industry development and upgrade (Kim and Zhang 2008). Therefore, unlocking the potential of these areas requires adopting a transformative approach to collectively address the institutional and infrastructural challenges facing the zones. Cross-border cooperation can overcome the locational disadvantages of these peripheries by pooling cross-border resources, capacities, ecosystems, and markets. But this requires a broad set of well-formulated strategic interventions.

Strategic Intervention 4: Promote Cross-Border Cooperation Programs to Build Production Capabilities of Micro, Small, and Medium-Sized Enterprises by Engaging the Private Sector

4.1   **Engage large subregional firms in promoting micro, small, and medium-sized enterprises.** According to the ASEAN website, MSMEs account for 88.8%–99.9% of total establishments and 51.7%–97.2% of total employment in ASEAN member states. Their development is the key to regional development. The local governments can collaborate with large regional firms through JBC to organize training in quality control, client-centric services, and compliance with domestic and internationally recognized standards and certifications for MSMEs to develop a business ecosystem in the region. These efforts may be initiated as part of corporate social responsibility. ASEAN countries have a long history of industrialization and have nurtured a

---

[29]   The study is jointly conducted by the University of Rostock, Germany and the CIMB ASEAN Research Institute.

strong private sector. The governments need to engage the private players in creating a viable investment condition in the subregion.

4.2 **Engage MSMEs associations.** Engaging MSME associations in the subregional program increases their opportunities and capabilities. They may identify cross-cutting constraints encountered across all sectors in the region and develop an agenda for addressing them and working with large firms to promote linkages between the two.

4.3 **Initiate industry-specific programs.** This strategy involves local governments, industry associations, and other development partners to target and develop the capacity of MSMEs through industry-specific joint entrepreneurship and management training programs based on their competitive advantages. The CIMT may spearhead such projects with funding committed by the local governments. A case in point is the halal industry, one of the key subregional industries. Box 1 highlights the importance of upgrading the MSMEs and the key actors in the halal food industry to compete in the world markets. This upgrade requires joint programs, which may be initiated in the subregion as pilot projects. Several such projects have been initiated in some European countries to strengthen the MSMEs sector in the cross-border regions, and evidence suggests that such programs affect the performance of these enterprises positively (Raposo et al. 2014).

Box 1. Halal Food Industry in the Subregion

Globally, the halal food industry is expected to reach $1.9 trillion by 2023, according to the State of the Global Islamic Economy Report 2018/2019. However, the export data of 2017 shows that the share of Malaysia in world exports stood at 0.7%, while that of Indonesia was 0.3%. In an interview by Food Navigator Asia, the chief executive officer of Malaysia External Trade Development Corporation attributes it to the dominance of micro, small, and medium-sized enterprises (MSMEs) in this sector, which have limited skills, knowledge of marketing, branding, and capacity to scale up. About 98% of firms in the industry are MSMEs that cannot leverage the elaborate ecosystem that the country has developed along with certification facilities. Indonesia, which had been mainly exporting raw materials due to the absence of certification facilities, has recently enforced Halal Law (17 October 2019), making certification of all halal products mandatory by the established Halal Products Certification Agency. However, this will require upgrading the capacity of MSMEs. Cross-border cooperation projects within the subregion need to synergize the existing capabilities and build on them, helping promote the region as a hub of halal products.

Source: Neo, P. 2019. Massive Potential: Why Are ASEAN Halal Food Exports Growing at a Slower Rate than Global Demand. *Food Navigator Asia*. 10 September. https://www.foodnavigator-asia.com/Article/2019/09/10/Massive-potential-Why-are-ASEAN-halal-food-exports-growing-at-a-slower-rate-than-global-demand?utm_source=copyright&utm_medium=OnSite&utm_campaign=copyright.

4.4 **Initiate pilot projects in the subregion for digital transformation.** Digital transformation is the rearrangement of customer relationships, operational processes, and business models to ensure new values for customers and employees driven by digital technologies, e-commerce, social media, big data, internet-of-things, artificial intelligence, augmented reality, chat box, smartphones, cloud computing, 3D printers, blockchains, etc. Digital technologies enable MSMEs to improve production processes, market intelligence, access to distant markets and knowledge networks at relatively low cost; and participate in international activity.

These technologies also allow them to scale up their activities without increasing fixed costs, improve their processes, and link them with networks and open innovation systems to improve their competitiveness (OECD 2018). MSMEs need to be integrated into the process of digital transformation, which requires a road map. A multipronged strategy needs to be drafted, including education and training, financial support, consultations, technological infrastructure, and policies and regulations. The digital FTZs are forward-looking in this direction, but they need to be associated with building capabilities of MSMEs to have far-reaching effects. The CIMT may start an initiative by engaging JBC and the national bodies to develop a road map and pilot projects.

Strategic Intervention 5: Promote Cross-Border Cooperation Programs to Build a Strong Technological Base

The architects of the IMT-GT Vision 2036 have envisaged an innovative subregion by 2036 with innovative agriculture and industry sector as two priority goals. However, one of the subregion's challenges is that there is no robust cross-border mechanism or program to promote active technology transfer, adaptation, and innovation. Rising research costs have made it increasingly difficult for individual developing countries or firms to conduct original research. Joint research capabilities may be promoted in the subregion to overcome financial constraints.

5.1 **Institute a research fund with contributions from the three governments and the private sector.** The research institutions, universities, and the private sector may be invited to apply for collaborative research projects, each for 3–4 years. The projects appraisal may be based on established criteria. These projects may focus on, among others, improving the productivity of rubber and palm plantations, greening these sectors, developing downstream products, and promoting diversification of the plantations. The precedence of the collaborative approach in R&D has already been set by the memorandum of understanding signed between IMT-GT universities for collaboration on the Super Fruit Project, Surath Red Goat, and other IMT-GT projects. However, these efforts need to be upscaled and institutionalized within the subregional framework and agenda. One example is the European Commission's Horizon 2020, a highly ambitious and collaborative R&D program that ensures high-class research, focuses on industrial leadership, and tackles societal challenges. The program aims at breaking down barriers to create a single market for knowledge, research, and innovation (Box 2).

5.2 **Strengthen knowledge transfers through faculty exchange and internship programs.** International internships are a very effective way to gain skills. A part of the research fund proposed in the previous paragraph may be used to fund prominent students or skilled young professionals in the target industries for internship programs. Applications may be invited every year to short-list the best ones for studies in some of the most research-oriented universities in the region and the world. The project may be instituted as part of the flagship program of university networks called UNINET. The Young Farmer Training Program, which promotes the participation of youths and new entrepreneurs in the subregion, may also be covered under this fund.

5.3 **Intensify efforts to build research and development alliances in the palm oil and rubber industries.** The region is dependent on two major agricultural products—rubber and palm oil, which are critical raw materials for many industries and have benefited millions of farmers and households in the subregion. Indonesia and Malaysia account for 85% of global palm oil production, with Indonesia taking the lead. Similarly, around 70% of natural rubber is

> ### Box 2. Horizon 2020: The Research Fund of the European Commission
>
> The European Commission initiated Horizon 2020 in 2014 for the joint promotion of research and innovation with nearly €80 billion of funding available over 7 years (2014–2020). The objective is to promote technological solutions for tackling the societal challenge of promoting economic growth and job creation. From time to time, there are calls for proposals from universities, research organizations, and private sector entities. A panel of independent specialists evaluates each proposal against a list of criteria to see if it should receive funding. Selection procedures are determined solely according to the criteria of quality and capability without considering geographical distribution. Small and medium-sized enterprises (SMEs) are encouraged to participate in collaborative projects as part of a consortium and benefit from support. A minimum amount of about €8.33 billion is allocated for SMEs for enabling industrial technologies. The emphasis is on the simplification and streamlining of the application and granting procedures. The procedures are even simpler for SMEs. With a high priority placed on science and technology through this and other such programs, the European Union has over performed the United States with respect to the performance of the science system (Frietsch, Rammer, and Schubert 2015). There is promising advancement in high-tech sectors of aerospace, biotechnology, computer hardware and services, health care equipment and services, internet, pharmaceuticals, semiconductors, software, telecom equipment, raw materials, added value manufacturing, and food4future.
>
> Sources: European Commission. Horizon 2020. What Is Horizon 2020? https://ec.europa.eu/programmes/horizon2020/en/what-horizon-2020; Frietsch, R., C. Rammer, and T. Schubert. 2015. Heterogeneity of Innovation Systems in Europe and Horizon 2020. *Forum.* 50 (1).

produced in this subregion, with Thailand taking the lead. However, these products are under scrutiny for their environmental effects, large-scale deforestation, land rights issues, and social abuses. Palm oil, the world's most versatile, economical, and widely used oil in both food and commercial production, is particularly controversial in Europe, which has put palm oil on the blacklist of biofuels to phase out by 2030. Multinational companies are increasingly committing themselves to source ecologically sustainable palm oil. While all three IMT-GT countries have well-developed certification institutions, there is a need for massive R&D efforts to improve yield, explore environment-friendly processing techniques, and develop downstream products for sustainable palm oil. Similar issues persist in rubber. In addition, natural rubber produced in these countries is facing tough competition with synthetic rubber. Many end users in the automotive, construction, and footwear industries have shifted their preferences to synthetic rubber due to its superior toughness, elasticity, high heat resistance, and abrasion resistance. With the advent of electric vehicles, the competition in the tire sector has further toughened. The three countries need to adopt joint mechanisms to compete internationally and establish the subregion as a sustainable and formidable hub of rubber and palm oil industries in these times of disruptive technologies. This strategy requires promoting regional research alliances in the private and public sectors. Research alliances can take various forms, including joint research agreements, technology sharing, bilateral technology flows, unilateral technology flows, and technology licensing.

5.4 **Form research alliances with international and extra-regional companies.** This strategy promotes international exchange of knowledge and technology transfers. Extra-regional cooperation positively impacts the firms' performance in border areas, which might have limited technological capabilities (Barzotto et al. 2019).

5.5 **Tighten sustainability certification criteria for palm oil to match international standards.**
Tightening the certification standards to match the internationally acceptable Roundtable
on Sustainable Palm Oil (RSPO) standards may help meet the criteria for sustainable and
climate-friendly palm oil production and procurement and ensure the competitiveness of
these countries in international markets. According to *Bangkok Post* (2013), Thailand has
already adopted the RSPO standards to enter the international markets, particularly European
markets. The other two countries may follow suit or bring their own standards closer to
RSPO standards.

Strategic Intervention 6: Engage Local Governments and the Private Sector to Strengthen Social Capital

6.1 **Institute small funds for building social capital.** Social capital is a critical success factor for
building cross-border production networks. Social capital means cross-border networks and
trust relationships between people (Sarmiento-Mirwaldt 2012). According to a large body
of literature led by Putnam, Leonardi, and Nanetti (1993), social capital precedes economic
development and is important in stimulating economic cooperation (Sertkaya and Özcan
2017). Realizing the importance of social networks, IMT-GT has also taken some initiatives
such as setting up an IMT-GT Plaza, initiating annual IMT-GT trade fairs, and creating JBC.
The UNINET Strategic Action Plan 2017–2021 provides strategic directions to promote
social capital. UNINET manages programs such as IMT-GT Summer Camp, Innovative
Competition on Smart Farming, Internship and Visiting Researcher Program at CIMT Office,
100 Million LED Bulb Campaign for ASEAN, Joint Conference on Bioscience, joint conference
on ICMSA, IMT-GT UNINET STEM, and IMT-GT Varsity Carnival. It is recommended to
institute small funds at the local government level to upscale, institutionalize, and broad
base these efforts and ensure their continuity. These funds may be used for projects that
bring people, businesses, and local governments together. They can fund business seminars,
conferences, sports festivals, cross-border market surveys by small firms, and travels to attend
important cross-border events. One example of best practice is the small funds maintained by
regional governments in the EU to promote social capital by funding cross-border programs
for fostering cross-border people-to-people contacts. Its administration is devolved to local
governments with simplified application procedures. The project managers apply for funding
and, before receiving the final payment, write the final report, which is submitted to the local
governments. There is evidence, albeit sparse, that the contribution of the small funds to
fostering cross-border social networks has been impressive (Sarmiento-Mirwaldt 2012).

Strategy: Promote Regional or Cross-Border Value Chains

Strategic Intervention 7: Leverage the Development Ladder Formed within the Subregion

The participation in the GVCs has been a central element of the industrial strategy of IMT-GT
economies, and economic zones have been the linchpin of this strategy. However, as shown in
Chapter 7, these economies seem to have hit a roadblock. The collaborative approach of promoting
regional and cross-border value chains in the IMT-GT could offer them an opportunity to
reengineer their growth processes, which requires repositioning the IMT-GT countries and areas to
leverage the development ladder in the subregion.

7.1   **Strategic global repositioning of IMT-GT countries and areas.** Malaysia leads in terms of industrial development and technological sophistication, with Malaysia-GT covering the most developed states of Selangor, Melaka, and Penang, followed by Sumatera in Indonesia and Southern Thailand, in that order. The development ladder (or flying geese pattern) within the subregion can be leveraged to foster RVCs. For this, Malaysia needs to assume the role of a leading goose with appropriate initiatives. In 1991, Malaysia set the vision of being a high-income knowledge-based nation by 2020. All subsequent medium-term plans have followed the strategies to achieve this vision. However, according to the United Nations Industrial Development Organization (UNIDO) database (Competitive Industrial Performance Index 2020), the share of high and medium industries in Malaysia's manufacturing value added has gradually declined from 57% in 1999 to 44% in 2017. To achieve the aspiration of being a high-income country, Malaysia needs to strategically focus mainly on high value-added activities such as high value-added products, R&D, branding, logistics, distribution, and services and let the processing activities pass on to the following geese. This has been done earlier by Japan, the Republic of Korea; Taipei,China; Singapore; and, most recently, the PRC. Malaysia can also address the challenge of excessive reliance on low-skilled foreign workers by moving up the economic ladder, which will help the other two countries reposition their growth triangle areas.

Strategic Intervention 8: Design Tailor-Made Trade and Investment Policies in the Subregion that can Generate Cross-Border Economic and Institutional Synergies

8.1   **Create a database on the business ecosystems in each of the three economies.** The first step toward cross-border chains is a broad understanding of the economic, institutional, and social forces shaping business ecosystems in each of the three countries and the existing value chains status within the country. This requires commissioned studies covering a wide range of activities, actors, and service suppliers; financing, skills, and factor availability; R&D institutions; and markets at the industry level.

8.2   **Compile the above information in a comparable framework.** This data should be made available on the website of CIMT and directly to the MSMEs associations. An ideal example is the US Department of State's Investment Climate Statements published every year, which is an effort to harmonize the national investment climate data for its investors to facilitate location decisions.

8.3   **Harmonize the data on product standards and rules and regulations.** The CIMT may institute a project with private sector partners to map the industry-specific rules and regulations in halal and other industries and services in the subregion to create a harmonized database on policies, technical standards, and rules and regulations, which is accessible on the CIMT website.

8.4   **Harmonize product standards and rules and regulations.** In the long run, the focus should be on harmonizing the policies, technical standards, and regulations for creating a single market and production base with a free flow of goods, services, investment, skilled labor, and capital, which the AEC recognizes as one of the four pillars of integration. Pilot testing of this aspiration in the subregion will significantly impact cross-border investment in manufacturing and services and relocation of activities.

Strategic Intervention 9: Plan Direct Policy Interventions to Promote Cross-Border Chains

9.1   **Identify the sectors where regional value chains and cross-border value chains can be set up.** The value chains look promising in agribusiness, rubber, palm, metal products, electronics, automotive, and related industries considering the factor endowment.

9.2   **Identify the structure of value chains of selected products.** Each industry has its own value chain. It is normally divided into stages, products, processes, and actors. Understanding the value chains provides a framework for assessing each country's strengths and comparative advantages in different segments. Table 21 and Table 22 present illustrative value chains in the rubber and palm oil industries, the subregion's largest industries. Each value chain is divided into three stages: upstream, midstream, and downstream.

Table 21. Value Chain of the Rubber Industry

Upstream		Midstream		Downstream
Plantation	Crude output	Refining	Further refined products	Rubber products
	Extruded materials	Latex	Latex concentrate	Manufacturing latex-based products: rubber gloves
			Value-added specialty rubber	Niche products: green tires, sealants, adhesives
		Coagulated rubber	Rubber blocks	Dry products, bridge bearings, car components, conveyor belts, tires, dock fenders, building materials
	Wood			

Source: Sharib, S. and A. Halog. 2017. Enhancing Value Chains by Applying Industrial Symbiosis Concept to the Rubber City in Kedah, Malaysia. *Journal of Cleaner Production.* 141 (10). pp. 1095–1108. https://doi.org/10.1016/j.jclepro.2016.09.089.

9.3   **Map the performance of the three countries in value chains segments of the selected industries.** The assessment may be carried out in the framework of the Porter's Diamond, according to which competitiveness of the countries in a particular industry depends on the market structure (the role of large vs. small and foreign vs. domestic actors), factor availability, demand conditions, related and supporting industries, technological capabilities, and government policies. Mapping these conditions and their linkages and interactions should inform the policies and joint actions. The objective is to identify the levers and challenges to be overcome to set up RVCs.

9.4   **Map the strengths and weaknesses of the three countries in each segment of the value chain.** Table 23 and Table 24 provide a broad illustrative assessment of the competitive strengths of the countries in different stages of the value chains of rubber and palm oil. There are apparent cross-country complementarities that can be leveraged to build cross-border value chains. Malaysia has lost comparative advantages in upstream industries with a shift toward midstream and downstream industries. However, it needs to strengthen its position in quality downstream products. Indonesia and Thailand have to catch up. Cross-border value chains

Table 22. Value Chain of Palm Oil

Upstream		Midstream	Downstream	Support Industries
Plantation	Crude output	Refining	Products	Complementary
Early stage	• CPO • CPKO	• Crude palm, olein/palm • Crude palm stearin/palm kernel stearin • RBD palm oil/olein/stearin	• Cooking oil, shortening, margarine, Vanaspati, frying fat • Cocoa butter substitute, dough fat, salad oil, confectionery fat, nondairy creamer • Chocolate products	• Bleaching earth, acids • Cartons, tins, drums, labels, adhesive tapes, plastics • Imported and locally made equipment • Shipping, tankers, storage, bulk pumping stations, services at ports
Middle state	• Increased supply of CPO/CPKO • Specialty fats (e.g., high carotenes, high lauric, high olein)	• Trans-fatty-acid-free POP • Red POP • Increased volume of current products	• Microencapsulated POP, emulsifiers, food ingredients, Powdered ice cream, salad dressing/oil • Low-calorie products, palm oil-based cheese, genetically modified oils/fats, vitamins E and B, carotenes • Pharmaceuticals and other nutrient products	• Competitively priced local products • Specialized packaging materials to meet consumer and environmental requirements • Locally made equipment for domestic use and export • Adequate dedicated services and facilities
High value added Cloning to get better pericarp breeding Mechanization			• Oleochemicals derivatives, biofuels, and renewable energy • Biotechnology and biomass-based products • Nutritional foods and ingredients • Biofertilizers	• Marketing, branding, logistics, packaging, R&D

CPKO = crude palm kernel oil; CPO = crude palm oil; POP = phytosterols oxidation product; R&D = research and development; RBD = refined, bleached, and deodorized.

Source: Author, based on various sources.

in these industries in midstream and downstream products with complementary resources, such as storage facilities, technology transfers, and technology development, may help build formidable regional industries through aggregation, branding, packaging, storage, and logistics facilities well developed in the region.

9.5 **Develop a strategic vision.** The promotion of cross-border cooperation requires planning, which in turn involves the choice of strategy. Three types of strategies may be identified: (i) horizontal (improving process, product, or volume within the existing nodes); (ii) vertical (upgrading by performing downstream activities, such as processing, grading, transporting, bulking up, or advertising); and (iii) a combination of the two. This sets the context of joint actions by identifying the areas of collaborative agreements.

Table 23. Competitive Strengths and Weaknesses of Indonesia, Malaysia, and Thailand in Rubber Industry Value Chains

Plantation	Upstream	Midstream Specialization	Downstream Strengths and Weaknesses
Indonesia	Largest area under plantation with relatively low productivity and low quality (Andoko 2019)	Refining	Footwear and other industrial products and tires (low value-added products)
Malaysia	High productivity but lagging behind Thailand	Latex	Dominant exporter of rubber gloves, latex threads, balloons, gloves, finger stalls, and foam Strong home-grown companies
Thailand	Upstream (plantation) technology transfers from Malaysia initially but has built strong technological capabilities with the highest productivity (Kawano 2019).	Coagulated rubber	Tires and other automotive parts Major producer of condoms Weakness: Most production is under the multinational corporations.

Sources: Author; Andoko, E. 2019. *Overview of Indonesian Current Issue and Government Strategy on the Rubber Commodity.* FFTC Agricultural Policy Platform, Food and Fertilizer Technology for the Asia and Pacific Region. https://ap.fftc.org.tw/article/1652; and Kawano, M. 2019. Changing Resource-Based Manufacturing Industry: The Case of the Rubber Industry in Malaysia and Thailand. In K. Tsunekawa and Y. Todo, eds. *Emerging States at Crossroads. Emerging-Economy State and International Policy Studies.* Singapore: SpringerOpen. https://doi.org/10.1007/978-981-13-2859-6_7.

Table 24. Competitive Strengths and Weaknesses of Indonesia, Malaysia, and Thailand in Palm Oil Industry Value Chains

Countries	Illustrative Assessment of Comparative Advantages in Palm Oil Industry
Indonesia	Indonesia is the largest producer of palm oil with the largest area. It also produces superior quality palm oil because oil palm fruits have to be processed within 24 hours to minimize the build-up of fatty acids, adversely affecting the quality of oil palm fruits. More oil can be extracted from high-quality fruits during processing. Similarly, the raw material, crude palm oil, also contains acid. It cannot be stored for long because the acid can increase. The higher the acid, the lower is the quality of palm oil. Being the largest producer, Indonesia has the advantage of processing it quickly and hence being the quality producer of palm oil. However, low productivity and underdeveloped downstream industries are major weaknesses.
Malaysia	Malaysia has lost revealed comparative advantage in crude and refined oil stages to Indonesia and may focus more on downstream industries through functional upgrading and cross-border cooperation (Nambiappan et al. 2016).
Thailand	In Thailand, consumption is directed to domestic markets. However, it has set the target of adopting the Roundtable on Sustainable Palm Oil standard to meet the international criteria to enhance its share in international markets.

Source: Author; and Nambiappan, B. et al. 2016. Revealed Comparative Advantage and Competitiveness of Malaysian Palm Oil Exports against Indonesia in Five Major Markets. *Oil Palm Industry Economic Journal.* 16 (1). pp. 1–7.

9.6 **Form digital consortia of industry associations, academic institutions, and research organizations in prominent industries.** Leverage technology revolution to form digital consortia of industry associations in selected industries across the subregion. The consortia will work closely with the governments of the three countries to develop the vision and strategic plans to promote shared development in these industries. Indonesia and Malaysia have collaborated at the government level to set up the Council of Palm Oil Producing Countries, an intergovernmental organization for promoting cooperation among palm oil-producing countries. Even though it focuses mainly on marketing, it sets a precedence for a collaborative effort in palm oil. In line with this, it is proposed to set up digital industry consortia to promote production and technological capabilities with industry partners who must coordinate with elaborate state bodies regulating these industries.

9.7 **Develop strategic short-, medium-, and long-term actions through collaborative efforts by industry consortia and state bodies.** Develop joint strategic master plans for targeted industries that must include

(i)   business-friendly policy environment;
(ii) harmonization of policies, regulations, and standards to create a single production and market base;
(iii) sustainability issues;
(iv) skills and training;
(v)   R&D agreements, technology licensing, bilateral or unilateral flows of technology;
(vi) financing mechanisms; and
(vii) marketing and distribution mechanisms.

Industry consortia can play an important role in developing these plans in collaboration with the relevant state bodies. The policies should be developed based on the broader strategies, both nationally and jointly, to leverage cross-border comparative advantages.

9.8 **Mainstream the joint strategic plans in national plans and programs.** It is crucial for the budgetary support and implementation of the joint mechanisms, as discussed in Chapter 7.

9.9 **Adopt a systematic approach to building the capabilities of regional firms to participate in regional value chains.** Develop implementation strategies of the strategic plan, including identifying projects, project funding, time frames, and possible outcomes. Partnerships may be developed between large and small firms, and regional and international organizations (or development partners) to create capacities to extend production networks beyond the national borders.

9.10 **Identify and encourage regional and domestic companies as anchor firms in targeted sectors.** Anchor firms are well-established influential businesses that have a significant capacity to multiply outputs and form value chains. Local governments, in collaboration with industry associations, can identify potential anchor firms, preferably domestic or regional, in designated target sectors for economic zones in the subregion. These firms can also be engaged in business planning exercises in the SEZs and economic zones to identify investment barriers and remove them.

Strategy: Improve Branding and Marketing of the Region

In today's competitive world, branding is important to significantly impact and to gain and sustain a sizable market share. It requires a cohesive strategic approach toward IMT-GT positioning as an attractive destination with projected and perceived values through joint marketing initiatives.

Strategic Intervention 10: Position the IMT-GT Region as an Investment Destination for Food, Palm, and Rubber Industries

10.1 **Position the subregion as a global hub of food, rubber, and palm industries.** The IMT-GT has a large agriculture sector. This sector needs to be leveraged to promote three major regional industries: food, palm oil, and rubber. The IMT-GT vision document also envisages them as priority industries in the subregion. A well-designed marketing program needs to position the subregion as a global hub of these industries. This strategic move is also important to address the negative image of rubber and palm oil industries and attract investors. Further, all three countries have focused on the halal industries by setting up dedicated economic zones. Malaysia has been the pioneer in recognizing halal as an engine of economic growth. It was the first country to have developed a halal master plan in 2006 and host an annual halal-only trade fair called Malaysia International Halal Showcase or MIHAS (ITC 2015). These advantages need to be leveraged through branding and well positioning of the halal products of the subregion.

10.2 **Engage investment promotion agencies.** The investment promotion agencies of each member state can develop a web page on IMT-GT subregional economic zones. The information on economic zones should be updated regularly.

10.3 **Develop an integrated information portal.** Link the national web pages with the IMT-GT website of the CIMT that serves as an integrated information platform on the subregional portal. Public relations activities, press releases, and research notes may be adopted as instruments to promote the subregional zones.

10.4 **Strengthen the IMT-GT website.** The IMT-GT website needs to be upgraded to provide more data and information regarding markets, production, and investment opportunities in the subregion. It is a powerful tool for branding and reaching out to regional and global investors. Member countries may commission research papers and policy briefs on market and production trends, and blogs on the latest developments in the regional industries, featuring entrepreneurs, their R&D, and other achievements. These may be uploaded on the IMT-GT website to make the subregion visible.

To summarize, the collaborative approach is critical for the success of economic zones in the subregion. This is because investors in economic zones assess the scale advantages to economize production, and, for this, they look beyond national borders to leverage the regional capabilities. According to the EU-ASEAN Business Sentiments Survey (EU-ASEAN Business Council 2019), European firms view ASEAN as the region of best economic opportunity. Yet, the slow progress in regional integration has dulled enthusiasm for the AEC among them, and they are now adjusting their business strategy according to local environments rather than regional synergies. These revelations underscore the need for proactive approaches to use the IMT-GT subregion to create conditions for capturing positive sentiments of these investors.

Competitive Approach: Strategies, Strategic Interventions, and Enabling Actions

Competition generates pressures and challenges in attracting investment and can benefit economic zones by driving their investment climate, growth, and efficiency. Thus, the collaborative approach should be combined with competitive strategies to expand and strengthen the SEZs and GEZs within the overall framework of the coopetition strategy. A two-pronged competitive strategy is recommended here: (i) improve the attractiveness of national SEZs, and (ii) maximize the domestic spillover effects.

Improve the Attractiveness of Special Economic Zones and Industrial Zones

SEZs' investment climate has three elements: micro, meso, and macro. All these dimensions must be addressed simultaneously to build competitive SEZs and other economic zones (Figure 13).

Figure 13. Enabling Conditions for Attractiveness of Economic Zones

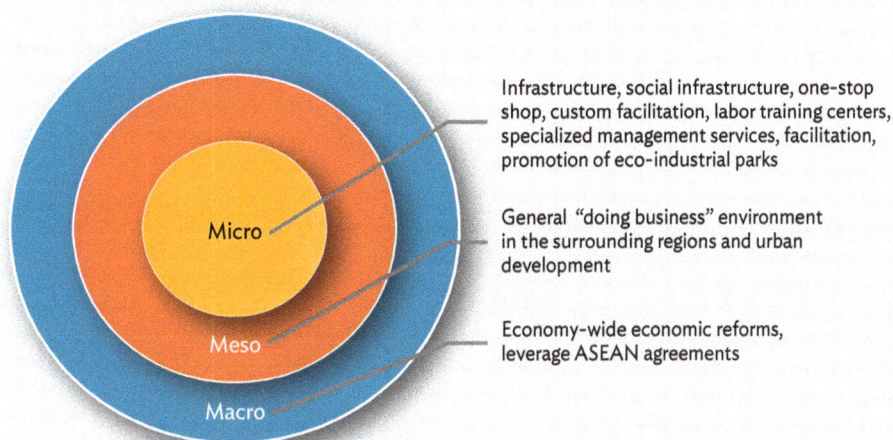

Micro — Infrastructure, social infrastructure, one-stop shop, custom facilitation, labor training centers, specialized management services, facilitation, promotion of eco-industrial parks

Meso — General "doing business" environment in the surrounding regions and urban development

Macro — Economy-wide economic reforms, leverage ASEAN agreements

ASEAN = Association of Southeast Asian Nations.
Source: Author.

Microclimatic Factors

Microclimatic factors refer to the investment climate prevailing in the SEZs and industrial zones, which depends on two sets of factors (i) structural, and (ii) legal and institutional. Structural factors constitute size, location, composition of economic activity, and development level. Legal and institutional factors comprise policies and operational practices adopted in the zones. Strategic intervention 11 captures the recommendations for upgrading the structural characteristics, while strategic interventions 12–15 focus on policies and practices.

Strategic Intervention 11: Promote Sustainable Economic Zones

11.1   **Promote logistics zones or parks.** A logistics park is an important logistics facility that can significantly impact not only economic efficiency in the movement of goods and commodities (as discussed above) but also the environment. It can, for instance, reduce carbon dioxide emissions and air pollution by combining multiple distribution centers and logistic operators into a single park (Zhang et al. 2017). There is a growing trend to introduce logistics parks in both the developed and developing countries. In the PRC, for example, the number of logistics parks stood at 1,638 by the end of 2017 compared with 1,210 in 2015, according to the fifth survey report conducted by the China Federation of Logistics & Purchasing. Of these logistics parks, 1,113 (68%) were operational; the rest were under construction or planning (Wang et al. 2020). In contrast, Malaysia has 14 operational free commercial zones (FCZs) within the subregion. The data on bonded logistics parks in Indonesia-GT are not available (overall, it has 91 bonded logistics parks), while Thailand develops logistics areas as part of the industrial estates and SEZs. It is recommended to fill the gaps in logistics facilities.

11.2   **Incorporate sustainability criteria in site selection.** In border areas, the proliferation of zones may cause irreversible destruction of ecosystems and biodiversity and in turn, environmental degradation and pollution. Thus, sustainability issues must be incorporated into site selection (Ahmed et al. 2020). Further, their establishment should be restricted to the ideal locations with a high probability of their success. There should also be an assessment of land availability in the existing zones before planning the new ones in less-than-ideal locations. Globally, the proliferation of SEZs is accompanied by a failure of several of them. One of the major reasons for this failure is setting up zones in less-than-ideal locations in the hope of attracting investment.

11.3   **Promote eco-industrial parks, particularly in rubber and palm.** Despite the economic benefits of palm oil and rubber industries, there have been negative social and environmental externalities such as displacement of rural communities, deforestation, soil erosion, and biodiversity loss. The food industry, particularly halal, is also associated with environmental degradation, causing depletion of natural resources and deterioration of ecosystems, social health, and livelihoods (Abdullah, Sabar, and Mustafar 2018). To maximize returns after discounting these negative impacts, the governments should adopt sustainable development strategies for these industries with a zero-waste approach through reduction, reuse, and recycling of waste and by-products. This approach is known by various names: 3Rs, industrial symbiosis, or circular approach. Eco-industrial parks are based on this approach and offer industries and organizations opportunities of sharing by-products generated in processing with other industries that develop niche business potential using these waste products. It is strongly proposed to develop eco-industrial parks to promote the three priority industries in the subregion.

11.4   **Promote environment-friendly infrastructure in the existing zones.** The economic zones need to have infrastructure focusing on the green conveyance; treatment, recycling, and reuse of wastewater (the management of sewage and waste); energy conservation building; solar-powered vehicles and buildings within the zones; and use of environment-certified equipment and appliances. The best global practices include the PRC's green SEZs, India's green SEZ guidelines, and Thailand's eco-industrial towns (EITs) initiative. These measures are needed to be complemented by training and skills development, as well as a virtual platform for the exchange of best-practice technologies.

11.5   **Apply the circular or industrial symbiosis approach in the rubber cities.** As discussed above, it is becoming increasingly urgent to erase the negative image of the rubber and palm oil industries. One proposal is to promote the rubber cities as eco-industrial parks (Chiu and Yong 2004). It is a low-hanging fruit because the rubber cities are already operational in Thailand and Indonesia. It will ensure the sustainability of rubber cities with efficient utilization of energy, water resources, and waste, as shown in Figure 14. This will also improve the image of the region's industry. The regulatory agencies of the three countries—the Malaysian Rubber Board, Rubber Authority of Thailand, and relevant agencies in Indonesia (Indonesia does not have a centralized agency)—may coordinate to develop a master plan in partnership with the consortium of industrial organizations.

Figure 14. List of Potential Industrial Symbiosis of Rubber

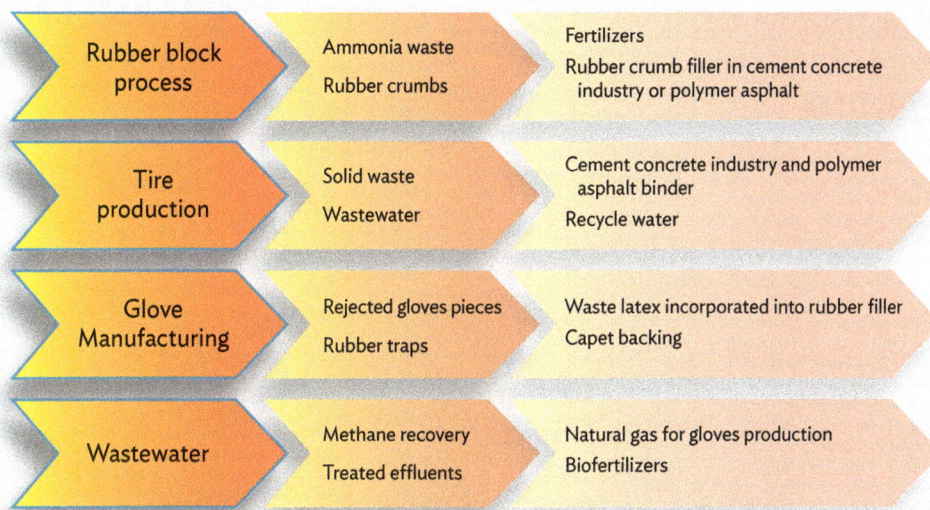

Rubber block process	Ammonia waste / Rubber crumbs	Fertilizers / Rubber crumb filler in cement concrete industry or polymer asphalt
Tire production	Solid waste / Wastewater	Cement concrete industry and polymer asphalt binder / Recycle water
Glove Manufacturing	Rejected gloves pieces / Rubber traps	Waste latex incorporated into rubber filler / Capet backing
Wastewater	Methane recovery / Treated effluents	Natural gas for gloves production / Biofertilizers

Source: Sharib, S. and A. Halog. 2017. Enhancing Value Chains by Applying Industrial Symbiosis Concept to the Rubber City in Kedah, Malaysia. *Journal of Cleaner Production.* 141 (10). pp. 1095–1108. https://doi.org/10.1016/j.jclepro.2016.09.089.

Strategic Intervention 12: Compensate the Locational Disadvantages through Strategic Master Planning of the Economic Zones

12.1   **Location-specific and innovative on-site infrastructure solutions may be critical in attracting investors.** Various infrastructure such as plug and play factories, transport, logistics, financial infrastructure, common facilities, green spaces, and connections to utilities need to be designed in the master plans. The physical infrastructure provided within economic zones must be able to compensate for what the location lacks. Sei Mangkei SEZ in Indonesia, for instance, has its own railway line that connects the SEZ with the Port of Kuala Tanjung, saving high logistics costs.

12.2   **For specialized zones, the master plan needs to cater to the target investor.** A case in point is food parks, which benefit from livestock and food testing, certification facilities, quality controls, warehousing, logistics, and R&D facilities. Similarly, other specialized zones have their own requirements related to facilities and infrastructure. Singapore's One-North Innovation

District, which caters to the biomedical science and high-tech industries, is designed to create an atmosphere of casual vibrancy, stimulating creativity and imagination (Cheong 2018). The Jurong Island petrochemical complex has common utilities, such as water and gas, supplied centrally to tenants in the complex. In India, the presence of environment-related infrastructure in pharmaceutical SEZs is a success factor in attracting foreign investors (Aggarwal 2012a).

12.3 **On-site social infrastructure.** The master plan of SEZs must compensate for the absence of social amenities such as food outlets and food courts, supermarkets, gymnasium, sports complex, housing, schools, and health care facilities in the border areas. Most economic zones in the subregion are typical industrial estates away from the cities. The presence of on-site or off-site social amenities may enhance their attractiveness.

12.4 **Training centers for labor.** One of the structural constraints on the border areas is the lack of relevant skilled or semiskilled workers and necessary technology support. A critical success factor is to have well-equipped skills training centers, which work closely with technical and vocational schools, colleges, and universities to provide skills training and technology support for the firms in the zones (e.g., in Pakistan). Zones may also have incubators to nurture new start-ups with certain seed money (as in the PRC).

12.5 **Off-site infrastructure.** As the focus is on on-site infrastructure, the development of off-site infrastructure is often neglected. Investors sometimes face huge bottlenecks in accessing ports, highways, and airports due to poor roads and logistics. Off-site connecting and logistics infrastructure and services are crucial for the success of zones in remote areas. According to Octavia (2016), the privately managed industrial estates prefer to operate in or around Greater Jakarta despite higher labor costs to access capital markets and superior infrastructure. High-class off-site connecting economic, financial, and technological infrastructure is a centripetal force critical in attracting investment in the economic zones.

Strategic Intervention 13: Provide Investor-Friendly One-Stop Services

13.1 **One-stop shop and custom facilitation.** Both Thailand and Indonesia provide one-stop shop services to investors. In Malaysia, MIDA and state investment agencies facilitate investors. Upgrading these services may further add value to economic zones in the subregion. Hawassa Industrial Park (SEZ) in Ethiopia, a successful venture, for instance, offers a one-stop institutional service center with banking, visa, and immigration facilities; import–export licenses; work permits; and customs clearance, all in one building within the zone to help speed up decision making and reduce setup costs. This differential approach for the subregional economic zones may cut transaction costs for the regional firms undertaking investment in these zones and facilitate cross-border value chains.

13.2 **Provide specialized management services.** Several zones provide value-added management services beyond the regular ones. Jebel Ali in Dubai, one of the most successful zones in the world, offers ready-to-use, fully furnished, and equipped offices with no setup cost; retail showrooms; and fully equipped business centers. Further, it offers its services as a development management consultant, whereby it assists the customer in developing the facility. It can also build and deliver the facility as per customer specification and budget or build the facility as per customer specification based on the long-term occupational lease.

These value-added services, which enhance the zone's attractiveness, may be identified and offered by the zone authorities in the peripheral areas of the IMT-GT.

13.3 **Digitization of services and transactions.** Even as the COVID-19 pandemic has taken a toll on the economies, it has had a catalytic effect on the economic sectors' digital transformation. Business models, customer behavior, and preferred interactions are dramatically changing and will continue to evolve even after the recovery. Underlying this shift is the need to go digital in all services and transactions with companies, assess long-term strategic plans, and explore new methods of facilitating economic zones management.

13.4 **Offer customized incentives in core and peripheral areas.** A differential approach in tax benefits across core and peripheral areas may also be adopted. While fiscal incentives in the core areas may be offered to high value-added industries, labor- or resource-intensive industries may be granted preferential tax treatment in the subregion. The differential tax incentive structure may contribute to eliminating competition for investment between the core and peripheral areas. Further, operating in a remote area may entail significantly higher production, transportation, and communications costs. Targeted tax incentives may encourage firms to invest in these areas. Finally, firms may find it difficult to hire a skilled labor force and may be incentivized to invest in training and skill development through tax benefits.

Meso Climatic Factors

Strategic Intervention 14: Improve General Investment Climate in Surrounding Areas of Economic Zones

14.1 **Improve regulatory institutions in the border regions.** Border areas have their own institutional disadvantages due to low-quality development. The key is to enhance the economic climate in these regions. Table 25 presents highlights from the regional enterprise surveys of the World Bank for Indonesia and Thailand. The purpose is to show how the investment climate in subregional areas is inferior to that in the core areas. Two subnational regions are selected in each country—Indonesia's Jakarta (the core) and North Sumatera (Indonesia-GT), and Central Thailand (core) and Southern Thailand (Thailand-GT). It shows that debottlenecking is required in the IMT-GT regions by improving infrastructure, governance, regulatory environment, and finance.

14.2 **Urban development in areas surrounding economic zones.** International experience suggests that if SEZs are located in backward areas with poor social and economic infrastructure and a lack of industrial culture, their performance is likely to be below expectation (Aggarwal 2005). Urban centers near the economic zones are critical to their success, ensuring more accessible and uninterrupted utilities, better services, availability of skilled labor, and quality of life for investors. A good practice is to develop the zones as part of the urban development program (Zeng 2016). Malaysia's spatial policy of "concentrated decentralization" is a good illustration of this practice.[30] Malaysia has been developing several zones under this framework, including Malaysia Vision Valley, Chuping Valley, and the East Coast Economic Region (ECER) SEZ. Thailand's model cities in Southern Thailand also plan to integrate industrial estates into these cities. A key lesson learned is that the economic zones need to be developed within the overall urban development context.

---

[30] Refer to p. 31, para. 2 for details.

Table 25. Doing Business Environment in Subregional Economies vs. National Capitals: Indonesia and Thailand

Doing Business Indicator	Indonesia		Thailand	
	Jakarta	Sumatera Utara	Central	South
Senior management time spent dealing with the requirements of government regulation (%)	1.6	0.1	0.1	3.4
% of firms visited or required to meet with tax officials	14.4	23.4	12.3	31.0
% of firms identifying tax rates as a major constraint	0.4	21.2	0	9.4
% of firms identifying tax administration as a major constraint	0.2	17.1	0	3.5
% of firms identifying business licensing and permits as a major constraint	0.4	19.3	0	9.5
% of firms experiencing electrical outages	16.1	11.4	4.1	13.0
No. of electrical outages in a typical month	0.2	0.5	0.1	0.7
Average duration of a typical electrical outage (hours)	2.7	17.4	1.3	2.0
% of firms identifying electricity as a major constraint	7.6	32.1	3.8	8.1
% of firms experiencing water insufficiencies	0.5	0.8	0.7	7.3
% of firms identifying transportation as a major constraint	7.6	29.0	0.6	7.4
% of firms identifying customs and trade regulations as a major constraint	2.0	19.3	0.3	1.1
% of firms identifying an inadequately educated workforce as a major constraint	3.3	10.5	3.3	6.0
% of firms identifying access to finance as a major constraint	3.8	12.8	0.9	2.6
% of firms expected to give gifts to public officials "to get things done"	37.7	73.6	–	–

– = not applicable.

Sources: World Bank. Enterprise Survey 2015: Indonesia. https://www.enterprisesurveys.org/en/data/exploreeconomies/2015/indonesia (accessed 27 January 2021); World Bank. Enterprise Survey 2016: Thailand. https://www.enterprisesurveys.org/en/data/exploreeconomies/2016/thailand (accessed 27 January 2021).

Macro Climatic Factors

Strategic Intervention 15: Expedite Global and Regional Integration Efforts for the Smooth Operation of Global Value Chains, Particularly during the COVID-19 Pandemic

15.1 **Establish ASEAN Economic Community.** A major push to the subregion may come from the achievement of the AEC itself. While the subregion is a building block and a testing lab for the AEC, it will benefit from progress in ASEAN integration. Macro-regionalism leads to more trust among the parties on both sides of the borders so that cross-border cooperation to address common policy challenges or manage shared resources becomes more likely

(Schiff and Winters 2002). Further, it can promote cross-border micro-regionalism in a top–down fashion through particular policies and incentives that target border areas (Lombaerde 2010). Thus, the ASEAN and IMT-GT subregional frameworks should be viewed as mutually reinforcing. While ASEAN has had phenomenal success in establishing ASEAN Free Trade Area, it fell short of its target of realizing the AEC by the end of 2015. The AEC agenda has been rolled out with a largely unfinished agenda (Menon and Melendez 2017). Nontariff measures and barriers to trade in service, labor mobility, and harmonization of rules persist, which may be affecting the performance of the subregional corridors and economic zones. Efforts should, therefore, be expedited to implement the AEC.

15.2 **Introduce broader economic reforms.** Although SEZs are designed to overcome institutional deficiency in the wider economy, in practice, their success is linked with the extent to which the host economies are globally integrated. Within the subregion, Malaysia—the best-performing economy in terms of various indicators of global integration (De Backer and Miroudot 2013, ADB 2019, ASEAN-Japan Centre 2019, WTO 2019)—also leads in various indicators of development (as shown in Chapter 7) and technological sophistication, with more than 44% of manufacturing value added accounted for by medium- and high-tech industries, as against 35% in Indonesia and 40% in Thailand (UNIDO Competitive Industrial Performance Index 2020). In contrast, Indonesia, with the lowest GDP per capita among the subregional countries, is poorly integrated into global supply chains, and its forward and backward linkages are further weakening (ADB 2019, ASEAN-Japan Centre 2019). Thailand lies in the middle in terms of both globalization and its economic performance. Acceleration in economic reforms at the macro level thus seems to be directly linked with the economic performance of these countries and has direct implications for the performance of economic zones.

15.3 **Provide greater autonomy to local governments.** SEZs are more likely to succeed in a decentralized political system because the local governments understand the local contexts better. In particular, the decentralization of financial powers can incentivize and empower the local government to provide good investment in SEZs to attract investment (Moberg 2018). The PRC is a classic example of success with a decentralized model of SEZs. Through fiscal decentralization, the central leadership provided local governments with the incentives and capacity to promote investments and industrial activities. It became instrumental in the success of SEZs (Zheng and Aggarwal 2020). Malaysia and Indonesia can test pilot the model in the subregional SEZs.

Improve Spillovers through Horizontal and Vertical Policies

Two complementary approaches may be adopted to maximize spillovers from economic zones within the national economy.

Strategic Intervention 16: Adopt a Vertical Approach to Maximize Spillover Effects

The vertical approach is a targeted approach of focusing on capacity building of domestic firms in those sectors that cater to SEZs by improving their market access, sales, product and services offerings, quality controls, financial management, and productivity. It is also known as the smart approach. The alignment of the production activities in the wider economy with those inside SEZs mutually reinforces investment within and outside the SEZs. The following enabling actions are proposed to adopt the vertical approach.

16.1   **Identify and promote the production of goods and services required by special economic zones.** The SEZ residents require a range of quality goods and services at competitive prices. The government needs to be proactive in promoting domestic enterprises to produce and supply them to SEZs' firms. Selected GEZs may be targeted to link them with the SEZs through this approach, driving the diversification of technological capabilities and skills base in the wider economy. The textile industry in an SEZ, for instance, needs dress materials, buttons, embellishments, machines, and equipment; human skills in cutting, designing, tailoring, and marketing; and a network of institutions supporting logistics services, financial services, testing and certification services, and R&D. Policy makers need to carefully assess these opportunities and build capabilities among MSMEs to cater to the requirements in SEZs. Taipei,China adopted this strategy successfully and became a powerhouse of MSMEs (Hidalgo et al. 2007).

16.2   **Link the subregional companies with extra-regional firms, particularly those participating in global value chains.** Lagging regions lack production and technological capabilities. They can benefit from extra-regional collaborations to build cooperative networks, which may be achieved by setting up virtual or physical knowledge networks. These networks can help set up contacts between the subregional and extra-subregional firms. The European Commission supports projects that involve the extra-regional collaboration of firms in the lagging regions through, for instance, the EU's Horizon 2020 and Interreg programs (Box 2). There are similar programs at the national levels in some European countries via initiatives such as the UK's Knowledge Transfer Network (Barzotto et al. 2019). In the IMT-GT subregion, such linkages may strengthen the firms' capabilities but, at the same time, can improve spillover effects within the subregion.

16.3   **Target subregional companies to link them with special economic zone companies.** In the initial stages, selected subregional companies may be targeted to be promoted through direct interventions. As firms are upgraded, a more general approach may be adopted. For instance, Taipei,China insists on localizing components and raw materials by MNCs to promote spillovers and offers non-fiscal incentives to domestic MSMEs to help them grow with MNCs.

16.4   **Develop skills required in special economic zones.** To bridge the demand–supply gap in skills, policy makers should map the demand for skilled workforce with supply, identify skills gap, and develop skills required in the SEZs. The zone companies with huge tax benefits may be encouraged to invest in skill development. The tax benefits may be conditional on companies investing a part of their revenue in research and skill promotion. Or the government can compensate the investor for the cost of constructing infrastructure and training workers in the region. Singapore follows this practice. Several low-income countries have also adopted these practices.

16.5   **Lower transaction barriers between special economic zones and domestic firms.** This promotes backward and forward linkages between them and improves capacity building outside the zones. In countries where government policy allows local entrepreneurs to supply SEZ producers with duty-free materials, significant backward linkages may be created. Similarly, the government policy of allowing companies to sell a part of the goods produced in SEZs to domestic tariff areas may lead to the creation of forward linkages.

Strategic Intervention 17: Complement the Vertical Approach of Promoting Targeted Sectors with a Horizontal Approach

17.1   **Build structural capabilities in the locations surrounding economic zones through strategic interventions.** Policy makers ought to complement the vertical approach with horizontal policies to create conditions for the cluster development by promoting entrepreneurship, subsidizing venture or other early-stage finance, building management capacity, and helping firms forge international links (Bresnahan and Gambardella 2004, Nathan and Overman 2013). Governments should also promote investment in skills, technologies, finance, R&D, and infrastructure in the wider economy to create conditions for spillovers from the SEZs. It must be noted that SEZs build on the existing capabilities; they do not build these capabilities afresh.

Chapter 9

Adoption of the Proposed Strategic Interventions and Enabling Actions into the IMT-GT Agenda and National Planning

Adopt a Holistic and Cross-Cutting Approach

The economic zones policy is cross-cutting. The success of subregional economic zones, in particular, hinges on many different cross-sector and cross-border interventions that go beyond ensuring a favorable business climate in them. The coopetition strategic framework proposed in Chapter 8 complicates the economic zones policy further. A wide-ranging cross-sector and border strategies are proposed, further broken down into strategic interventions and enabling actions. This chapter focuses on the adoption of the policy prescriptions into the IMT-GT and national development agendas. Its contention is fourfold.

- **Adopt a holistic and integrated approach** that requires adopting all the broad policy prescriptions simultaneously as a package. A piecemeal approach cannot be effective.

- **Break down the strategic interventions into three time frames: short, medium, and long terms.** Short-term programs are incremental actions that do not require an extensive preparatory effort (CIMT 2017b). Medium-term interventions focus on the existing pipeline projects that do not require consensus before they can be implemented. Both short- and medium-term actions are low-hanging fruits. Long-term actions require a long process of negotiation and consensus building before they can be implemented.

- **Use a cross-sector approach and mainstream all proposed strategic interventions and enabling actions** for economic zones into the relevant sectoral or thematic strategies of the development plans, and the seven working groups of IMT-GT on (i) agriculture and agro-based industry; (ii) tourism; (iii) halal products and services; (iv) transport and ICT connectivity; (v) trade and investment; (vi) human resource development, education, and culture; and (vii) working group on the environment.

- **Design special programs and initiatives** to implement them effectively in the subregion, i.e., complement mainstreaming with a targeted approach.

Map Strategic Interventions and Enabling Actions with Sectoral Strategies and Working Group Agenda

Indonesia, Malaysia, and Thailand adopt different planning frameworks depending on their strategic thrusts, but they all cover three basic themes: economic, social, and environmental. Economic development includes macroeconomic goals and strategies on the one hand and sectoral development planning on the other. Sectoral development planning covers agriculture, industry, infrastructure, transport, finance, trade, services, research and innovation, and regional equity. Table 26 and Table 27 map the collaborative and competitive strategic interventions and enabling actions proposed above with sectoral or thematic strategies in the development plans on the one hand and working groups agendas and time frames on the other hand. The serial numbers given to strategic interventions and enabling actions in the tables match those in Chapter 8. Mapping of strategic interventions and enabling actions with sectoral strategies and working groups agendas is a first step toward adopting the strategic framework proposed here into planning. The mapping should be followed by targeted programs and initiatives for the subregion in each thematic area.

Table 26. Mapping of the Collaborative Strategies of Economic Zones with Thematic or Sectoral Areas of the National Plan Agendas and Working Groups

Strategy	Strategic Intervention	Enabling Action	Working Group	National Plan	Time
Implement subregional economic corridors effectively	1. Mainstream the IMT-GT Vision agenda, objectives, and strategic approaches into national plans and programs	1.1 Mainstream the IMT-GT Vision agenda of regional cooperation 1.2 Mainstream the objectives and spatial approach of the IMT-GT	WGTI	Macro-economic objectives	MT
	2. Improve physical connectivity through efficient and integrated physical infrastructure	2.1 Expedite the completion of IMT-GT projects 2.2 Develop a pipeline of physical connectivity projects 2.3 Constitute a Project Selection Committee to strengthen the project selection process 2.4 Adopt an ex ante approach in developing a pipeline 2.5 Develop techno-analytic criteria for project assessment	WGTIC	Transport and infrastructure	LT
	3. Remove impediments to mobility	3.1 Pilot test ASEAN agreements on transport facilitation in the subregion 3.2 Pilot test trade facilitation agreements in the subregion 3.3 Relax labor mobility 3.4 Ensure seamless mobility within the subregion in the long run beyond the ASEAN agreements	WGTI	Transport and trade	ST to MT LT

continued on next page

Table 26 *continued*

Strategy	Strategic Intervention	Enabling Action	Working Group	National Plan	Time
Augment regional capabilities through cooperative strategies	4. Promote cross-border cooperation programs to build production capabilities of MSMEs with the private sector participation	4.1 Engage large subregional firms in promoting the ecosystem for production 4.2 Engage MSMEs associations 4.3 Initiate industry-specific programs 4.4 Initiate pilot projects in the subregion for digital transformation	WGTI WGHAPAS WGAA WGHRDEC CIMT JBC	MSMEs development	LT
	5. Promote cross-border cooperation programs to build a strong technological base	5.1 Institute an IMT-GT research fund with contributions from the governments and private sector 5.2 Strengthen knowledge transfers through faculty exchange and internship programs 5.3 Intensify efforts to build R&D alliances in palm oil and rubber industries 5.4 Form international research alliances 5.5 Tighten the certification criteria for palm oil	WGHRDEC WGHAPAS WGAA CMGF JBC	Agriculture industry R&D	MT to LT
	6. Engage local governments and the private sector to strengthen social capital	6.1 Institute small funds for building social capital	WGHRDEC CIMT JBC	Human capital	ST
Promote regional or cross-border value chains	7. Leverage the development ladder formed within the subregion to foster cross-border and regional value chains	7.1 Strategic global repositioning of IMT-GT countries and areas	WGTI	Industry	LT
	8. Design tailor-made trade and investment policies in the subregion that can generate cross-border economic and institutional synergies	8.1 Create a database on the business ecosystems in each of the three economies 8.2 Compile the above information in a comparable framework 8.3 Harmonize the data on product standards and rules and regulations 8.4 Harmonize product standards and rules and regulations	WGTI	Industry Industrial policies	MT to LT

continued on next page

Table 26 *continued*

Strategy	Strategic Intervention	Enabling Action	Working Group	National Plan	Time
	9. Plan direct policy interventions to promote cross-border chains	9.1 Identify the sectors where RVCs and cross-border value chains can be set up 9.2 Map the structure of value chains of the selected product 9.3 Map the performance of the three countries in value chains segments of the selected industries 9.4 Map the strengths and weaknesses of the three countries in each segment of the value chain 9.5 Develop a strategic vision 9.6 Form digital consortia of industry associations, academic institutions, and research organizations in prominent industries 9.7 Develop strategic plans for short-, medium-, and long-term actions through collaborative efforts by industry consortia and state bodies 9.8 Mainstream the joint strategic plans in national plans and programs 9.9 Adopt a systematic approach to building capabilities of regional firms to participate in regional value chains 9.10 Identify and encourage regional and domestic companies as anchor firms in targeted sectors	WGHAPAS WGAA WGHRDEC JBC CIMT WGTIC	Industry Balanced regional growth MSMEs Industrial policies	MT to LT
Improve branding and marketing of the region	10. Position the IMT-GT subregion as an investment destination for food, palm, and rubber industries	10.1 Position the subregion as a global hub of food (halal), rubber, and palm industries 10.2 Engage investment promotion agencies 10.3 Develop an integrated information portal 10.4 Strengthen the IMT-GT website	WGTI CIMT	Industry and industrial policies	MT

ASEAN = Association of Southeast Asian Nations; CIMT = Centre for IMT-GT Subregional Cooperation; CMGF = Chief Ministers and Governors Forum; IMT-GT = Indonesia–Malaysia–Thailand Growth Triangle; JBC = Joint Business Council; LT = long term; MSMEs= micro, small, and medium-sized enterprises; MT = medium term; R&D = research and development; RVC = regional value chain; ST = short term; WGAA = working group on agriculture and agro-based industry; WGHAPAS = working group on halal products and services; WGHRDEC = working group on human resource development, education, and culture; WGTI = working group on trade and investment; WGTIC = working group on transport and ICT [information and communication technology] connectivity.

Source: Author.

Table 27. Mapping of the Competitive Strategies of Economic Zones with Thematic and/or Sectoral Areas of the National Plan Agendas and Working Groups

Strategy	Strategic Intervention	Enabling Action	Working Group	Thematic Area in Plans	Time
Improve the attractiveness of SEZs and industrial zones	**Micro Climate** 11. Promote sustainable economic zones	11.1 Promote logistics zones or parks 11.2 Incorporate sustainability criteria in site selection 11.3 Promote eco-industrial parks, particularly in rubber and palm 11.4 Promote environment-friendly infrastructure in the existing zones 11.5 Apply the circular or industrial symbiosis approach in the rubber cities as a starting point	CMGF WGTI	Environment and sustainable development	MT to LT
	12. Compensate the locational disadvantages through strategic master planning of the economic zones	12.1 Location-specific innovative on-site infrastructure solutions may be critical in attracting investors 12.2 For specialized zones, the master plan needs to cater to the target investor 12.3 On-site social infrastructure 12.4 Training centers for labor 12.5 Off-site infrastructure	WGTI, WGT (tourism zones)	Industry services Industrial policy	LT
	13. Provide investor-friendly one-stop services	13.1 One-stop shop and custom facilitation 13.2 Provide specialized management services 13.3 Digitization of transactions and governance	WGTI, WGT (tourism zones)	Industry Services Industrial policy	ST to MT
	Meso Climate 14. Improve the general investment climate in economic zones	14.1 Improve regulatory institutions in the border regions 14.2 Urban development in areas surrounding economic zones	WGTI WGTIC	Industry services Regional development Industrial policy	LT
	Macro Climate 15. Expedite global and regional integration efforts for the smooth operation of GVCs	15.1 Establish ASEAN Economic Community 15.2 Introduce broader economic reforms.	WGTI	Trade	MT to LT

continued on next page

Table 27 *continued*

Strategy	Strategic Intervention	Enabling Action	Working Group	Thematic Area in Plans	Time
Improve spillovers through horizontal and vertical policies	16. Adopt a smart approach to maximize spillover effects	16.1 Identify and promote the production of goods and services required by SEZs 16.2 Target domestic support companies 16.3 Develop skills required in SEZs 16.4 Lower the transaction barriers between SEZs and domestic firms	WGTI	Industry	MT to LT
	17. Complement the smart approach of promoting targeted sectors with a horizontal approach	17.1 Build structural capabilities in the location surrounding SEZs through strategic interventions 17.2 Link the subregional companies with extra-regional firms	WGTI	Industry	MT to LT

ASEAN = Association of Southeast Asian Nations, CMGF = Chief Ministers and Governors Forum, GVC = global value chain, LT = long term, MT = medium term, SEZ = special economic zone, ST = short term, WGT = working group on tourism, WGTI = working group on trade and investment, WGTIC = working group on transport and ICT [information and communication technology] connectivity.

Source: Author.

Promotion of the IMT-GT Rubber Cities

Of late, efforts to promote the IMT-GT rubber cities have been accelerated. In the 12th IMT-GT meeting in Medan, Indonesia in August 2019, the working group on trade and investment agreed to form a project implementation team (PIT) taking into consideration the 12th Strategic Planning Meeting in Kota Bharu, Kelantan in March 2019 and the workshop on developing rubber cities in the IMT-GT, Putrajaya, Malaysia in May 2019. The PIT has already been constituted, which, together with the cooperation from the private sector, can provide a platform for developing the rubber cities. The working group has also set the targets to (i) promote regional consumption of rubber for stabilizing the price of rubber, (ii) utilize rubber products in the infrastructure and consumable sectors, (iii) transform the subregion from a low value-added commodity producer to a high value-added rubber products manufacturing area, and (iv) promote exports of high value-added rubber products.

Several proposals were made in the workshop on developing rubber cities, one of which was designing tailor-made concept development for the rubber cities in addition to harmonization of labor standards, mutual recognition of test laboratories, collaboration in R&D, etc. In line with this proposal, the present study proposes to develop the rubber cities as eco-industrial parks, the development of which needs to be based on a systematic and holistic approach informed by an in-depth analysis of the structure of the rubber industry globally and regionally and involving the participation of the private sector to establish the subregion as a hub of rubber products. Some steps in developing rubber eco-industrial parks and cross-border value chains have been suggested in Table 28 with strategic themes and enabling actions. The enabling actions correspond with those proposed in Chapter 8 and summarized in Table 26 and Table 27 with the same serial numbers. Descriptions of these interventions have been provided in a separate column.

Table 28. Strategies for Rubber Cities

Strategic Themes	Enabling Actions	Description
Institutional support	9.6 Form a consortium of companies in the rubber industry by engaging the JBC, CIMT, WGTI, and state bodies.	• The consortium should have membership from industry organizations, academic institutions, research organizations, financial institutions, and small industries associations. • It should closely work with the project implementation team on IMT-GT Rubber City, which is formally established as a platform for collaboration between the private and public sectors.
Mapping the rubber value chains in the three countries	9.2 Map the value chains of the selected industries. 9.3 Map the performance of the three countries in value chains segments of the selected industries. 9.4 Map the strengths and weaknesses of the three countries in each segment of the value chain.	• Commission a study for a comprehensive mapping of value chains with stages, actors, products, processes (raw material, imports, exports, and consumption), institutional structure, support industries, and services for each stage. • SWOT analysis of the countries is provided in each segment.
Collaborative strategic plan	9.5 Develop a strategic vision. 9.7 Develop strategic plans. 9.8 Mainstream the joint strategic plans in national plans and programs. 9.9 Adopt a systematic approach to building capabilities of regional firms to participate in regional value chains. 9.10 Identify and encourage regional and domestic companies as anchor firms in targeted sectors.	• The strategic plan may be developed by the relevant authorities in collaboration with the consortium of industries. It should cover business-friendly policy environment, harmonization of policies and regulations and standards to create a single production and market base, sustainability issues, skills and training, R&D agreements, technology licensing, bilateral or unilateral flows of technology, financing mechanism, and marketing and distribution mechanisms.
Harmonization of standards and policies in rubber cities	8.1 Create a database on the business ecosystems in each of the three economies. 8.2 Compile the above information in a comparable framework. 8.3 Harmonize the data on product standards and rules and regulations. 8.4 Harmonize product standards and rules and regulations.	• In the short term, compile the information on rules and policies. • In the medium term, harmonize the data. • In the long term, harmonize the standards and policies in the cities.
Building technology alliances for developing downstream industries	5.3 Intensify efforts to promote the formation of R&D alliances in the rubber industry involving private companies and government agencies to leverage the technological gaps within the region. 5.4 Form international research alliances.	• R&D alliances can take various forms, from inter-firm to inter-governmental. • These alliances help in upscaling technological efforts. • R&D alliances can be forged with multinational companies and at governmental levels.

continued on next page

Table 28 *continued*

Strategic Themes	Enabling Actions	Description
Master planning of the rubber cities	11.4 Promote environment-friendly infrastructure in the existing zones. 11.5 Apply the circular or industrial symbiosis approach in the rubber cities.	• The strategic vision of the rubber cities is to develop a sustainable, innovative, and integrated hub of rubber industries.
Customized design of the rubber cities	12.2 The master plan needs to cater to the target investor. 12.3 Training centers for the labor 12.4 Off-site infrastructure including logistics.	• Identify the on-site, off-site, and social infrastructure requirements, depending on the locational factors.
Branding and marketing of the region	10.1 Position the rubber cities as a global hub of rubber industries. 10.2 Engage investment promotion agencies. 10.3 Develop an integrated information portal. 10.4 Strengthen the IMT-GT website.	• Marketing of the industry should be strengthened.

CIMT = Centre for IMT-GT Subregional Cooperation; IMT-GT = Indonesia–Malaysia–Thailand Growth Triangle; JBC = Joint Business Council; R&D = research and development; SWOT = strengths, weaknesses, opportunities, threats; WGTI = working group on trade and investment.

Source: Author.

Chapter 10
The Implementation Strategy

Implementation is turning strategies and plans into actions to accomplish strategic objectives and goals. Chapters 8 and 9 present recommendations for policy development and adoption, which can be translated into reality only through effective implementation strategies of the three member countries. The focus should be on overcoming structural and institutional barriers, increasing the pace of implementation, and reducing implementation costs. This strategy calls for an integrated approach toward implementation, covering a range of implementation issues.

Institutional Approach

Strategic Intervention 18: Introduce Evolutionary Changes in the Institutional Framework for Subregional Economic Zones

18.1 **Set up a sub-working group for economic zones within the working group of trade and investment.** The working group on trade and investment has been mandated to implement three priority strategies: simplify technical, administrative, and regulatory barriers to trade and investment; improve logistics services; and increase trade and investment promotion activities. While implementing the first two strategies focuses on regulatory reforms, the third strategy requires simplification of investment procedures, trade fairs, promotion of MSMEs, and the assessment of special incentives in the subregion. These strategies are based on the horizontal approach. The SEZs are, on the other hand, an element of the vertical policy approach. The proposed subgroup on economic zones within this working group would thus focus on the business conditions and regulatory reforms in economic zones and coordinate with all other working groups to promote sustainable economic zones within the subregion through the coopetition strategy.

Strategic Intervention 19: Broad-Base Stakeholders' Participation in Decision Making

Typically, the underlying principle of a subregional program is to promote bottom-up processes in contrast with macro-regional programs, such as ASEAN, which require a top–down approach. However, the subregion's institutional structure has been modeled after ASEAN's. Indeed, the institutional arrangement is pragmatic, flexible, and incremental, maintaining respect for countries' differing needs and sensitivities. But it is central government-centric with the dominant presence of national agencies (ADB 2016, Appendix 1). The CIMT plays the role of a coordinator providing little inputs for capacity building. There are forums of local governments and private businesses, but their participation is yet to be inclusive and outcome-oriented. In contrast to the bottom-up approach for project selection as emphasized by the IMT-GT Implementation Blueprint 2017–2021, the framework for project selection, design, implementation, monitoring, and evaluation as outlined in the IMT-GT Project Manual (ADB 2016) shows the dominance of the national agencies in the process. While the top–down approach offers some benefits in terms of autonomy and flexibility, it is time-consuming and costly and can produce suboptimal outcomes (UNESCAP 2019). Moreover, these countries are part of many bilateral, regional, and multilateral arrangements that have placed a heavy burden on scarce technical, human, and bureaucratic resources at the national level. The best practice for the subregion's institutional structure is to delegate greater powers and responsibilities to the local governments, with the national nodal agency as coordinator. However, since any drastic change in the organizational structure is not foreseen, a second-best approach may be adopted, which requires mainstreaming the role of local governments and the private sector in program implementation.

19.1 **Mainstream local governments and the private sector in all three stages of the project cycle: design, implementation, and monitoring.** In the current institutional framework for IMT-GT, the role of local governments and the private sector is limited to proposing the projects along with other stakeholders. It is recommended that their role be broad-based. A major challenge is the lack of financial and technical capacities of the local governments, which can be attributed to the lack of capacity building opportunities and empowerment. Thus, a vicious circle is created, which can be overcome by making the local governments' roles more effective at the subregional level. Their capacity and involvement need to be strengthened through direct participation in the subregional processes. Thailand sets a good practice example, where the CMGF secretariat located in Prince Songkhla University has a clear mandate from the Government of Thailand to support and empower the local governments of Thailand growth triangle. The CMGF secretariat conducts structured trainings for local governments, such as developing project proposals for submission to relevant IMT-GT forums and national government. It monitors the implementation progress and evaluates the impacts of Thailand growth triangle projects. The objectives are to consolidate the local governments' positions for elevation to the Government of Thailand and IMT-GT official meetings and serve as a central pool for Thailand-GT (CIMT 2017a). The proposal is to extend such practices to the other two countries. With an ambitious decentralization program, Indonesia has already set the targets of greater participation of local governments and the private sector in the subregional program. However, it needs to be translated into reality. Malaysia can follow suit. Institutionalizing local governments and private sector participation at various decision-making stages is an achievable goal, which can go a long way for an effective implementation of the subregional program.

19.2 **Engage the private sector and local governments in various other strategic interventions.** The JBC should proactively support the industry associations of both small and large companies in setting up industry consortia to develop industry-specific strategic plans and ensure their implementation to promote regional capabilities and cross-border chains. Similarly, intergovernmental cooperation at the local level may be promoted in the development of subregional SEZs, with continuous monitoring of their performance by the country secretariat.

19.3 **Extend the role of the CIMT.** The research and technical wings should be incorporated into the CIMT. CIMT's research outputs can inform the secretariat's inputs. It can also advise on projects, compile primary and secondary databases, and continuously analyze the data to produce research outputs. The research wing can invite interns and visiting scholars from different member states based on well-established selection criteria to engage and connect the researchers' community across the three countries. The technical wing can play an important role in the PSC and contribute to assessing technical eligibility or feasibility and environmental impacts of the projects. It can also have experts who strengthen and continuously update the CIMT website to make it more substantive and informative (strategic intervention 10). Finally, the CIMT needs to work closely with the JBC to engage the private sector in implementing the proposed strategic interventions.

Human Resource Management Approach

Strategic Intervention 20: Capacity Building Initiatives for Bureaucrats

It is generally difficult to implement cross-national policies because the implementing officials are trained and shaped to view the policies from the national perspective. They need to have a greater understanding of the philosophy and prerequisites underlying regional policies and projects. Therefore, implementing regional policies requires tremendous managerial and technical skills, bringing the concept of learning, training, and incentive structures to the center of implementation.

20.1 **Training programs for upgrading bureaucratic capabilities.** Training programs should be organized to build institutional capabilities and develop competencies and capabilities to create a conducive culture for implementing the subregional programs and economic zones within them. An evaluation study of the ADB training programs makes several recommendations to improve the effectiveness of these programs (Independent Evaluation Department 2011). These recommendations include (i) developing better mechanisms for needs assessment, (ii) establishing better control over the selection of participants (they must satisfy the minimum standards set by ADB), (iii) using various instructional tools, (iv) developing post-training participants' networking and knowledge exchange, and (v) developing follow-up sessions. It is generally assumed that the training programs offered to participants contribute to broader organizational and institutional capacity development in their home countries (Independent Evaluation Department 2011). However, there are no automatic knowledge spillovers. Follow-up actions must be taken for knowledge dissemination and to build institutional capabilities. For instance, virtual or physical presentations by the participants may be organized at the institutional level with invitees not only from the SEZ implementing authority but also from other departments.

20.2 **Autonomy.** Implementing agencies (for example, the national secretariats) must be given the means, including the necessary authority, autonomy, and resources, to achieve the specified objectives. There is robust evidence that granting bureaucrats more autonomy is positively associated with the effectiveness of bureaucracies (Rasul, Rogger, and Williams 2017).

20.3 **Accountability.** All participants in the implementation process should be accountable to the implementing agencies. Their roles and relationships with implementing agencies must be clearly understood. They should know to whom and for what they are accountable. They should know the key activities that must be undertaken, the processes to organize them, the time frame to deliver, and the criteria for evaluating their performance.

Cost Management Approach

Strategic Intervention 21: Risks Management Strategy

21.1 **Develop mechanisms to manage social and environment costs.** Economic zones are getting bigger, and their establishment may have wide-ranging social costs such as land dispossession, unfair compensation, inadequate resettlement and rehabilitation packages to the affected people, and aggravation of poverty (Regondi, George, and Pillay 2013; McMichael and Healy 2017). Public opinion must be shaped and formed so that social stability is not affected adversely and to minimize the social cost. It is important to build trust and place the SEZ program within the overall development program. Small viable projects may be initiated, to begin with. Further, the border zones may inflict direct costs on the environment, such as depletion of natural resources, deforestation, biodiversity loss, and ecosystem degradation. An effective solution to the cross-border management of natural and environmental resources within the subregion requires joint efforts by all governments concerned based on mutual trust and cooperation.

21.2 **Strengthen border security measures.** As discussed in Chapter 7, there are security-related risks due to the facilitation of mobility within the economic corridors. The subregional bodies, along with the local governments and private sector, may develop comprehensive border management strategies and action plans that must incorporate counterterrorism measures. Security arrangements require reorganization of border protection agencies, strict enforcement of the law, and enhanced intergovernmental cooperation to promote awareness, knowledge, and capacity to deal with organized crimes and extremism. It also requires implementing border community policing programs and remote border area surveillance programs (Gerstein et al. 2018).

21.3 **Develop mechanisms to deal with special economic zone-related fraud, tax avoidance, and money laundering.** There is a possibility of misuse of SEZs for money laundering, tax avoidance, trafficking of counterfeit and piracy products, narcotics, smuggling, and financing of terrorism. These risks arise due to inadequate anti-money laundering mechanisms; relaxed oversight by competent domestic authorities; weak procedures to inspect goods, and inadequate record keeping and ICT systems; and the lack of adequate coordination and cooperation between zone and customs authorities. The risks are heightened in border economic zones. Thus, awareness should be created in the private sector and relevant competent authorities such as SEZ administrators, customs authorities, and bank regulators to better identify the cases of SEZ misuse by criminals. A stronger focus on training programs on these issues is essential to raise awareness of the potential misuse of SEZs. There is also a clear need to improve cooperation between competent authorities at the national and international levels, as the exchange of information is a key element in identifying illicit activities (e.g., fraud schemes) using SEZs. Finally, several organizations have developed reference tools for addressing some of these issues, including Caribbean Financial Action Task Force guidelines (2001) and the World Customs Organization instruments and standards. These may be used as a guide for building measures to counter these risks (Financial Action Task Force 2010).

21.4 **Macro management.** Unsound monetary or fiscal policies can lead to a bloated fiscal deficit, which can cause inflation, affecting the producer in terms of higher local costs, difficulty in planning, and currency depreciation. The success of economic zones depends on the prudent macro management of the economy.

21.5 **External shocks management.** Business cycles and alternating periods of recession and recovery are integral to all free market economies. During downturns, exports, and investments slow down, affecting SEZs. Currently, the COVID-19 pandemic has disrupted GVCs and affected the zones rather adversely. There should be strategies to manage these external shocks, which should include the following:

- diversification of economic activities, export destinations, and FDI source countries within the SEZs;
- promotion of the clustering of both domestic and foreign firms within SEZs;
- provisions of flexibility in the rules regarding domestic market sales during crises to provide support to SEZ tenants;
- a focus on improving the business climate in SEZs during a crisis;
- vigorous marketing of SEZs; and
- flexibility in the criteria for approving economic activity in the zones during the crisis.

The COVID-19 pandemic, for instance, has led to a sharp increase in the demand for food, medicines, vaccine, testing kits, scientific and laboratory equipment, rubber gloves, and personal protective equipment. Promoting such activities in the zones may have favorable economic and social impacts. Indonesia, Malaysia, and Thailand, which already have their respective competitive advantages in such products, can leverage them by forming an alliance and cross-border value chains and establishing themselves as global suppliers. The provision of operational flexibilities in managing the external risks may thus pay off.

Establish an Effective Monitoring and Evaluation Framework

The IMT-GT Implementation Blueprint 2017–2021 has mandated result-based monitoring to capture the outputs, outcomes, and impact of the IMT-GT projects. Under the framework as outlined in the Project Manual (ADB 2016), the CIMT is tasked to ensure that all IMT-GT project proposals it receives and processes must include a section on results-based management framework with specific, measurable, achievable, relevant, and time-bound indicators, as well as data sources and risks and assumptions. Evaluation, an integral part of the IMT-GT project cycle, has two dimensions: self-evaluation by the project manager and independent evaluation by an external party. However, there are challenges in the M&E process in the subregion that need to be addressed to make it more effective. Building an M&E system requires the following essential strategic interventions.

Strategic Intervention 22: Generate Relevant Databases

22.1 **Strengthen database management.** The most critical element of an M&E framework is collecting and analyzing quality data to generate insights for policy makers into the program's success. The term "quality data" is defined by seven dimensions: relevance, accuracy, comparability, coherence, timeliness, clarity, and completeness (de Vries 2002). ADB assisted the countries in producing an IMT-GT statistical booklet compiling the aggregate subregional data and facilitated the development of a sustainable time series database for IMT-GT as the first step toward quality data management. It also provided technical support to CIMT to manage the statistical database in coordination with the Working Group on Trade and Investment. Further, to ensure comparability and coherence of the data compiled and published by the national statistical systems and international organizations, ADB provided support in developing a statistical metasystem framework with a set of selected indicators used to publish a statistical brochure for the 2017 IMT-GT Summit. However, its continuity could not be maintained.[31] Thus, the data gathered and compiled at the subregional level are not necessarily in the standardized format ADB assisted in developing. Indeed, countries are increasingly moving toward standardization of data, but the cross-country data are currently not strictly comparable due to the use of different variable definitions, concepts, units, and classifications, as well as the differences in collection and processing approaches. The study proposes developing a homogenized system of definitions and classification to have meaningful data. It is also necessary for the countries to adopt standard classifications such as the System of National Accounts 2008, International Standard Industrial Classification, and Harmonized System of trade classification, ensuring that data across countries can be aligned and compared.

22.2 **Institutionalize mechanisms.** The IMT-GT's statistical working group comprises national statistics organizations from the member countries (with subnational and national representation). The working group is in charge of (i) compiling the aggregate subregional data, (ii) managing the sustainable time series database, and (iii) producing the annual statistical brochure. However, the data management system is yet to be institutionalized. Further, the database needs to be made available on the website of CIMT. Mekong Institute, for instance, provides data on key variables pertaining to the Greater Mekong Subregion on its website.

22.3 **Create an economic zones database.** There is an explosion of economic zones in the three countries, not only in the national cores but also in the IMT-GT subregion and other border and backward areas. However, there are no systematic databases on the number, size, and location of SEZs or GEZs. Some exceptions include data on industrial estates and KEKs in Indonesia and industrial estates and SEZs in Thailand. Recently, MIDA has also posted on its website the data on 247 economic zones in the country. However, the data are not comprehensive. Further, the data on key performance indicators such as size, job creation (direct and indirect), revenue growth, and exports are almost completely missing. As suggested, these databases can offer policy makers insights into what works and what does not, and help them in better planning. Currently, much of the information pertains to expected gains. There are insufficient data on actual performance. Gathering quality data is crucial for building and sustaining outcome-based M&E systems for economic zones. It may be enabled by the following actions:

- Consolidate general information on SEZs and other industrial zones at the national level (size, year of establishment, location, and composition).
- Update information on their current operation status (such as approved, under construction, operational).

---

[31] In 2019, the countries, led by the CIMT, took lead in preparing an updated statistical database. However, the task remains unfinished as of date.

- Set key performance indicators with respect to inputs, activities, outputs, outcomes, and impacts and generate data on them with clarity of their measurement. The performance indicators may include land occupancy, sectoral composition, FDI, total investment, origin of investment, employment, exports, production, etc.
- Update the performance data regularly.
- Provide links on the CIMT website as suggested in strategic intervention 10.

Strategic Intervention 23: Strengthen the Monitoring and Evaluation Framework for Economic Zones

23.1 **Monitoring and evaluation framework for economic zones.** Each of the three countries may institute its own M&E framework to gauge the impact and success of the economic zones program. This requires a database covering various aspects of the zone functioning as suggested above, and an institutional mechanism to monitor them regularly. The data should be made public for greater transparency. Occasionally, there should be an evaluation of the investment in these industrial areas. There is a range of methodologies available for evaluation (Mackay 2007). The most appropriate ones may be identified and adopted depending on the availability of information, M&E objectives, evaluation indicators, data availability, and human resources.

23.2 **Reorient the perspective toward the monitoring and evaluation framework.** One of the problems is that the M&E process is designed as a mechanical exercise aimed at senior officials. Its role in providing policy insights into the roadblocks and possible solutions is less appreciated. There is a need to change this perspective. M&E should be seen as a means to learn from past or current experiences; improve the design, implementation, planning, and allocation of resources; and demonstrate results as part of accountability to key stakeholders. Its importance in improving the project implementation must be made clear to all those engaged in this exercise.

23.3 **Dissemination of the results.** It is important to engage all relevant stakeholders, not just funders and senior management, to disseminate results to mainstream various stakeholders into the program and motivate them. It is also important that the findings become a regular part of planning, rather than a one-off exercise.

23.4 **Follow-up actions.** M&E is worthwhile only to the extent the IMT-GT decision makers use it for follow-up actions. Regular monitoring and updating the status of evaluation should be mandated for follow-up actions.

Adoption of the Implementation Strategy

Table 29 summarizes the implementation of the strategic approaches alongside strategic interventions and enabling actions needed for the desired outcomes. The strategic interventions and enabling actions are represented by the same serial numbers as assigned to them in Chapter 10. The table maps the working groups and the government agencies that need to collaborate closely to adopt these strategies into policies and deliver the desired results.

Table 29. Mapping of the Competitive Strategies of Economic Zones with Thematic and/or Sectoral Areas of the National Plan Agendas and Working Groups

Strategic Approach	Strategic Interventions	Enabling Actions	IMT-GT Setup	Government Agencies
Institutional approach	18. Introduce evolutionary changes in the institutional framework for subregional economic zones	18.1 Set up a sub-working group for economic zones within the WGTI	WGTI and national secretariats	Nodal ministries
	19. Broad-base stakeholders' participation in decision-making	19.1 Mainstream local governments and the private sector in all three stages of the project cycle: design, implementation, and monitoring 19.2 Engage the private sector and local governments in various strategic interventions as proposed above 19.3 Extend the role of CIMT		
Human resource management approach	20. Capacity building initiatives for bureaucrats	20.1 Training programs for upgrading bureaucratic capabilities 20.2 Autonomy 20.3 Accountability	WGTI CIMT	Economic zones, regulatory bodies, and relevant department or ministries
Cost management approach	21. Risks management strategy	21.1 Develop mechanisms to manage social and environment costs 21.2 Strengthen border security measures 21.3 Develop mechanisms to deal with SEZ-related fraud, tax avoidance, and money laundering 21.4 Macro management 21.5 External shocks management	WGTI	Ministries or departments of environment Law enforcement agencies Economic zone authorities and planning bodies
M&E framework for economic zones	22. Generate relevant databases	22.1 Strengthen database management 22.2 Institutionalize mechanisms 22.3 Create economic zones database	WGTI CIMT Statistical working groups	Badan Pusat Statistik, Indonesia Department of Statistics, Malaysia NESDC, Thailand
	23. Strengthen the M&E framework	23.1 M&E framework for economic zones 23.2 Reorient the perspective toward the M&E framework 23.3 Dissemination of the results 23.4 Follow-up actions	WGTI CIMT Statistical working groups	SEZ and GEZs, regulatory bodies, and relevant ministries

CIMT = Centre for IMT-GT Subregional Cooperation, GEZ = general economic zone, IMT-GT = Indonesia–Malaysia–Thailand Growth Triangle, M&E = monitoring and evaluation, NESDC = National Economic and Social Development Council, SEZ = special economic zone, WGTI = working group on trade and investment.

Source: Author.

Chapter 11
Conclusion

Since the early stage of development, the IMT-GT member countries (Indonesia, Malaysia, and Thailand) have been following the objective of balanced regional development alongside that of national economic growth, with manufacturing being the central element of their development strategy. The aim has been to promote industrial development and equally distribute economic prosperity across the provinces and states through an active policy of developing industrial estates and SEZs supported with wide-ranging investment programs. The top–down development strategy with SEZs and other industrial estates as the linchpin facilitated the insertion of these countries into global value chains, which resulted in rapid economic growth and development, transforming their economic base from agriculture to export-oriented manufacturing. However, in this development process, many peripheral backward areas were further marginalized, with most investment and economic activity getting attracted to a few economic cores, such as Jakarta and Batam in Indonesia, West Coast in Malaysia, and Bangkok and the Eastern Seaboard in Thailand.

In the early 1990s, these countries initiated the IMT-GT subregional program as a potentially effective mechanism to stimulate economic activities and employment generation in the peripheral areas by deepening subregional cooperation. Based on the spatial approach that accords a high priority to the development of regional and cross-border production networks using economic corridors, and SEZs and other production sites as the key tools, these initiatives signaled a shift from the inward-looking old approach to regional development to a new one based on cross-border economic cooperation and regional integration through economic zones. In principle, this approach is based on three premises. First, globalization processes have made development more localized and complex with the increasing importance of local specificities and competitive advantages. The spatial approach to the subregional program can turn the national peripheries into cross-border growth centers by strengthening local specificities, empowering local actors, creating connectivity among them, and facilitating cross-border production networks through regional integration. Second, political borders disrupt economic spatiality. The subregional priority economic corridors restore cross-border economic spatiality and create conditions for the success of economic zones by aggregating and complementing resources and markets, enhancing the capacity of clusters within the subregion. Third, the top–down approach of augmenting regional capabilities has not proven to be effective. The subregional programs set the contexts in which local governments and the private sector can play an important role in designing and shaping the policies at the local level itself by strengthening the capabilities of the local actors and fostering local partnerships of organizations to design their own programs.

Notwithstanding the strong economic foundations, subregional programs are informal; they are not binding and cannot be enforced. Their success depends on a long-term vision, strong political will, and collective ownership, all of which should be backed by generous financial resources. This, in turn, requires the integration of subregional agendas into national development planning. Unless the subregional initiatives are integrated into national development agendas, they may lose out to other plan priorities and may not receive wide governmental support beyond specific line ministries and resource commitments for the program. The alignment of the subregional economic zone program with the national strategy can help leverage synergies across different programs and development agencies. The explorations of this study indicate that the subregional agenda is yet to be fully mainstreamed into national and subnational development strategies. It is also found that the number and types of economic zones proliferated in the IMT-GT economic corridors with the commitment of massive resources to their development. But this has not yielded the expected results.

The study argues that a renewed thrust on zones programs from the perspective of regional integration can infuse a new dynamism to economic growth by debottlenecking these regions' growth potential. It will not only turn the marginalized border areas into growth centers but also upgrade the central cores where diseconomies have kicked in. There are challenges in this experimentation. The study identifies the challenges facing subregional economic zones and proposes to adopt a coopetition strategy for promoting economic zones in the subregion, which combines the elements of collaboration with that of the competitive approach. The key argument is that the subregion is a transborder hybrid zone of special and general economic zones, the success of which depends on the local capabilities and competitiveness and not just the facilities and incentives provided within these economic zones. It proposes to generate and augment regional synergies by adopting the collaborative approach through (i) the promotion of cross-border connectivity and mobility of people, goods, and freight; (ii) the development of regional capabilities covering the competitiveness issues like innovation, networking, quality of human capital, knowledge infrastructure, finance, and entrepreneurship with particular focus on the policies for small and medium-sized enterprises; (iii) a targeted approach in promoting cross-border production networks leveraging the development ladder present in the subregion, and (iv) branding and marketing of the subregion. The study proposes to adopt a multipronged competitive strategy alongside the collaborative initiatives for improving the attractiveness of the zones and their spillovers. It underscores the need to incorporate sustainability issues in-site selection and master plans of SEZs.

Further, the study argues that the adoption of the strategic intervention into planning requires mainstreaming of the proposed strategic interventions and enabling actions for economic zones into the relevant sectoral or thematic strategies of the development plans, and the agendas of various working groups. This requires sustained large public investment in wide-ranging projects in the region. A piecemeal approach may not be effective. The generic framework proposed in the study is used to make some specific recommendations for promoting the rubber cities. Finally, the study proposes an implementation strategy that creates conditions to effectively implement the policies with thrusts on institution building with local governments and the private sector assigned a pivotal role. To conclude, a shift to new growth paradigms requires integrating the subregional agenda into national and subnational plans and translating the goals into reality with a sequence of strategic actions based on joint initiatives to achieve them.

References

Aggarwal, A. 2005. *Performance of Export Processing Zones: A Comparative Analysis of India, Sri Lanka and Bangladesh. New Delhi Working Papers*. No. 155. New Delhi: Indian Council for Research on International Economic Relations.

____. 2010. Economic Impacts of SEZs: Theoretical Approaches and Analysis of Newly Notified SEZs in India. *Munich Personal RePEc Archive*. No. 20902. http://mpra.ub.uni-muenchen. de/20902/.

____. 2012a. *Social and Economic Impact of SEZs in India*. Delhi: Oxford University Press.

____. 2012b. *Asian Survey*. 52 (5). pp. 872–899.

____. 2017. Towards an Integrated Framework for Special Economic Zones (SEZs): A Dynamic Institutional Approach. *Copenhagen Discussion Paper*. No. 64. Copenhagen: Asia Research Centre, Copenhagen Business School.

____. 2019. Leveraging SEZs for Regional Integration in ASEAN: A Synergistic Approach. *Asian Survey*. 59 (5). pp. 795–821.

Ahmed, W. et al. 2020. Sustainable and Special Economic Zone Selection under Fuzzy Environment: A Case of Pakistan. *Symmetry*. 12 (2).

Ajanant, J. 1987. Trade Patterns and Trends of Thailand. In C. I. Bradford, Jr. and W. H. Branson, eds. *Trade and Structural Change in Pacific Asia*. University of Chicago Press.

Aji, A. et al. 2020. The Ministerial Regulation Position in the Hierarchy of Legislation in the Indonesian Legal System. *International Journal of Advanced Science and Technology*. 29 (2). pp. 2214–2224

Akinci, G. and J. Crittle. 2008. Special Economic Zone: Performance, Lessons Learned, and Implication for Zone Development. *Foreign Investment Advisory Service Occasional Paper*. Washington, DC: World Bank.

Amin, K. 2016. New Regulation Aims to Attract Investment to Industrial Zones. *The Jakarta Post*. 7 January. https://www.thejakartapost.com/news/2016/01/07/new-regulation-aims-attract-investment-industrial-zones.html.

Amir, S. 2013. *The Technological State in Indonesia: The Co-constitution of High Technology and Authoritarian Politics.* London and New York: Routledge.

Ananta, A., M. Soekarni, and S. Arifin, eds. 2011. *The Indonesian Economy: Entering a New Era.* Singapore: Institute of Southeast Asian Studies.

Anderson, J. E. and E. van Wincoop. 2004. Trade Costs. *Journal of Economic Literature.* 42 (3). pp. 691–751.

Andoko, E. 2019. *Overview of Indonesian Current Issue and Government Strategy on the Rubber Commodity.* FFTC Agricultural Policy Platform, Food and Fertilizer Technology for the Asia and Pacific Region. https://ap.fftc.org.tw/article/1652.

Arifin, J., M. A. Taufiqulhakim, and T. V. Salsabila. 2020. *The Implementation of ASEAN Single Window in Indonesia as an Effort to Facilitated the Flow of Import and Export in Indonesia.* https://www.researchgate.net/publication/338479459.

Arvis, J.-F. et al. 2016. Connecting to Compete 2016: *Trade Logistics in the Global Economy— The Logistics Performance Index and Its Indicators.* Washington, DC: World Bank.

Ascani, A., R. Crescenzi, and S. Iammarino. 2012. Regional Economic Development: A Review. *SEARCH Working Paper.* No. WP01/03.

ASEAN. 2015. *ASEAN 2025: Forging Ahead Together.* Jakarta: The ASEAN Secretariat.

ASEAN-Japan Centre. 2019. *Global Value Chains in ASEAN: A Regional Perspective.* PAPER 1 (Revised). Tokyo: ASEAN Promotion Centre on Trade, Investment and Tourism.

Asian Development Bank (ADB). 2015. *IMT-GT Implementation Blueprint 2012–2016: Mid-Term Review.* Manila.

———. 2011. Independent Evaluation Department. 2011. *Special Evaluation Study: Performance of the Asian Development Bank Institute: Research, Capacity Building and Training, and Outreach and Knowledge Management.* Manila: ADB.

———. 2016. *IMT-GT Project Manual.* Manila.

———. 2018. *Strategic Framework for Special Economic Zones and Industrial Zones in Kazakhstan.* Manila.

———. 2019. *The Evolution of Indonesia's Participation in Global Value Chains.* Manila. Co-published by Islamic Development Bank.

Athukorala, P. C. and S. Narayanan. 2018. Economic Corridors and Regional Development: The Malaysian Experience. *World Development.* 106 (C). pp. 1–14.

Aziz, A. 2018. Business as Usual for Malaysia's Economic Corridors, Says Guan Eng. *The Edge Markets.* 6 December.

Bangkok Post. 2013. Univanich Begins RSPO Palm Oil Exports. 26 August. https://www.bangkokpost.com/business/366379/univanich-begins-rspo-palm-oil-exports.

Barbieri, P. et al. 2020. What Can We Learn about Reshoring after COVID-19? *Operations Management Research*. 13. pp. 131–136. https://doi.org/10.1007/s12063-020-00160-1.

Barzotto, M. et al. 2019. Enhancing Innovative Capabilities in Lagging Regions: An Extra-Regional Collaborative Approach to RIS3. *Cambridge Journal of Regions, Economy and Society*. 12 (2). pp. 213–232. https://doi.org/10.1093/cjres/rsz003.

Berawi, M. A., P. Miraj, and H. Sidqi. 2017. Economic Corridor of Industrial Development in Indonesia. *In IOP Conference Series: Earth and Environmental Science*. 109. IOP Publishing.

Berg, C. N. et al. 2017. Transport Policies and Development. *The Journal of Development Studies*. 53 (4). pp. 465–480.

Bernama. 2019. Bukit Kayu Hitam Integrated Logistics Hub to Cost RM200 Mil. Focus Malaysia. 3 December. https://focusmalaysia.my/mainstream/bukit-kayu-hitam-integrated-logistics-hub-to-cost-rm200-mil/.

Brandenburger, A. M. and B. J. Nalebuff. 1996. *Co-Opetition*. New York: Currency Doubleday.

Bresnahan, T. and A. Gambardella, eds. 2004. *Building High-Tech Clusters: Silicon Valley and Beyond*. Cambridge University Press.

Brunner, H.P. 2013. What Is Economic Corridor Development and What Can It Achieve in Asia's Subregions? *ADB Working Paper Series on Regional Economic Integration*. No. 117. Manila: Asian Development Bank.

Capello, R. 2009. Regional Growth and Local Development Theories: Conceptual Evolution over Fifty Years of Regional Science. *Géographie, Économie, Société*. 11 (1). pp. 9–21.

Centre for IMT-GT Subregional Cooperation (CIMT). 2017a. *IMT-GT Vision 2036*. Putrajaya, Malaysia.

CIMT. 2017b. *IMT-GT Implementation Blueprint 2017–2021*. Putrajaya, Malaysia.

Chen, D. et al. 2019. Optimizing Multimodal Transportation Routes Considering Container Use. *Sustainability*. 11 (19), 5320. https://doi.org/10.3390/su11195320.

Cheong, T. E. 2018. The Key Success Factors of Special Economic Zones. *Surbana Jurong*. 7 June. https://surbanajurong.com/perspective/the-key-success-factors-of-special-economic-zones/.

Chimhowu, A. O., D. Hulme, and L. T. Munro. 2019. The 'New' National Development Planning and Global Development Goals: Processes and Partnerships. *World Development*. 120. pp. 76–89.

Chiu, A. S. F. and G. Yong. 2004. On the Industrial Ecology Potential in Asian Developing Countries. *Journal of Cleaner Production*. 12 (8–10). pp. 1037–1045.

Choy, T. 2018. *Can Batu Kawan Industrial Park be the Silicon Valley of the East?* 12 September. Penang Institute. https://penanginstitute.org/publications/issues/can-batu-kawan-industrial-park-be-the-silicon-valley-of-the-east/.

Cusin, J. and E. Loubaresse. 2018. Inter-Cluster Relations in a Coopetition Context: The Case of Inno'vin. *Journal of Small Business & Entrepreneurship*. 30 (1). pp. 27–52.

Damuri, Y. R., D. Christian, and R. Atje. 2015. *Kawasan Ekonomi Khusus dan Strategis di Indonesia: Tinjauan atas Peluang dan Permasalahan* (Special Economic and Strategic Zones in Indonesia: A Review on Opportunities and Challenges). Jakarta: Center for Strategic and International Studies.

De Backer, K. and S. Miroudot. 2013. Mapping Global Value Chains. *OECD Trade Policy Papers*. No. 159. Paris: OECD Publishing.

De Vries, W. 2002. Dimensions of Statistical Quality: A Discussion Note about the Quality Initiatives of Some International Organisations. Inter-agency Meeting on Coordination of Statistical Activities. New York. 17–19 September. https://unstats.un.org/unsd/accsub/2002docs/sa-02-6add1.pdf.

Dosch, J. 2013. *The ASEAN Economic Community: The Status of Implementation, Challenges and Bottlenecks*. Kuala Lumpur: CIMB ASEAN Research Institute.

Econ. 2020. Cabinet Nods to Plan for Bt18.7 Bn Economic Zone in Songkhla. *The Nation Thailand*. 21 January. https://www.nationthailand.com/business/30380887.

Econ. 2019. Border Trade Drops 2.97 per cent in First 11 Months of Year. *The Nation Thailand*. 25 December. https://www.nationthailand.com/business/30379834.

EU-ASEAN Business Council. *2019. 2019 EU-ASEAN Business Sentiment Survey*. https://14b6ea15-d0b2-4a66-9bfb-e8396fd5ddf4.filesusr.com/ugd/63371b_2605df6085c3460eac6b017ed3cf7099.pdf.

Eurofound. 2019. *Reshoring in Europe: Overview 2015–2018*. Publications Office of the European Union, Luxembourg.

European Commission. 2017. *What is an EU Macro-Regional Strategy?* https://ec.europa.eu/regional_policy/sources/cooperate/macro_region_strategy/pdf/mrs_factsheet_en.pdf.

Excell, C. and E. Moses. 2012. Can Access to Information Protect Communities from Pollution? A Lesson from Map Ta Phut, Thailand. *World Resource Institute*. Blog. 28 September. https://www.wri.org/blog/2012/09/can-access-information-protect-communities-pollution-lesson-map-ta-phut-thailand.

Farole, T. 2011. *Special Economic Zones in Africa: Comparing Performance and Learning from Global Experience.* Washington, DC: World Bank.

Fernandez, A.-S., F. Le Roy, and D. R. Gnyawali. 2014. Sources and Management of Tension in Co-Opetition Case Evidence from Telecommunications Satellites Manufacturing in Europe. *Industrial Marketing Management* 43 (2). pp. 222–235.

Financial Action Task Force (FATF). 2010. Money Laundering Vulnerabilities of Free Trade Zones. Paris: FATF/Organisation for Economic Co-operation and Development.

Free Malaysia Today. 2019. Penang Airport, Subang, Port Kelang to be New Digital FTZ. 15 July. https://www.freemalaysiatoday.com/category/highlight/2019/07/15/penang-airport-subang-port-kelang-to-be-new-digital-ftz/.

Frietsch, R., C. Rammer, and T. Schubert. 2015. Heterogeneity of Innovation Systems in Europe and Horizon 2020. *Forum.* 50 (1).

Gern, K-J and S. Mösle. 2020. The Impact of the COVID-19 Pandemic on the Global Economy: Survey-Based Evidence from Free Zones. *Kiel Policy Brief.* No. 139. Kiel Institute for the World Economy (IfW).

Gerstein D.M., Atler A., Davenport A.C, Grill B., Kadlec A. Young W. 2018. Managing International Borders: Balancing Security with the Licit Flow of People and Goods. *Perspective.* Rand Corporation.

Global Business Guide Indonesia. 2014. A Look into Indonesia's Special Economic Zones. 2 April. http://www.gbgindonesia.com/en/main/business_updates/2014/upd_a_look_into_indonesia_s_special_economic_zones.php.

Gnyawali, D. R., J. He, and R. Madhavan. 2008. Co-opetition: Promises and Challenges. In C. Wankel, ed. *21st Century Management: A Reference Handbook.* London: Sage Publications. pp. 386–398.

Gordon, I. R. and P. McCann. 2000. Industrial Clusters: Complexes, Agglomeration and/or Social Networks? *Urban Studies.* 37 (3). pp. 513–532.

Government of Japan, Ministry of Land, Infrastructure, Transport and Tourism. *An Overview of Spatial Policy in Asian and European Countries.* Malaysia: Country Profile. https://www.mlit.go.jp/kokudokeikaku/international/spw/general/malaysia/index_e.html.

Government of Indonesia, Ministry of Industry. 2016. *Industry Facts & Figures.* Jakarta.

Government of Indonesia, Ministry of National Development Planning. 2015. *National Medium-Term Development Plan (RPJMN) 2015–2019.* Jakarta.

Government of Indonesia, Ministry of National Development Planning. 2020. *National Medium-Term Development Plan (RPJMN) 2020–2024.* Jakarta.

Government of Indonesia, Office of Assistant to Deputy Cabinet Secretary for State Documents & Translation. 2019. Govt Inaugurates Tanjung Kelayang SEZ in Bangka Belitung. *Cabinet Secretariat of the Republic of Indonesia*. 14 March. https://setkab.go.id/en/govt-inaugurates-tanjung-kelayang-sez-in-bangka-belitung/.

Government of Malaysia. 1966. *First Malaysia Plan 1966-1970*. Kuala Lumpur. https://www.pmo.gov.my/dokumenattached/RMK/RMK1.pdf.

Government of Malaysia. 2011. *Eleventh Malaysia Plan 2016-2020: Anchoring Growth on People*. Prime Minister's Department. Putrajaya. https://policy.asiapacificenergy.org/sites/default/files/11th%20Malaysia%20plan.pdf.

Government of Malaysia, Federal Department of Town and Country Planning. 2010. *National Physical Plan-2*. Kuala Lumpur.

Government of Malaysia, Ministry of Economic Affairs. 2017. *Mid-Term Review of the Eleventh Malaysia Plan 2016-2020: New Priorities and Emphases*. Kuala Lumpur.

Government of Malaysia, Ministry of International Trade and Industry. Digital Free Trade Zone Fact Sheet.

Government of Malaysia, Office of the Prime Minister. 1971. *Second Malaysia Plan 1971-75*. Kuala Lumpur. https://www.pmo.gov.my/dokumenattached/RMK/RMK2.pdf.

Government of Thailand, Board of Investment. 2008. *Thailand Investment Review*. 20 April.

Government of Thailand, National Economic Development Board, Office of the Prime Minister. 1961. *First National Economic and Social Development Plan (1961-1966)*. Bangkok.

Government of Thailand, National Economic and Social Development Board, Office of the Prime Minister. 1987. *Sixth National Economic and Social Development Plan (1987-1991)*. Bangkok.

Government of Thailand, National Economic and Social Development Board, Office of the Prime Minister. 2017. *Twelfth National Economic and Social Development Plan (2017–2021)*. Bangkok.

Government of Thailand, National Economic and Social Development Board, Office of the Prime Minister. 2018. *National Strategy, 2018–2037*. Bangkok. http://nscr.nesdb.go.th/wp-content/uploads/2019/10/National-Strategy-Eng-Final-25-OCT-2019.pdf.

Grabowski R. and S. Self. 2020. Industrialization and Deindustrialization in Indonesia. *Asia & the Pacific Policy Studies*. 7 (1). https://doi.org/10.1002/app5.295.

Hadiputranto, Hadinoto & Partners. 2015. *Government Introduces Regulatory Framework on Bonded Logistic Centers*. https://www.bakermckenzie.com/-/media/files/insight/publications/2015/12/government-introduces-regulatory/al_jakarta_bondedlogisticcenters_dec15.pdf?la=en.

Hai, W.S. 2019. E&E Industry – the Golden Goose of Malaysia. *The Star*. 13 July. https://www.thestar.com.my/business/business-news/2019/07/13/ee-industry--the----------golden-goose-of-malaysia.

Halimatussadiah, A. 2020 Mainstreaming the Sustainable Development Goals into National Planning, Budgetary and Financing Processes: Indonesian Experience. *MPDD Working Paper Series*. WP/20/06. Macroeconomic Policy and Financing for Development Division, UNESCAP Bangkok.

Haryana, A., D. W. Prabowo, Y. Nuryati, R. T. Cahyono, and R. B. Setiawan. 2017. *Evaluation of the Benefits of Bonded Logistic Center in Supporting Industry Competitiveness*. In A New Paradigm in Trade Governance to Increase Domestic Efficiency and to Strengthen Global Competitiveness. The Proceeding of the International Conference and Call for Paper on Trade. Jakarta. 5–6 September.

Henkins S., M.A Boyd and Martin A. 2020. Southeast Asia after the Caliphate: Identifying Spatial Trends in Terrorism and Radicalization in Malaysia *De Gruyter*, published online: 24 August 2020. https://doi.org/10.1515/spp-2020-0001.

Hidalgo, C. A. et al. 2007. The Product Space Conditions the Development of Nations. *Science*. 317 (5837). pp. 482–487.

HKI. 2015. *Indonesia Industrial Estate Directory 2015/2016*. Jakarta: Industrial Estate Association of Indonesia. http://investindonesia.tw/upload-file/Indonesia-Basic-Information-Industrial-Estates.pdf.

_____. 2019a. *Indonesia Industrial Estate Directory 2018/2019*. Jakarta: Industrial Estate Association of Indonesia. https://www.scribd.com/document/452854705/Buku-HKI-23-lowres-pdf.

_____. 2019b. *Indonesia Industrial Estates Directory 2018-2019. Province Overview: West Sumatra Province*. https://industrialestateindonesia.com/files/provinces/kYEKIYaxiySza5JYGobSGQJmdpYMGMp3zryloePX.pdf.

H.N., Oyos Saroso. 2013. Tanggamus Builds SE Asia's Largest Maritime Zone. *The Jakarta Post*. 28 June.

Hoekman, B. and A. Nicita. 2010. Assessing the Doha Round: Market Access, Transactions Costs and Aid for Trade Facilitation. *The Journal of International Trade & Economic Development*. 19 (1). pp. 65–79.

Hoekman, B. and A. Nicita. 2011. Trade Policy, Trade Costs, and Developing Country Trade. *World Development*. 39 (12). pp. 2069–2079.

Howlett, M. and M. Ramesh. 2003. *Studying Public Policy: Policy Cycles and Policy Subsystems*. Toronto: Oxford University Press.

Hummels, D. 2007. Transportation Costs and International Trade in the Second Era of Globalization. *Journal of Economic Perspectives*. 21 (3). pp. 131–154.

Humphrey, D. D. 1962. Indonesia's National Plan for Economic Development. *Asian Survey*. 2 (10). pp. 12–21.

Hussey, A. 1993. Rapid industrialization in Thailand 1986-1991. *Geographical Review*. 83 (1). pp. 14–28.

Hutchinson, F. E. and T. Chong, eds. 2016. *The SIJORI Cross-Border Region: Transnational Politics, Economics, and Culture*. ISEAS-Yusof Ishak Institute.

Indonesia Investment Coordinating Board. 2016. *FAQ: Frequently Asked Question on Investment*. Jakarta.

Indriani, R. N. 2019. Indonesia Has Science Techno Parks: Ministry Official. *ANTARA News*. 25 April.

Industrial Estate Authority of Thailand (IEAT). Rubber City Industrial Estate. About. https://www.ieat.go.th/en/rubbercity.

IEAT. 2017. I-EA-T 4.0: *IEAT Annual Report 2017*. Bangkok. https://www.ieat.go.th/assets/uploads/cms/file/201810181619451881906406.pdf.

International Monetary Fund. 2020. The Great Lockdown: Worst Economic Downturn since the Great Depression. Press release no. 20/98. 23 March.

InvestPenang. Electrical & Electronics (E&E). https://investpenang.gov.my/electrical-electronics/.

Islam R. and El Madkouri, F. 2018. Assessing and ranking HALMAS parks in Malaysia: An application of importance-performance analysis and AHP. *Journal of Islamic Marketing*. 9 (2). pp. 240–261.

The Jakarta Post. 2019. Govt to Allow More Self-Managed Bonded Zones to Boost Exports, investments. 23 September. https://www.thejakartapost.com/news/2019/09/23/govt-to-allow-more-self-managed-bonded-zones-to-boost-exports-investments.html.

Javorcik, B. 2020. Global Supply Chains Will Not Be the Same in the Post-COVID-19 World. In R. E. Baldwin and S. J. Evenett, eds. *COVID-19 and Trade Policy: Why Turning Inward Won't Work*. CEPR Press. London: Centre for Economic Policy Research. pp. 111–116.

Jessop, B. 2003. The Political Economy of Scale and the Construction of Cross-Border Micro-Regions. In F. Söderbaum and T. M. Shaw, eds. *Theories of New Regionalism*. London: Palgrave Macmillan.

Jomo, K. S., ed. 2013. *Industrialising Malaysia: Policy, Performance, Prospects*. Routledge.

Kam, W. P. and N. K. Kee. 2009. *Batam, Bintan and Karimun: Past History and Current Development towards Being a SEZ*. Singapore: National University of Singapore, Asia Competitiveness Institute.

Kasahara, S. 2013. The Asian Developmental State and the Flying Geese Paradigm. *UNCTAD Discussion Paper*. No. 213. Geneva: United Nations Conference on Trade and Development.

Kawano, M. 2019. Changing Resource-Based Manufacturing Industry: *The Case of the Rubber Industry in Malaysia and Thailand*. In K. Tsunekawa and Y. Todo, eds. Emerging States at Crossroads. Emerging-Economy State and International Policy Studies. Singapore: SpringerOpen. https://doi.org/10.1007/978-981-13-2859-6_7.

Kelly, M., P. Yutthaphonphinit, S.-A. Seubsman, and A. Sleigh. 2012. Development Policy in Thailand: From Top-Down to Grass Roots. *Asian Social Science*. 8 (13). pp. 29–39.

Kim, J. Y. and L.-Y. Zhang. 2008. Formation of Foreign Direct Investment Clustering—A New Path to Local Economic Development? The Case of Qingdao. *Regional Studies*. 42 (2). pp. 265–280.

Krainara, C. and J. K. Routray. 2015. Cross-Border Trades and Commerce between Thailand and Neighboring Countries: Policy Implications for Establishing Special Border Economic Zones. *Journal of Borderlands Studies*. 30 (3). pp. 345–363.

Krugman, P. R. 1992. Does the New Trade Theory Require a New Trade Policy? *The World Economy*. 15 (4). pp. 423–442.

Krugman, P. 1991. Increasing Returns and Economic Geography. *Journal of Political Economy*. 99 (3). pp. 483–499.

Kuchiki, A. and M. Tsuji, eds. 2011. *Industrial Clusters, Upgrading and Innovation in East Asia*. Edward Elgar Publishing.

Kwanda, T. 2000. Pengembangan Kawasan Industri di Indonesia. *DIMENSI Journal of Architecture and Built Environment*. 28 (1).

Lombaerde, P. D. 2010. How to 'Connect' Micro-Regions with Macro-Regions? A Note. *Perspectives on Federalism*. 2 (3).

Lowe, E. A. 2001. *Eco-Industrial Parks: A Handbook*. Manila: ADB.

Mackay, K. R. 2007. *How to Build M&E Systems to Support Better Government*. Washington, DC: World Bank.

Malaysian Investment Development Authority (MIDA). Infrastructure Support. https://www.mida.gov.my/setting-up-content/infrastructure-support/.

_____. 2018a. MVV 2.0 Will Be Rejuvenated to Promote Hi-Tech Industries.

_____. 2018b. Mida Invest Series: Unfolding States' Business Potential. A Briefing by Kelantan State Economic Development Corporation. 8 February 2018.

McMichael, C. and J. Healy. 2017. Health Equity and Migrants in the Greater Mekong Subregion. *Global Health Action*. 10 (1).

Meesook, O. A., P. Tinakorn, and C. Vaddhanaphuti. 1987. *Thailand: The Political Economy of Poverty, Equity and Growth*. Washington, DC: World Bank.

Menon, J. 2018. Assessing ASEAN's Economic Performance. *Asian Development Bank*. Op-Ed/Opinion. 17 April. https://www.adb.org/news/op-ed/assessing-asean-s-economic-performance-jayant-menon.

Menon, J. and A. C. Melendez. 2017. Will 2025 Be the Final Deadline for the ASEAN Economic Community? *Asia Pathways*. Blog. Asian Development Bank Institute. https://www.asiapathways-adbi.org/2017/07/will-2025-be-the-final-deadline-for-the-asean-economic-community/.

Miller, R. and Cote, M. (1985) *Growing the Next Silicon Valley*, Harvard Business Review July/August, pp. 114–123.

Miroudot, S. and H. Nordström. 2019. Made in the World Revisited. *EUI Working Paper*. RSCAS 2019/84. Florence: European University Institute.

Moberg L. 2018. *The Political Economy of Special Economic Zones: Concentrating Economic Development*. Routledge.

Moser H. 2019. Reshoring Was at Record Levels in 2018. Is It Enough? *Industry Week*. https://www.industryweek.com/the-economy/article/22027880/reshoring-was-at-record-levels-in-2018-is-it-enough.

Myrdal, G. 1957. *Economic Theory and Underdeveloped Regions*. London: University Paperbacks, Methuen.

Nambiappan, B. et al 2016. Revealed Comparative Advantage and Competitiveness of Malaysian Palm Oil Exports against Indonesia in Five Major Markets. *Oil Palm Industry Economic Journal*. 16 (1). pp. 1–7.

Narita, V. 2015. Can Science and Technology Parks Boost the Economy? *The Jakarta Post*. 13 November. https://www.thejakartapost.com/news/2015/11/13/can-science-and-technology-parks-boost-economy.html.

Nasution, A. 2016. Government Decentralization Program in Indonesia. *ADBI Working Paper*. No. 601. Tokyo: Asian Development Bank Institute. https://www.adb.org/publications/government-decentralization-program-indonesia/.

Nathan, M. and H. Overman. 2013. Agglomeration, Clusters, and Industrial Policy. *Oxford Review of Economic Policy*. 29 (2). pp. 383–404.

NESDC. 2020. *Special Economic Zones SEZs Development Progress*. July 2020. Office of the National Economic and Social Development Council. Bangkok.

Nee, E. A. 2019. Eight e-Fulfilment Projects, more to Come. *The Sun Daily*. 10 July. https://www.thesundaily.my/business/eight-e-fulfilment-projects-approved-more-to-come-EM1086644.

Ng, Audrey. 2019. Bringing Batam into the Next Phase. *The Business Times*. 29 August.

Noer, J. et al. 2019. Implementation Model of Integrated Industrial Estate Development Policy for Tukak Sadai Port in South Bangka Regency, Bangka Belitung Islands Province, Indonesia. *International Journal of Science and Society*. 1 (3). pp. 251–260.

Octavia, J. 2016. *Rebuilding Indonesia's Industrial Estates*. Transformasi, Center for Public Policy Transformation. Policy brief 2016/01.

Oh, D.-S. and I. Yeom. 2012. Daedeok Innopolis in Korea: From Science Park to Innovation Cluster. *World Technopolis Review*. 1 (2). pp. 141–154.

Organisation for Economic Co-operation and Development (OECD). 2016. *OECD Economic Surveys: Indonesia*. Paris.

———. 2018. *Strengthening SMEs and Entrepreneurship for Productivity and Inclusive Growth*. Key Issues for SME Ministerial Conference. Mexico City. 22–23 February.

Ortiz-Guerrero, C. E. 2013. The New Regionalism: Policy Implications for Rural Regions. *Cuadernos de Desarrollo Rural*. 10 (70). pp. 47–67.

Parpart, E. 2016. Thai-Malaysian Border Trade Ready to Move to the Next Level. *Bangkok Post*. 17 October. https://www.bangkokpost.com/tech/1112357/thai-malaysian-border-trade-ready-to-move-to-the-next-level.

Peng, T. J., M. H. Yen, and M. Bourne. 2018. How Rival Partners Compete Based on Cooperation? *Long Range Planning*. 51 (2). pp. 351–383.

Perkmann, M. 2002. *The Rise of the Euroregion. A Bird's Eye Perspective on European Cross-Border Co-Operation*. Lancaster, UK: Department of Sociology, Lancaster University. https://www.lancaster.ac.uk/fass/resources/sociology-online-papers/papers/perkmann-rise-of-euroregion.pdf.

Phasukavanich, C. 2003. *The Pace of Thailand through the Year 2020: A Presentation by Chakramon Phasukavanich*. Bangkok. 20 May.

Pombhejara, V. N. 1965. The Second Phase of Thailand's Six-Year Economic Development Plan, 1964-1966. *Asian Survey*. 5 (3). pp. 161–168.

Porter, M. E. 1998. Clusters and the New Economics of Competition. *Harvard Business Review*. 76 (6). pp. 77–90.

Putnam, R. D., R. Leonardi, and R. Y. Nanetti. 1993. *Making Democracy Work: Civic Traditions in Modern Italy*. Princeton, New Jersey: Princeton University Press.

PwC. Indonesia: Corporate - Tax Credits and Incentives. https://taxsummaries.pwc.com/indonesia/corporate/tax-credits-and-incentives.

Quium, A. 2019. Transport Corridors for Wider Socio-Economic Development. *Sustainability*. 11 (19). pp. 1–23.

Raposo, M. L, J. J. M. Ferreira, and C. Fernandes. 2014. Local and Cross-Border SME Cooperation: Effects on Innovation and Performance. *Revista Europea de Dirección y Economía de la Empresa*. 23 (4). pp. 157–165.

Rasiah, R. 1996. The Changing Organisation of Work in Malaysia's Electronics Industry. *Asia Pacific Viewpoint*. 37 (1). pp. 21–38.

———. 2019. Industrial Diversification in Malaysia. Presentation prepared for the UNIDO Workshop, Promoting Export Diversification in the CAREC Region. Ulan Bator, Mongolia. 16–17 May.

Rasiah, R., V. Crinis, and H.-A. Lee. 2015. Industrialization and Labour in Malaysia. *Journal of the Asia Pacific Economy*. 20 (1). pp. 77–99.

Rasul, I., D. Rogger, and M. J. Williams. 2017. *Management and Bureaucratic Effectiveness: A Scientific Replication in Ghana and Nigeria*. Policy Brief. No. 33301. London: International Growth Centre.

Raza-Ullah, T., M. Bengtsson, and S. Kock. 2014. The Coopetition Paradox and Tension in Coopetition at Multiple Levels. *Industrial Marketing Management*. 43 (2). pp. 189–198.

Regmi, M. B. and S. Hanaoka. 2012. Assessment of Intermodal Transport Corridors: Cases from North-East and Central Asia. *Research in Transportation Business and Management*. 5. pp. 27–37.

Regondi, I., G. George, and N. Pillay. 2013. HIV/AIDS in the Transport Sector of Southern Africa: Operational Challenges, Research Gaps and Policy Recommendations. *Development Southern Africa*. 30 (4-05). pp. 616–628.

Rothenberg, A. D. et al. 2017. When Regional Policies Fail: An Evaluation of Indonesia's Integrated Economic Development Zones. *RAND Working Paper*. No. WR-1183. Santa Monica, CA: RAND Corporation.

Rothenberg, A.D. and D. Temenggung. 2019. *Place-Based Policies in Indonesia: A Critical Review*. Background paper for the Urbanization flagship report Time to ACT: Realizing Indonesia's Urban Potential. Washington, DC: World Bank.

Roy Chaudhury, D. 2019. Eyeing Southeast Asia, India Builds Port in Indonesia. *Economic Times*. 20 March. https://economictimes.indiatimes.com/news/defence/eyeing-southeast-asia-india-builds-port-indonesia/articleshow/68490478.cms?utm_source=contentofinterest&utm_medium=text&utm_campaign=cppst.

Rubber Journal Asia. 2019. Latex: Asian Rubber Industry Beats the Odds. September.

Sarmiento-Mirwaldt, K. 2009. The Small Projects Fund and Social Capital Formation in the Polish-German Border Region: An Initial Appraisal. *Regional Studies.* 46 (2).

Schiff, M. and L. A. Winters. 2002. Regional Cooperation, and the Role of International Organizations and Regional Integration. *Policy Research Working Paper.* No. 2872. Washington, DC: World Bank.

Sertkaya, B. and G. Özcan. 2017. The Importance of the Social Capital with Regard to Economic Development: An Evaluation on the Developed and the Developing Countries. *Bulletin of Economic Theory and Analysis (BETA) Journals.* 2 (1). pp. 63–78.

Sharib, S. and A. Halog. 2017. Enhancing Value Chains by Applying Industrial Symbiosis Concept to the Rubber City in Kedah, Malaysia. *Journal of Cleaner Production.* 141 (10). pp. 1095–1108. https://doi.org/10.1016/j.jclepro.2016.09.089.

Sihotang, J. W., M. S. D. Hadian, and D. Muslim. 2019. A New Perspective in Science and Technology Park Model (STPM) for Eco-Social Development Using Penta-Helix Concept: Case Study in Sumedang Regency. *Earth and Environmental Science.* 248. IOP Publishing.

Sinaga R. Humang W.P. and Kurniawan A. 2018 Potential cargo demand of Kuala Tanjung Port as international hub port in Western Indonesia, *MATEC Web of Conferences* 181, 09001 (2018).

Sivananthiran, A. 2009. Promoting Decent Work in Export Promotion Zones in Indonesia. *ILO Working Paper.* Jakarta: International Labour Organization.

Söderbaum, F. 2004. Theorizing the New Regionalism Approach. In *The Political Economy of Regionalism.* International Political Economy Series. London: Palgrave Macmillan.

Statista. Number of People Employed in the Electrical and Electronic Products Industry in Malaysia from 2015 to 2019. https://www.statista.com/statistics/809680/annual-employment-in-the-electrical-and-electronic-products-industry-malaysia/.

SteadieSeifi, M. et al. 2014. Multimodal Freight Transportation Planning: A Literature Review. *European Journal of Operational Research.* 233 (1). pp. 1–15.

Sulistyawati I., A. Sulistiyono, and M. N. Imanullah. 2019. Implementation of Bonded Zone Facilities in Indonesia. *International Journal of Research and Innovation in Social Science (IJRISS).* (III) III. pp. 162–167. https://www.rsisinternational.org/journals/ijriss/Digital-Library/volume-3-issue-3/162-167.pdf.

Tantanasiriwong, K. 2016. *The Role of Institutions for the Development of Science Parks: The Case of Regional Science Parks in Thailand.* Master's thesis. KTH Industrial Engineering and Management.

Tatiana, Y., M. Firdaus, H. Siregar, and H. Hariyoga. 2015. Determinant Factors of Agricultural Industry Investment in Province Bengkulu, Indonesia. *International Journal of Sciences: Basic and Applied Research*. 23 (2). pp. 312–323. https://pdfs.semanticscholar.org/8e83/f27a24a1268f34b0105e4cb58de8ed939420.pdf.

TB Supply Base Sdn. Bhd. About. https://www.tbsb.my.

Temenggung, D. 2013. Policies to Promote Development and Integration of Lagging Regions: The Indonesian Experience. In T. Farole, ed. *The Internal Geography of Trade: Lagging Regions and Global Markets*. Washington, DC. World Bank. pp. 209–227.

Theparat, C. 2020. State to Set Up SEZ Supervisory. *Bangkok Post*. 13 January. https://www.bangkokpost.com/business/1834304/state-to-set-up-sez-supervisory.

Tijaja, J. and M. Faisal. 2014. Industrial Policy in Indonesia: A Global Value Chain Perspective. *ADB Economics Working Paper Series*. No. 411. Manila: ADB.

Tridech, C. 2016. *Regional Science Parks: A Step Forward to Innovation Ecosystem in Thailand*. 33rd IASP World Conference on Science Parks and Areas of Innovation. Moscow, Russia. 19–22 September.

Umezaki, S. 2019. Transport Facilitation in the Era of the ASEAN Economic Community. In M. Ishida, ed. *Cross-Border Transport Facilitation in Inland ASEAN and the ASEAN Economic Community*. Economic Research Institute for ASEAN and East Asia. http://hdl.handle.net/11540/9808.

United Nations Conference on Trade and Development (UNCTAD). 2019. *World Investment Report 2019: Special Economic Zones*. Geneva.

____. 2021. *Investment Trends Monitor*, 24 January 2021. Geneva.

United Nations Economic and Social Commission for Asia and the Pacific (UNESCAP). 2017. *Enhancing Regional Economic Cooperation and Integration in Asia and the Pacific*. Bangkok.

____. 2018. *Trade Facilitation and Paperless Trade Implementation in APEC Economies: Results of the UN Global Survey 2017*. Bangkok.

____. 2019. *Establishing Science and Technology Parks: A Reference Guidebook for Policymakers in Asia and the Pacific*. Bangkok.

UNESCAP and ADB. 2019. *Asia-Pacific Trade Facilitation Report 2019: Bridging Trade Finance Gaps through Technology*. Manila.

UNESCAP-World Bank Trade Cost Database. https://www.unescap.org/resources/escap-world-bank-trade-cost-database (accessed 1 December 2020).

United Nations Industrial Development Organization (UNIDO). Competitive Industrial Performance Index 2020 (accessed 1 December 2020).

———. 1997. Industrial Estates: Principles and Practices. Vienna.

———. 2015. *Economic Zones in the ASEAN: Industrial Parks, Special Economic Zones, Eco Industrial Parks, Innovation Districts as Strategies for Industrial Competitiveness.* Hanoi.

———. 2019. *Eco-Industrial Parks: Achievements and Key Insights from the Global RECP Programme 2012–2018.*

United States (US) Department of State. 2019a. *Investment Climate Statements 2019: Indonesia.*

———. 2019b. *Investment Climate Statements 2019: Malaysia.*

Wang, L. et al., eds. 2020. *Contemporary Logistics in China.* Singapore: Springer Singapore.

Wicaksono, T. Y., C. Mangunsong, and T. Anas. 2019. Failure of an Export Promotion Policy? Evidence from Bonded Zones in Indonesia. *ERIA Discussion Paper Series.* No. 2018-16. Jakarta: Economic Research Institute for ASEAN and East Asia.

Wijeratne D., N. Plumridge, and S. Raj. 2019. Sustaining Southeast Asia's Momentum: How the 10 Countries of the Vibrant ASEAN Region Can Avoid the Threat of Slower Growth. *WORLD VIEW.* 94. 12 February. https://www.strategy-business.com/article/Sustaining-Southeast-Asias-Momentum?gko=32ad4.

Wilson, L. S. 1996. *Federal-State Fiscal Arrangements in Malaysia: State Revenue Equalization in Malaysia.* John Deutsch Institute for the Study of Economic Policy, Queen's University.

Winosa, Y. 2019. Indonesia's First Halal Industrial Zone to Start Development early 2020. *Salaam Gateway.* https://www.salaamgateway.com/story/indonesias-first-halal-industrial-zone-to-start-development-early-2020.

Workman, D. 2019. Malaysia's Top Ten Exports. *World's Top Exports.* http://www.worldstopexports.com/malaysias-top-10-exports/.

World Bank. Enterprise Survey: Indonesia, 2015. https://www.enterprisesurveys.org/en/data/exploreeconomies/2015/indonesia.

———. Enterprise Survey: Thailand 2016. https://www.enterprisesurveys.org/en/data/exploreeconomies/2016/Thailand.

———. 1992. Export Processing Zones. *Policy and Research Series.* No 20. Washington, DC.

———. 2013. Decentralization. *Brief.* 6 June. https://www.worldbank.org/en/topic/communitydrivendevelopment/brief/Decentralization.

____. 2021.Global Economy to Expand by 4% in 2021; Vaccine Deployment and Investment Key to Sustaining the Recovery Press release no. 2021/080/EFI 5 January.

World Bank, ADB, Japan International Cooperation Agency, Department for International Development. 2018. *The WEB of Transport Corridors in South Asia.* Washington, DC: World Bank.

World Trade Organization (WTO). 2007. Indonesia Trade Policy Review 2007.

____. 2019. Technological Innovation, Supply Chain Trade, and Workers in a Globalized World. *Global Value Chain Development Report 2019.* Geneva. https://www.oecd.org/dev/Global-Value-Chain-Development-Report-2019-Technological-Innovation-Supply-Chain-Trade-and-Workers-in-a-Globalized-World.pdf.

____. 2020. Trade Falls Steeply in First Half of 2020. Press Release. World Trade Organization. 22 June. https://www.wto.org/english/news_e/pres20_e/pr858_e.htm.

Zeng, D. Z. 2016. Special Economic Zones: Lessons from the Global Experience. *PEDL Synthesis Paper Series.* No. 1. Private Enterprise Development in Low Income Countries.

Zhang, D. et al. 2017. Optimal Investment Timing and Size of a Logistics Park: A Real Options Perspective. *Complexity.* https://doi.org/10.1155/2017/2813816.

Zheng, Y. and A. Aggarwal. 2020. Special Economic Zones in China and India: A Comparative Analysis. In A. Oqubay and J. Y. Lin, eds. *The Oxford Handbook of Industrial Hubs and Economic Development.* Oxford University Press. pp. 607–622

www.ingramcontent.com/pod-product-compliance
Lightning Source LLC
Chambersburg PA
CBHW061234270326

41929CB00031B/3488